A House Next Door to Trauma

of related interest

Past Trauma in Late Life
European Perspectives on Therapeutic Work with Older People
Edited by Linda Hunt, Mary Marshall and Cherry Rowlings
ISBN 1 85302 446 5

Children of Social Trauma
Hungarian Psychoanalytic Case Studies
Terez Virag
ISBN 1 85302 848 7

Living Through Loss
A Training Guide for Those Supporting People Dealing with Loss
Fay W. Jacobsen, Margaret Kindlen and Allison Shoemark
ISBN 1 85302 395 7

Good Grief 1
Exploring Feelings, Loss and Death with Under 11s, Second Edition
Barbara Ward and Associates
ISBN 1 85302 324 8

Good Grief 2
Exploring Feelings, Loss and Death with Over Elevens and Adults
Barbara Ward and Associates
ISBN 1 85302 340 X

Children, Bereavement and Trauma
Nurturing Resilience
Paul Barnard, Ian Morland and Julie Nagy
ISBN 1 85302 785 5

Psychodrama with Trauma Survivors
Acting Out Your Pain
Peter Felix Kellermann and M.K. Hudgins
ISBN 1 85302 893 2

The Social Symbolism of Grief and Mourning
Roger Grainger
ISBN 1 85302 480 5

A House Next Door to Trauma

Learning from Holocaust Survivors
How to Respond to Atrocity

Judith Hassan

Jessica Kingsley Publishers
London and New York

First published in the United Kingdom in 2003
by Jessica Kingsley Publishers Ltd
116 Pentonville Road
London N1 9JB, England
and
96 West 35th Street, 10th fl.
New York, NY 10001-2299
www.jkp.com

Copyright © 2003 Judith Hassan

Library of Congress Cataloging in Publication Data
Hassan, Judith, 1946-
    A house next door to trauma : learning from Holocaust survivors how to respond to atrocity / Judith Hassan.
       p. cm.
    Includes bibliographical references and index.
    ISBN 1-85302-867-3 (pbk. : Alk. paper)
     1. Holocaust survivors--Mental health. 2. Psychic trauma--Patients--Care. I. Title.

RC451.4.H62 H37 2002
616.85'21--dc21   2002034071

British Library Cataloguing in Publication Data
A CIP catalogue record for this book is available from the British Library

ISBN 1 85302 867 3

Printed and Bound in Great Britain by
Athenaeum Press, Gateshead, Tyne and Wear

This book is dedicated
to the memory of my mother and father
Else and Frank Hassan

Contents

Acknowledgements

I want to thank Jewish Care for their outstanding support in encouraging me to develop these specialist services. I am grateful for their generosity in giving me the time to write this book. My sincere thanks go to Jeremy Oppenheim, Chief Executive of Jewish Care, Michael Goldmeier, Chairman of Jewish Care, and Simon Morris, Director of Community Services, who have all played a crucial role in both strengthening the services and endorsing me in my multifaceted tasks. Particular mention goes to Melvyn Carlowe, former Chief Executive of Jewish Care, who believed in my capacity to undertake my work with survivors, as well as steering me into documenting it through my writing. My consultants, Sonny Herman and John Bridgewater, are given special mention within the text of the book for their invaluable contribution. I could not have undertaken this work alone, and recognise the part played by the teams I have worked with, both past and present.

I particularly wish to thank Pamela Mendel for her skill, patience, support and good humour while typing my manuscript and co-ordinating with the publishers on all practical matters associated with the book.

I am extremely grateful to Gideon Taylor, Executive Vice President of the Conference on Jewish Material Claims Against Germany, Inc., for the generous grant enabling me to write my book, in addition to the ongoing funds towards the services for survivors. My sincere thanks go to Moshe Jahoda, Associate Vice President of the Claims Conference, for his valuable advice and his support for the concept of writing this book, as well as the interest he has shown in connection with the services for survivors.

I extend my thanks to Dr Zvi Feine, Deputy Director of the American Joint Distribution Committee (JDC) (Israel), who has known my work over several years, and enthusiastically supported my documenting it in book form; I extend my thanks for the support of Ted Comet, Honorary Executive Vice President of the American Joint Distribution Committee (JDC – Israel), who has known my work over several years and enthusiastically supported my documenting it in book form; and to the Wiener Library (London) for endorsing the grant application to the Claims Conference.

I am most grateful to Elie Wiesel for his endorsement of my book, and for guiding my writing through reference to his outstanding literature. I also wish to acknowledge the very positive co-operation and encouragement I have received from the staff at Jessica Kingsley Publishers. This has been an essential ingredient in bringing my book to fruition.

To all my organisational partners, both here and abroad, I owe my appreciation. The role of the Association of Jewish Refugees and World Jewish Relief (WJR) are particularly noteworthy. Special mention goes to Janet Cohen, Chairman of the Jewish Refugee Committee (part of the WJR), for her unstinting, practical, professional and personal commitment to our shared projects, including the work with the Bosnian refugees.

I also pay tribute to the late Professor Shamai Davidson for the special way he helped me, in our frequent discussions over a number of years, to engage in the world of severe suffering and its aftermath. Even today, his words are ever present in my mind as I continue to implement his wise counsel.

For all those who have shown interest and enthusiasm for me to write this book, including my family, Ann-Marie, Bryan, Nick and Kate, friends and colleagues, they may never know how much they have helped me to reach my goal. I greatly value the part played by Peter Speyer in guiding my thinking and my writing at key moments during the development of my book.

My deepest thanks go to the survivors themselves: both those who speak in the text of this book and those from whom I continue to learn daily about my work. The book would have remained as empty pages without the life-force which has emerged from these human encounters.

Preface

The 'Other World' of the Survivors' Suffering

Working with survivors and refugees who have suffered extreme trauma is a dynamic and ever-evolving process. Those of us who have not been subjected to uprooting, persecution, torture and massive losses can only see shadows or glimpses of these unimaginable experiences. Try as we may to empathise with people who have witnessed indescribable horror; who have reached what Amery (1999) calls 'the mind's limits', both physically and mentally; who have encountered what Herzog (1982) calls a 'world beyond metaphor' (pp.103–19), we can never imagine what it must be like to have gone through such hell.

The language of trauma cannot evoke the degradation, dehumanisation, powerlessness and starvation characteristic of extreme suffering such as that found in the Nazi Holocaust. The fragility of language and the limitation of what can be tolerated in our conceptual thinking tend to render the words to describe these horrific memories void and redundant.

The inadequacy of communication in the reality of today's world brings with it the potential danger of a wide gulf emerging between those who have suffered severe trauma and those who wish to reach out and help them.

This book will explore ways of reconstructing a language through which the whispering voices of those who have suffered can be heard.

When I started my work with refugees from Nazi persecution twenty-five years ago, I found myself in a wilderness of ignorance and lack of interest in the professional world regarding the re-emergence of trauma forty years after the event. Now, twenty-five years on, there is a plethora of literature on the subject of trauma. The reader shifts backwards and forwards as different theories are tossed around in an angry sea of confusion. There are pressing needs in dealing with refugees worldwide, and with the aftermath of war.

There is an urgency to develop a body of knowledge, to provide a secure base on which to build effective ways of working – yet the complexity of trauma defies such clear-cut definition. The subject of extreme trauma is by its nature chaotic. Those who are victims have had their value systems violated; those at the mercy of totalitarian regimes lose their trust in others and their sense of self. What does it really mean to have experienced severe suffering, and then be thrown into another alien environment? What does it feel like to lose everything one held dear and important in one's life?

In the darkness, in the chaos of this upside-down world, there is a chink of light – a way through the labyrinth – but there are no short cuts. The faint-hearted may not wish to enter this space, as they cling on desperately to their familiar theories and practices. The sometimes overwhelming sense of powerlessness and de-skilling which we experience in our work with severely traumatised people may be too great a threat to our professional sense of identity.

However, my aim in this book is to encourage those who wish to work in this specialised area to travel with me on this journey, as I have done for many years with the survivors and refugees themselves. Seeing this learning experience as a partnership of discovery is how my work evolved. There are no experts among the professionals – no-one who has all the answers. We can, however, learn new ways of responding; we can tap into our creative minds; we can develop a different language; we can find strengths in ourselves to journey beyond what is familiar and safe in our quest for understanding. This takes courage and confidence, but the determination to adapt to new ways of working can be personally and professionally liberating.

My wish to pass on what I have witnessed and learned has more than one motivation. There is a clear desire to widen the spectrum of professionals who are able to develop such work, and thereby alleviate the suffering and pain of so many people. There is also a personal reason for doing so. I have found that the survivors of extreme trauma want the world to know what happened so that it should never happen again. They bear witness to these events and thereby speak for those who were murdered or killed. The closeness to natural death of the survivor or refugee increases the urgency of this task. The dead reside in the survivors' voices.

Over the years I have been listening to and working with survivors, I have in a sense become a witness in my own right to the horrors that have been recounted to me as therapeutic facilitator. In my role as supervisor of the therapists in my team, the reflective process encountered in the supervision has held up a mirror to the world the survivors were recreating in the here and now of their sessions. As Director of the services for survivors and refugees, I had to ensure that these eye-witness accounts were recorded and kept for posterity. It has been my responsibility to make a link between the past, the present and the future.

The book becomes my testimony, my account of the difficult but also profoundly moving experience of working with those who have been to hell and back. On a daily basis I have witnessed the pain they carry, but I have also seen life emerge from the ashes which threatened to 'bury' them in the aftermath of destruction.

The survivors themselves are integral to this book. Remaining close to them during the writing process maintains the dynamic and practical focus of the book. The therapeutic encounters which are interspersed throughout the book are vignettes which give passion to my writing. The survivors have shaped the way I work and respond to trauma. I am their messenger in conveying their story about what seems to help them, no matter how late this is addressed in their lives. By making these encounters with survivors central to the book, I am also emphasising the particularness of the Nazi Holocaust, with its systematic, scientific precision of the annihilation process, as well as the 'high culture' of the German perpetrators who were responsible for the genocide.

The book is not meant to be a theoretical or academic exercise. It offers a pragmatic guide, starting with the very basic questions: 'Where do I begin?' 'How do I prepare myself for this work?' It follows a sequential process, opening up the mind of the reader as he/she passes through from experiential sensitisation to the subject of severe suffering in war, towards an understanding of trauma in its myriad of component parts. The centrepiece of the book focuses on a particular therapeutic model which has evolved from my listening to several hundred survivors about what seems to help them to live with their trauma. The model is based on a social centre – the Holocaust Survivors' Centre (HSC) – side by side with Shalvata – a centre in which survivors can speak with specialised therapeutic workers about the trauma they continue to carry inside themselves. The combined therapeutic options in these two centres represent symbolically the two worlds of darkness and light, despair and hope, destruction and regeneration. The model looks at how the two worlds may be bridged through translating the concepts of the trauma into a meaningful therapeutic language, whether this be through the social programme of the HSC, or the therapeutic work undertaken in Shalvata, or the crossover between the two. The model traces the shift from modest beginnings to a complex structure and infrastructure which supports these services for survivors. This includes organisational and managerial issues, often missing in descriptions of therapeutic work.

What is unique about this book is the opportunity it allows for an unfolding story of a particular experience of war trauma. The length of time I have been working with Holocaust survivors, plus the depth of my involvement, means that outcomes can be observed from the interventions which have been made. It allows me to ask questions from the survivors about the usefulness of the services to them, and whether they notice differences in how they live with their trauma. Many books on war trauma that I have read have been collections of chapters by different authors about individual experiences of working with the aftermath of war. Conclusions are different from the cross-section of settings and approaches. What are missing, as Bracken and Petty (1998) conclude at the end of their book on war trauma, are 'studies that attempt to make more serious analysis of the effectiveness of trauma programmes' (p.189). That being so, this longitudinal account finds its rightful place in the understanding of those professionals who are trying to alleviate the suffering of people traumatised by war. For that reason I wish to pass on what I have learned. I make no claims to impose this model over any other way of working, but only offer a point of reference from which adaptations can be made.

The impact of developing services for the Holocaust survivors not only has an effect on *their* lives, but has influenced the way *I* respond to suffering in a wider context. The positive and hopeful feedback from the survivors gives me more confidence to respond to more recent trauma, namely that of the Bosnian refugees, with whom I have worked for the past seven years. The lessons I learned from the Holocaust survivors have direct relevance to how I am able to respond in more meaningful ways to the integration of the refugees in our community. Living next to the survivors' trauma for so long fine-tuned my hearing to the 'cries' of refugees from Bosnia. I have interwoven the development of my work with the Bosnian refugees, adapting the model, allowing for differences, but nevertheless responding in a more informed way to their needs because of the lessons I have learned from the Holocaust survivors.

Finally, brief work with the co-ordinator of a project for Rwandan refugees has opened a door to the connectedness of this work to asylum seekers currently arriving in the UK and elsewhere. The suffering of those close to us makes us conscious of the suffering of those with whom we are not as yet familiar. A house next door to trauma becomes a metaphor for that heightened awareness of suffering. The end of the journey opens up a new beginning in which the legacy left behind by the Holocaust survivors will live on long after they have ceased to exist.

PART I

Facing the Dark Shadow

Introduction

Beginning this journey into the world of extreme suffering presents us immediately with a paradox and dilemma. As non-survivors who wish to work with those who survived starvation, dehumanisation and torture, we need to immerse ourselves in that 'other world' to which we will always remain outsiders. Exposure to the survivors' suffering may increase our risk of suffocation in the filth and excrement which characterised life in extremity. However, if we save ourselves from exposure to that 'other world', we cannot begin to get closer to those who have been forced to experience first-hand the horrors that accompany victimisation under tyranny.

Those who were 'selected' had no choice in their passage from the world of the living to a world of death and destruction. They had no way of knowing what to expect, what they would feel or how they would cope. The mind tried in vain to make sense of what was happening as people were herded into cattle wagons, as people around them were shot and beaten, as neighbours who were once trusted friends started hurling stones at them and vandalising their property. There was a sense of foreboding – no-one was safe. Life was no longer governed by the same set of values that had existed up until the onset of the trauma.

So much literature describes in graphic detail the sickening stench of the prisoners' own journey on their way to the hell they were about to encounter. As the journey unfolds in the pages of this book, so reference will be made to these essential texts. They make difficult reading. However, our task at this stage of the journey is to open the door just enough for us to acknowledge the abnormality of that 'other world' which, to use Daniel Bar-On's (1999) words, is 'indescribable' and 'undiscussable'. The choice remains for the reader as to whether the door is closed again, or opened wider, in order to pass through.

To work with survivors of extreme trauma, we are challenged to pass through the door. However, we must first prepare ourselves. We need to be sure that we are willing to get closer to an understanding of extreme trauma; that we are strong enough personally to be touched by the pain of the survivors' suffering; that we are prepared to have our professional assumptions questioned; that we can open ourselves up to the complexity of trauma and equip ourselves for the journey ahead.

To begin to address the indescribable, we first have to communicate in a language we understand. The story that follows uses words that are familiar to describe a situation that is unknown to us. We are led into a world in which we can assume nothing.

Chapter 1

Opening the Door to the World of Extreme Trauma

The alarm rang loudly. Was it already morning? In this twilight zone I was aware it was time to get up. I opened my eyes. Had I made a mistake? Had I set the alarm incorrectly the night before? Through the curtain in my bedroom, only darkness lurked outside. I checked the time. The clock read 7.15am I turned on the radio. After some minutes the announcer confirmed it was 7.20am. It was the middle of summer. The sky, normally bright, remained menacingly dark. My heart started to beat faster. I quickly got out of bed and went to the window. Cars were passing as usual and everyone seemed to be going about their daily business. No-one else seemed to have noticed that the day had not dawned. On the radio, 'Thought for the Day', the weather forecast, the news, all met my ears with regular precision and regularity. Everything else seemed perfectly normal.

Whom should I phone? Would they think I had lost my mind; should I just pretend that everything was all right and continue on my route to work? I looked in my diary. It was mapped out with meetings which would take me through the day. It wasn't day though; it was night. All the assumptions that had governed my thinking were thrown into chaos. I was confronting something I could never have imagined.

I had studied philosophy and was familiar with the need to question my beliefs and the complacency attached to them. Even my existence was put under the microscope: did I exist or not? A useful exercise for the mind at the time, sharpening the powers of logic and conceptual thinking. As an academic exercise, it was fascinating. As a reality of what was happening in the here and now, it was terrifying. I felt a kind of paralysis. There was an overwhelming sense of fear and aloneness. I wanted to scream and make everyone take notice of this dark shadow which was engulfing the outside world. What did it mean? Did it herald the end of the world? Or was it a vision which only I could see and, if so, why should that be?

I had achieved much academically and in my career and thought I had the skills to deal with situations of stress and trauma. I felt lost in this now unknown world which I could not understand. Memories came back from my childhood – vivid memories of the emptiness, fear and confusion surrounding childhood grief. No-one talked; no-one explained what had happened. The finality was as inexplicable as the dark cloud outside. Would the cloud ever lift? Would the darkness ever give way to light?

In this shadowy world were only glimpses of the world we see in daylight. In the 'normal' hours of darkness, our mind's eye compensates for the silhouettes and fragments which make up the reality of night. When the daylight returns, we are reassured that all is well and the apparent fragments are still part of a whole. Only the darkness made them appear broken and disconnected.

We need to feel secure in the knowledge that the daylight world is the real world; that we are not being deceived by what we see; that it is not an illusion. The foundation on which we build our world must be as sure as day follows night.

It was that security which was being threatened. I peeped out again from behind the curtain. The sky remained dark. Was this really happening to me, or was I witnessing something from another time, and another place? This latter realisation, this boundary between dreaming and awakening, was suddenly transformed by a sound familiar to me which I thought I had already heard – the sound of my alarm clock. It was indeed 7.15am And the light was streaming into my room.

As I emerged from my bed, I felt a duality of emotion. First, a tremendous sense of relief that the day had in fact dawned. At the same time, a weightiness hung upon my shoulders in the aftermath of the fear which had threatened to overwhelm me in my dream.

In this nightmare I have described, some of the essence of a world which cannot be explained is contained. It is a world which defies the logic and continuity symbolised by the concept of day following night. There are rules but no-one is sure what they are. Our assumptions are invalidated, and factual evidence becomes meaningless.

When we are in pain, it always feels worse at night. We often feel alone, frightened, longing for the daylight to come. Those who experience severe trauma may see the dawn break, but it is as though the darkness continues and, with it, the fear, pain and feeling of abandonment.

> Never shall I forget that night, the first night in camp, which has turned my life into one long night, seven times cursed and seven times sealed... Never shall I forget that nocturnal silence which deprived me, for all eternity, of the desire to live... Never shall I forget these things, even if I am condemned to live as long as G-d Himself. Never! (Wiesel 1981, p.45, first published 1958)[1]

The suffering does not end when the victims of war are 'liberated'. It does not end when the displaced and uprooted find havens to flee to. The impact of trauma is profound. It creates wounds which cannot necessarily be seen. The effect of the suffering is often silent and buried until the means are found for a story to be told.

Though there can be no comparison in terms of suffering between this nightmare in the dream and the daytime reality of extreme trauma, it nevertheless can serve as an introduction to preparing the worker to think beyond the assumptions that govern our waking lives. However, these are abnormal circumstances we are now addressing, in which everything is thrown into disarray. Patrick Bracken (Bracken and Petty 1998), who has worked in Africa with victims of torture, writes: 'By showing that the discourse on trauma has been organised around certain assumptions, I hope I will show how it is also limited by these assumptions' (p.42). As outsiders to the suffering, there is a tendency to promote myths about what really happened in the trauma. For example, survivors of the Holocaust have been described as going 'like a lamb to the slaughter' (Isaiah: Chapter 53, Verse 7). Why was there so little resistance? In reality, those who were starving, weak, humiliated and tortured, as well as having no weapons, had no way of resisting openly. If prisoners did escape, the punishment for those left behind was brutal. Yet there was resistance. Those who worked as slave labourers, making weapons in the ammunition factories in the death camps, may have used sabotage to ensure the weapons would not work. Small acts of kindness from one prisoner to another could also be seen as a small victory over Hitler's plan to reduce the prisoners to animals.

It is in the minutia, in the detail, as we search and seek out what we do not know, that we engage in the world of suffering. 'Helping agencies have a duty to recognise suffering, but are there to attend to what the people carrying the suffering meant to signal by it' (Summerfield 1998, p.34).

In the maelstrom of this topsy-turvy world of trauma, we can begin to distinguish the individual. No two survivors or refugees are the same. What happened to them before, during and after the trauma is different for each of them. They coped and adapted in a variety of ways. Early experiences of childhood; whether they remained with their families during the trauma; the social, political and cultural context of the trauma; the age they were at the time of the trauma; the level of suffering in the trauma; their religious faith during the trauma; and what happened to them after the trauma – all affected their responses later on. As Derek Summerfield writes, 'There is no such thing as a universal trauma response, and we must take a relativistic approach' (Summerfield 1998, p.31).

This helps us to identify with survivors of trauma as human beings. They are just like you and me, but with one main difference. They have confronted horror face to face. Steven Spielberg, in his film *Schindler's List*, and Claude Lanzmann, in his documentary *Shoah*, have helped to personalise the experience of suffering. Each character has a name and a story to tell. We need to remain passive and listen, as each one informs us about what happened. The grandchild of one of the survivors I see, in describing her trip to Auschwitz-Birkenau with her grandmother, wrote, 'I have the same brown eyes as my grandmother, but they have not seen what she has seen.'

To expose ourselves to pain and suffering, we need to look inwards on ourselves as further preparation to undertake this work.

Endnote

1. Excerpts from *Night* by Elie Wiesel, translated by Stella Rodway. Copyright © 1960 by MacGibbon & Kee. Copyright renewed © 1988 by The Collins Publishing Group. Reprinted by permission of Hill and Wang, a division of Farrar, Straus and Giroux, LLC. Permission to reprint is also granted by Sheil Land Associates Ltd, London.

Chapter 2

Personal Preparation to Confront the Dark Shadow

Survivors and refugees I have encountered have frequently said to me that when they wanted to talk about their suffering in the Holocaust, whether they were in therapy or in any social situation, there seemed to be a reluctance to touch the subject. One survivor I met had suffered severely in a death camp and unusually had physical signs of the brutality – her fingers had been mutilated through frostbite from the extreme cold she had to endure. When she tried to tell people the real reason why she was handicapped, they did not respond. She learned to tell another story – namely, that she had been in an accident. The response was then one of sympathy rather than revulsion.

This blocking off and avoidance of the pain of a person who has suffered has contributed to what became known as a 'conspiracy of silence' (Danieli 1984) between the listener and the speaker. On the one hand, the survivor may feel no-one can ever really understand what he/she has been through, so why bother to speak about it? On the other hand, the non-survivor feels impotent as a sense of grief and loss threatens to overwhelm him/her.

The avoidance of asking the pertinent questions is part of what Robert Krell calls 'a self-protective strategy' (Krell 1989, p.217). Sometimes the survivor is blamed for the 'failure of treatment'. This 'self-protection,' he says, 'may not differ greatly from other painful subjects avoided by therapists for fear of revelations about experiences for which treatment responses are primitive or inadequate. In recent times, the dimensions of sexual abuse have become known because therapists began to pose the pertinent questions' (p.217).

To try to address this complex feature in our work, it is important to understand our personal views in relation to the concept of the victim and the traumatised. This may help us to avoid making inappropriate therapeutic responses. My opening remark in training professionals to work with survivors and refugees is to ask the question, 'How do you understand the term "survivor"?' The responses range from seeing survivors as vulnerable, pathetic victims to people with enormous strength and superhuman qualities. To the former, we may feel pity for their suffering and wish to make reparation in some form. To the latter, we may feel inadequate or in awe and consequently impotent to help them.

To see the traumatised person only as victim brings with it a sense that the survivor is so fragile that he/she would fall apart if the trauma was brought into the conversation. There may also be a sense of guilt on the part of the listener due to the fact that he/she has not suffered in a similar way to the survivor of the trauma. Yael Danieli (1989), who has focused on the 'counter-transference' themes of therapists, writes that there may be a fear that the therapist will be 'drawn into a vortex of such blackness that I may never find clarity and may never recover my own stability so that I may be helpful to this patient' (p.14).

Such fear is also bound up with what Robert Krell (1989) calls the rage of the survivor. It is a rage 'too great for vengeance. It is so enormous, survivors must settle for justice.' Krell, who is himself a survivor, advocates that the 'expression of rage, properly directed, is itself, healing' (pp.218–19). This rage needs a conduit. This will be looked at later when the focus shifts to ways of dealing with these overwhelming emotions through our specialist services. Suffice to say at present, whoever wishes to work with the severely traumatised must have the courage to address this question, and develop a more appropriate strategy to face it, rather than avoid it.

As I began entering this world of extreme trauma, I felt an immense sense of isolation. I began to ask myself the questions, 'Who am I?' 'What is it in me that is being drawn towards this suffering?' 'What am I?' My training and professional role were now under scrutiny. 'Why me?' There were so many other therapists who could undertake this work: why did I have to focus on it?

These existential questions helped me to address some of the contributing factors from my own background and life which were predisposing me to find the inner strengths to venture into the unknown. An opportune meeting with

Dr Shamai Davidson, a psychiatrist working in Israel with Holocaust survivors, helped in this process of introspection. The understanding and warmth I received from him, the very particular way that he listened to my fears and confusion, served as a model for my encounters with survivors and refugees. I no longer felt on my own – someone else understood the process I was going through. This support is a basic prerequisite for all those wishing to embark on such work.

My personal connection with those who have been persecuted and uprooted comes from my mother's experience as a refugee from Nazi persecution. However, she was already in her thirties when she arrived in Britain in August 1939 and had therefore experienced a stable and happy home life for many years before Hitler came to power. Despite her losses, despite the incarceration of my grandparents in a camp in France (Gurs), despite the murder of many family members in Auschwitz, the Holocaust was never an over-evident aspect in our lives. My father was English, and my mother adapted herself to life in England in such a way that German was never spoken at home. All that remained was her accent, her Gothic script and her wonderful recipes tasting of times past. This food turned into nourishment for the mouths of other dislocated people – refugees my father brought home as part of his work in the Jewish community. Refugees from other persecutions in Iraq and Egypt, as well as from Germany who came here on the Kindertransport (whereby 10,000 endangered children were brought to the UK in 1938 and 1939), were regularly welcomed into our home, some staying with us for many years. This exposure as a child to people who had suffered, and the supportive response of my mother, perhaps unconsciously guided me into my work many years later.

My grandfather, who lived in our home during his last years, was haunted by memories of his time in the camp. As his mind wandered, it lodged itself in the trauma of both his and my grandmother's suffering. The repetition of these events in his life also impacted on me as an adult. The way my mother converted her suffering into something positive, by caring for others who had suffered, became a beacon of light for me. It allowed me to see the vision of extending such care to a wider community of survivors and refugees.

This motivation, however, was not the whole story. There remained the problem of what Klaus Hoppe calls the 'danger of over-identification' of the helper. 'Over-identification includes feeling overwhelmed by pity and one's own guilt feelings' (1989, p.41). Certainly, in my early days of working with severely traumatised survivors, there was a wish to make reparation for their suffering, by helping them in practical ways to try to make their lives a little easier as they were growing older. Such approaches, while useful on one level, nevertheless focused on the dependence and vulnerability of the person seeking help, thereby reinforcing his/her image as victim and myself as saviour. This may have made me feel better, but pertinent questions remained unanswered about the hidden agendas of these survivors and refugees.

Acknowledging the traumatised person's past, acknowledging the suffering, acknowledging also the strengths which have brought him/her to this moment in time allows the subject of trauma to be raised. It is then up to the person who has suffered as to how he/she wishes to proceed with it. To be able to convey empathy without an over-identification with the sufferer requires a delicate balance.

This raises the question of whether you have to be Jewish to work with Holocaust survivors. Is it better or worse in terms of identification to be a child of survivors and offer therapy? Similarly, can someone from a Serb background work with Croats? Can someone who is white work with a black population? Can someone from a different political regime – for example, a democratic one – work with people who have been under a Communist regime?

In my experience of working in a Jewish organisation, there is an expectation that the therapeutic staff are Jewish. In terms of the Race Relations Act, we are allowed to mention this specifically in our advertisements. However, this does not mean that non-Jewish people cannot work with survivors from the Holocaust. Indeed, there are some survivors who would not use a Jewish service, either because they lost their sense of belonging to Judaism in the Holocaust and felt G-d had abandoned them, or they were converted to Christianity to save their lives. Alternatively, they may feel animosity towards the Jewish community for not having done enough to help them when they needed it. Other, more orthodox Jewish survivors may feel the services at Jewish Care are too 'secular' for them.

However, to work with Holocaust survivors, as a Jew, makes demands on the professional to look at his/her own identity. Paul Marcus (1989) has noted:

> Issues of Jewish identity, faith in G-d, involvement in organised religion, intermarriage, and other issues of self-definition after the Holocaust, are particularly painful for the survivor or child of a survivor patient to work through, when the therapist[s] themselves have their own unresolved conflicts and blind spots about their own Jewish identity. (pp.41–2)

If the professionals cannot get beyond their own ambivalence towards their Judaism, then therapeutic aspects related to mourning, such as saying Kaddish (Jewish prayers for the dead) for those family members of the survivor who have been murdered, or dealing with memorial stones to be consecrated for those annihilated, may never be dealt with.

I have the unusual and positive experience of being line-managed by a non-Jew, at the same time as having a Rabbi as my consultant. I will say more about this later.

In the job description for a specialist worker working with Holocaust survivors, technical competence and professional qualification is only part of the equation in relation to the suitability to do such work. In the interview situation we have to assess whether someone has the inner strength not only to confront trauma, but also to deal with the turbulent process of unlearning familiar ways of working. Has someone come from a situation in which he/she was an 'expert' and will now find him/herself having to adopt a position of humility and not knowing? What do you do and how do you feel when 'a survivor has just told you of witnessing the death of his children? Which of us wants to step into the abyss with the survivor and into such depths of anguish and rage that one can do nothing but weep?' (Krell 1989, p.218).

How have the helpers dealt with trauma in their lives? What coping mechanisms have they adopted? What support networks do they have, both in the work situation and outside? What interests or hobbies do they have which will serve as a balance to the stressful nature of the work? How able are they to draw boundaries between working and not working? Are they rigid or flexible types of people? How do they feel about working informally and socially with people as well as in a counselling/therapy role?

Personally, I have managed to stay in this specialised work for this long because I have balanced my deep commitment to working with survivors with strategies that offer me either alternative involvement or diversion from the trauma. I endeavour to keep to working hours and not take work home with me. Even in the writing of this book, I have a designated workday for this purpose, with the support of Jewish Care, my employer. I have come to know my own threshold of pain; I take care not to overstep it.

In a similar vein, I pursue this balance in my recreational life. So many films, plays, books and television programmes are devoted to the theme of the Holocaust that it would be easy to become obsessed with the subject. While these are important developments in educating a wider audience, my own equilibrium is maintained through immersing myself in other worlds of creative work. My passion for opera, theatre, film and music can lift me from the dark shadow I witness in my work. These recreational interests also bind me to the survivors, who use similar strategies to lighten the darkness in their lives. The space outside of work, whether recreational, familial or social, helps to reinforce the strength which emanates from the world of life and the living, of which I am a part. It is an essential strategy for 'survival' for those who work daily with people who have suffered severe trauma.

Taking care of ourselves and finding meaning in our lives brings a positive force into our work. In my experience, survivors seem to know very quickly whom they feel can help them. Much of this emanates from the worker – the interest shown in the survivor, and the personal information given of him/herself. For example, survivors pick up rapidly if the helper sees him/herself as the authority – as the one who has the power and control. Such characteristics are an anathema for people who have been victimised.

We have to continue to ask ourselves the question – why am I attracted to working with traumatised people? For example, those attracted to work with elderly people, which is often seen as the least desirable of the helping professions, may do so to have power over a vulnerable group, rather than for caring reasons. Those who are vulnerable, who do not wish to draw attention to themselves, can be prey to being further victimised in a therapeutic context. The screening process in appointing specialist staff to work with ageing survivors and refugees must therefore address these difficult issues.

Knowing ourselves, honestly facing who we are, is not an optional extra. Joan Freyberg (1989) has pointed out that those working intensively with traumatised people need supervision and support 'in order to deal with their difficulties in facing their inner terror when they listen to the gruesome stories about when Hansel and Gretel were really pushed into the oven' (p.95). To do the work properly, the worker must be affected by what he/she hears. At times of great difficulty, support must be available. If not, burn-out would result quite rapidly. Alternatively, defence mechanisms would emerge to block off the pain.

Looking inwardly on ourselves, acknowledging the need to be professionally challenged, begins to wear down some of the veneer which protects us. In the face of the complexity of trauma, we must learn to be humble. However, in reassessing our competence to undertake this specialised work, we need more information before we can proceed to adapt our ways of working. We now turn to the complexity of trauma as a guide to some of the issues we need to take into account.

Chapter 3

The Complexity of Trauma

Having raised an awareness of how our personal issues impact on our ability and aptitude to work with severely traumatised people, we can now turn our attention to how trauma affects the lives of the traumatised long after the horror has ceased. Each one of us will have faced some trauma in our lives, and can thereby understand something of the impact it can make – but what of severe or prolonged trauma such as that encountered during the Nazi Holocaust? To address this question, we first need to look at the complexity of trauma. Rather than trying to define trauma, I would like to break down trauma into some of its component parts. This process will help the reader to shift his/her thinking towards the practical responses which need to be made that are meaningful to those who have undergone the trauma. This aspect will be dealt with in Part II.

The effects of loss, grief and mourning in relation to trauma

Let us start with the familiar. It is difficult for us to go through life without experiencing one or more of the following: loss of health, a bereavement of someone close to us, loss of work, divorce or moving house, to name but a few. Most of us would be aware of the processes of mourning as described by Bowlby (1982). He differentiated four main phases of mourning: numbing, yearning and searching, disintegration and despair, and finally reorganisation. These responses are seen on a continuum, fluctuating back and forth among the phases over a period of weeks or months, and vary from person to person.

When losses are massive, and when grief work is interrupted by the trauma itself, the outcome may be different. The final stage may never be reached. The survivors of the trauma may remain locked in their grief, with this 'unfinished business' staying with them for many years after the event.

If we take, for example, prisoners in the death camps during the Holocaust, any expression of grief would have been life-threatening. As Brainin and Teicher (1997) observed, 'Grief was a luxury that one could afford only under relatively secure conditions. During the period of imprisonment, it could not find its ritualised framework' (p.91). For these camp survivors, grief became suspended. There was no ritual for burying the dead, no formalised way of saying goodbye or letting go. When they emerged from the camps, this grief was confirmed rather than resolved. The often hopeless searching for lost relatives and communities reinforced the reality that all was indeed lost.

Post-war experiences in displaced persons camps, or the continuing persecution for those who remained in Poland, did nothing to create an environment in which any 'healing' could take place. *The Truce*, a film based on Primo Levi's (1965) book about his return to Italy after Auschwitz, graphically illustrates the chaos in Europe after the war. Liberation did not mean freedom. The dead were not buried, but were carried inside the survivors. Many survivors have described this phenomenon to me as being like a stone lodged in their bodies.

We did not know then what we know now about the impact of such massive losses over time. Expression of grief after the war was discouraged. There was a sense that it was best to leave all the horror behind. However, we now realise that if this grief work is not completed, it can re-emerge even forty or fifty years after the trauma has ceased.

In a survey I carried out in the early 1980s among GPs working in areas highly populated by refugees and survivors of the Holocaust, responses were overwhelmingly negative on the subject of developing therapeutic services for ageing survivors. First, they were not even aware of how many of their patients were traumatised in the Holocaust. Second, they felt that the past should be forgotten, and it was already too late to deal with it. The survivors should be left to die quietly. The naivety of these responses did not deter me. I continued to gain first-hand evidence from the survivors about their wish to address their unfinished grief in the latter part of their lives.

The effects of age in relation to trauma

This subject will be looked at in two parts:

- the age of the person when the trauma began
- how the ageing process contributes to the re-emergence of trauma in later life.

The age at which the trauma began

Natan Durst (1995) and Judith Kestenberg (Kestenberg and Brenner 1986) concur that, generally speaking, the younger the child was when he/she went through the trauma, the greater the effect in later life. For a child on his/her own in the Holocaust, the sense of deprivation (physical and material) and abandonment by parents was so great that his/her secure base, as Bowlby (1982) termed it, was threatened (Attachment Theory). Among all the multiple losses child survivors experienced, they also share with each other the burden of dealing with a lost childhood (Fogelman 1991).

Kestenberg and Brenner (1986) paint a vivid picture of what it meant for a child to be under Nazi rule:

> Under Nazi rule, adults and children were subjected to a curious mixture of rules, routines and sudden changes, difficult to understand…the degradation of parents whose values were shattered, resulted in a confusion over 'who to listen to', the adult relatives and teachers, the Nazis or the street-wise older children. The usual pattern of listening to an adult took on a bizarre twist. Obedience could result in getting caught, being deported or dying; at other times, strict obedience to parents' directions were necessary to avoid the same dangers… The trust of the child in the traditional protection of the family and the authorities was severely undermined. (pp.310–311)

To understand what child survivors went through we have to immerse ourselves in this trauma. We have to prepare ourselves to confront these extremely painful stories. Much is made these days of the effect on a child of the loss of a parent, as seen in the work of Dora Freeman Black (Black and Urbanowicz 1983). Children need to be listened to and helped in their grief. Multiply this many times over and we hear the voices of children who came unaccompanied on the Kindertransports having to leave their families behind, not really knowing that they would never see them again. We hear children who were 'hidden' in the Holocaust, some of whom had to endure abuse, including sexual abuse, by those who were hiding them. Such disturbing details were also revealed in a BBC Radio 4 series about evacuee children in Britain during the war. In addition, we hear the children who were living wild in the forests of Europe, scavenging for food in order to stay alive.

Perhaps the depths of this descent into the hell-hole of suffering can be found in Paul Valent's book *Child Survivors – Adults Living with Childhood Trauma* (1993). Eva, a child survivor, described her experiences as a twin in Auschwitz, and the horror she felt when remembering that Mengele made the children play 'The Farmer Had a Wife' (p.26). One child would be placed in the centre and asked to choose another child, unaware that the chosen child was to be taken for experiments. These so-called 'medical' experiments, carried out on twins in Auschwitz, test to the limit our capacity to stay with the pain. It changes our perception of the world and how we relate to it. The extent of man's inhumanity to man is embodied in it, and needs recognition by those who will encounter the severely traumatised.

In another hell-hole, Bergen-Belsen, some children remained with their families in the camp. One such person I have encountered felt that the presence of his parents formed a buffer, or protective shield, against the hostile world of the camp. Another child survivor, who remained with her sisters in Auschwitz, felt that this was one of the factors that helped her survive, even though only the Nazis decided who should live and who should die. Such differences in experiences need to be noted, rather than taking age as a separate indicator as to the potential impact of the trauma.

Similarly, children's experiences at home, and their relationship to the parents prior to the trauma, seemed to make differences in terms of the impact of the trauma. What happened to these children after the war also served to either exacerbate the effects of the trauma or soften it. However, we can make no assumptions about what we feel to be mitigating factors. For example, we may think that a reunion between a 'hidden' child and his/her original family after the war would have brought longed-for relief. Our experience in working with this group of children traumatised in the Holocaust led us to hear accounts of the additional trauma for some of them when their families claimed them. Some who had been converted to Catholicism to save their lives then faced confusion in their identity when their Jewish families wanted them to re-adopt their religious practices.

The accounts of evacuee children (Charles Wheeler, BBC Radio 4, 1999) also indicated that some of them had grown used to the relative luxury encountered during their evacuation, compared to the poverty they were forced to return to in the East End of London after the war. Some Kindertransport children were placed in families who looked after them well and allowed some bonding and attachment to take place, and this seemed to help to counterbalance the impact of the separation from the families they left behind. Others who were less fortunate felt an intense and ongoing sense of isolation and loss, as recounted in ...*And the Policeman Smiled* (Turner 1990).

Whatever the individual circumstances, the suffering of children who have been traumatised affects us deeply. They differ from adult survivors of trauma in that their emotional foundations were only just being formed. Their developmental immaturity leaves many of them vulnerable to additional traumas in life. We need to pay special attention to their 'missing years' of childhood; the years which they feel were stolen from them. In understanding their trauma we are more likely to cater for their particular needs in the therapeutic services we provide. Such knowledge has encouraged us to work more sensitively with those more recently traumatised. The importance of keeping families together after the Bosnian war has become an important focus in the work the Jewish Refugee Committee has undertaken in addressing the emotional impact of the trauma. By keeping families together it is hoped that we can prevent the long-term vulnerabilities which emerged for the children who were left alone to cope with their trauma.

How the ageing process contributes to the re-experiencing of trauma in later life

If old age is seen as a time of consolidation and a preparation for letting go, what happens if the past cannot be consolidated into the present? What happens when the past that is reflected back is so full of trauma that remembering it is a nightmare? What happens when the notion of growing old is equated with extermination in gas ovens rather than natural death?

As we grow older under 'normal' circumstances, we have more time to reflect on what has happened in our lives. When we retire from work, when children have left home, and our days tick by ever more rapidly, we tend to drift in and out of events we have experienced. As Jean Amery (1999) writes, 'For ageing makes us dependent to an increasing degree on the memory of the past' (p.57). In comparison to a young person, he maintains, 'the credit of the person who is aging depletes. His horizon presses in on him, his tomorrow and day-after-tomorrow have no vigor and no certainty. He is only who he is' (p.58).

This rather sad image seems bound up in Amery's own experience in the Holocaust. He felt similarly to Alfred Mombert (Amery 1999), the seventy-year-old poet he met in Gurs internment camp. The dislocation and trauma in which everything was taken away from them by the Nazis, as Mombert described, was as though 'everything flows off me like a great rain... Everything had to remain behind, everything' (p.59). It led Amery to conclude that 'one ages badly in exile' (1999, p.60).[1]

However, what is felt by Jean Amery and other exiled and displaced people is echoed over and over again in accounts of other traumas which re-emerge in later life. This seems to be true whether they were war veterans, evacuees, Holocaust survivors or those who have been sexually abused. Details of this can be found in Hunt, Marshall and Rowlings's (1997) book on *Past Trauma in Late Life*. Linda Hunt emphasises that 'at least 10% of the population over 60 years of age may be suffering some continuing difficulty resulting from earlier traumatic experience' (pp.8–9). This being so, those who work professionally with people in the last phase of their lives have to be vigilant in picking up the links between present difficulties and past trauma.

The mechanisms involved in delayed trauma

Trauma delayed through misdiagnosis and misunderstanding

My own experience with Holocaust survivors gives some insight into the mechanisms involved in the delayed effect of trauma. After the war, the survivors themselves seemed to be ambivalent about remembering the past. In a sense their existence and the meaning of their lives was linked to their need to remember not only for themselves but also for those who perished. They needed to bear witness to what had happened. Davidson (1981, pp.55–63) highlighted the conflict between the survivors' sense of duty to remember and a wish to forget the horrors of what happened.

As so little was done about helping them to bear witness, these memories were repressed, as their energy became focused into making lives for themselves both at work and in raising their families. Many survivors achieved extremely well, and to the outside world it appeared, on the whole, that the trauma had been overcome.

It was not recognised that as we grow older we tend to have less control over what we want to remember. One survivor described this process to me as her 'nights beginning to invade her days'. The nightmares which had contained the horror became increasingly part of her daytime reality.

With Alzheimer's disease or dementia, this process could become even more difficult and, consequently, more distressing. This is the theme of Elie Wiesel's book *The Forgotten* (1992). It is the story of Elhanan, a Holocaust survivor who is losing his memory. He tells his son Malkiel, 'Try to remember what I tell you, because soon I won't be able to tell you anything' (p.27); '…soon I will be absent from myself. I'll laugh and cry without knowing why…' (p.62). 'Soon,' says Elhanan, 'I will envy the prisoner. Though his body is imprisoned, his memory is free. Whereas my body will always be free, but…' (p.61).[2]

The reliving of past trauma in the present is often triggered by a current loss. Loss of work (retirement), loss of health (illness), loss of someone close (bereavement) can all act as powerful stimuli for remembering the massive losses experienced in the trauma, irrespective of what the trauma was. The following illustration will address this phenomenon.

AN EARLY ENCOUNTER WITH A REFUGEE FROM NAZI PERSECUTION

Erna was a refugee in her eighties when I first met her. Most of her family perished in the Holocaust. She came to Jewish Care asking for a volunteer to help her to move house. On first contact it seemed to me that her level of anxiety was excessive for the request she was making. This was conveyed to her and we agreed to meet over a period of time to try to understand what had brought her to me at that moment in time. After all, she said she had managed for over eighty years.

However, before our meeting, she was involved in a road accident and was admitted to hospital. I continued to see her there. Erna refused to be operated on for a fractured leg and, indeed, refused all treatment for infection. In desperation, the staff called in a psychiatrist who diagnosed her as paranoid schizophrenic, without taking her background into account.

During her time in hospital, as she lay helpless and vulnerable and unable to move, she began to talk to me about her past, particularly her persecution under the Nazis. Her current helplessness seemed to reactivate similar feelings she had about being unable to save her mother, whom she had left behind, from being killed. She began to mourn for her mother which she said she had never done before.

Though she displayed considerable hostility with paranoid features towards the hospital staff, she allowed me to continue to see her regularly. Our relationship was not without difficulty, and I felt I was always walking a fine line between colluding with her paranoid feelings and becoming yet another persecuting 'Nazi' in her eyes by differentiating myself from her. However, I seemed to convey to her a sense that she was heard and believed and some feeling of trust developed.

I continued to see her weekly over one-and-a-half years. The move, which had brought her to me initially, turned out to be an eviction – a traumatic enough event at any time but, for her, it was also a reminder of her enforced 'eviction' from Germany as a refugee. Erna was able to share with me her real fear of breaking down mentally and being admitted to a psychiatric hospital. This did not happen, though she came very close to it. She made a successful move to new accommodation, thereby avoiding the trauma of eviction.

However, once the crisis was over, Erna's defences re-emerged. What she found so difficult to acknowledge was that, through our relationship, I had become significant to her. Once more in control of events, she defended herself against feelings of vulnerability and helplessness, first by trying to use my sessions with her to do practical tasks which the local authority worker was already doing and, second, by rejecting me altogether. Dr Hillel Klein (1968) has noted that this 'fear of getting to love someone' (p.233) is not uncommon in survivors of the Holocaust.

Understanding the reality base of her 'paranoia', rather than labelling her as psychiatrically ill, allowed us an opportunity to struggle with the fears and anxieties I had initially felt at our first meeting. Erna was a highly intelligent, articulate woman who internalised something from what transpired in our sessions. Despite a great deal of denial concerning the connections made between current and past trauma, we were able to work through some of the 'unfinished business' which had contributed to her vulnerability and sense of aloneness.

Entering into Erna's world gave me a unique opportunity to learn how to relate to someone who, in another setting, would be labelled as paranoid and consequently seen as having an impaired ability to relate. Erna had been touched by a 'mad' environment under the Nazis. She may have had some disturbance prior to this period, but there is no doubt that the reality of what she experienced affected her ability to trust. Despite her 'paranoia', she had amazing support from neighbours and friends as well as social services. There was a warmth that emanated from her and I tended to build on these strengths.

I could so easily have just seen Erna as yet another victim of Nazi persecution, perhaps feeling that her behaviour was understandable considering the trauma she had been through. Consequently, I might have tried to make reparation to her through practical provision and giving as much emotional comfort as possible. However, I believe it was the struggle and fight that constituted our work together that helped Erna to break out from the 'victim' category. It may have helped her to experience again a feeling of being in control of events so that her current trauma did not overwhelm her.

The re-emergence of trauma many years later is often so overwhelming that it has frequently been described as pathological. When I began my work with refugees and survivors in the mid-1970s, there was a sense that they had been damaged irreparably by their experiences. This view was partly due to the fact that compensation claims to Germany emphasised the need to look for causal connections between current emotional difficulties and the experiences in the Holocaust. The professionals were looking for 'sickness' to justify the claims. A medical model was developed known as survivor syndrome, and it was this model, with its classifications of symptoms and syndromes, which heavily influenced the thinking about 'treatment' responses. Diagnosis became the primary focus rather than understanding the nature of extreme experience, and the resultant 'prognosis' was a largely negative one.

The work of Bruno Bettelheim (1943, 1971), as well as Krystal and Niederland (Krystal 1968; Krystal and Niederland 1971), reinforced this pessimistic view on the possibility of healing the survivors. The latter emphasised survivor guilt as a major pathogenic force in severely traumatised survivors. Those who were seen as being unable to complete their mourning, because of their need to bear witness repeatedly to those heinous crimes, were diagnosed as neurotic at best, or pathological at worst. 'Identification with the aggressor' became the terminology or shorthand which rescued the diagnostician from a sense of failure to comprehend what really happened in the trauma.

The medical model then became applied to psychoanalytic treatment. Robert Krell (1989) believes the assumptions made from psychoanalytic knowledge about the experience of extreme trauma are 'badly flawed' (p.216). Steinberg (1989) also noted that an attempt to fit survivors into existing therapeutic frameworks found that the 'fit is not quite right'. There seemed to be little meeting point between the therapists, who tried to 'treat' survivors, and the survivors themselves, who wished to remain free from the labels which were being attached to them. The survivors I have spoken to feel deeply that they do not wish to be perceived as mentally ill. They want to be listened to, to be believed and to be seen as individuals – each on a continuum of pre-Holocaust and post-Holocaust experiences which influenced how they responded.

The basic misunderstanding in these attempts to deal therapeutically with the effects of severe trauma has been highlighted through work such as Victor Frankl's (1987) *Man's Search for Meaning*. Frankl, a Holocaust survivor himself, emphasised that it was the environment in the camps which was abnormal; the survivors' reaction to it was normal. This shifts the balance away from a pathological interpretation of the behaviour to a recognition of the severity of the trauma itself, and the inadequacy of explaining this away by professional terminology.

Marcus and Rosenberg (1988) also developed this thinking further by their critical survey of the different interpretations of the concept of survivor syndrome. 'They themselves raise serious objections to its legitimacy. They argue that the acceptance of the concept of survivor syndrome has led to viewing the survivor as so damaged that a cure is doubtful, or impossible' (p.15). They feel the term 'damaged' is inappropriate.

This does not mean that the survivors emerged from their ordeal unscathed. In my experience, they are the first to recognise the scars which they still carry with them. Some may have had experiences prior to the Holocaust which contributed to emotional problems later.

Others may have had diagnosed mental health problems prior to the Holocaust. For the vast majority, however, the emotional repercussions of the severe trauma do not need to result in needing psychiatric help, or even medical help, but an opportunity to have their trauma recognised within the context in which it happened. How they coped, sometimes without violating their own values, should be an area of study and learning for professionals.

This somewhat sedate presentation of the change in emphasis in our work with severely traumatised people masks the enormous impact which such changes potentially leave in their wake. The inadequacy of psychoanalytical and psychodynamic models in working with survivors of unimaginable horror has caused immense unease in the professional world. More and more literature is emerging which demands that we rethink our familiar theories and practices, *Healing their Wounds* (Marcus and Rosenberg 1989a) being a good example.

This debate has been raging for years and yet, even today, it appears as if it has all been enacted in silence. Just as the survivors from the Holocaust felt that their experiences fell on deaf ears, so it would seem to hold true of the professional world too. The evidence of this can be found in the more recent diagnostic term 'post traumatic stress disorder' (PTSD). Is this a new phenomenon? On closer examination, it would seem to be very similar to survivor syndrome and shell shock before it. Why has no connection been made, and why have the lessons which have emerged gone unheeded?

Falling back on the familiar at times of therapeutic impotence would seem to be a repeated theme. Psychiatric terminology brings order to the chaotic aftermath of trauma. It helps the therapist to feel safer in a world in which he/she is unfamiliar. PTSD is presented as a 'new discovery'. When talking about the effects of the Vietnam war, Robert Krell (1989) points out that the lessons which emerged from working with Holocaust survivors have not been taken on board, and the 'professional "unawareness" continues' (p.217).

I do not feel it is my task to go into further detail in order to make a comparative study of survivor syndrome and PTSD. In my view the fundamental flaw is in all such classifications – namely, that extreme suffering cannot be reduced to simplified categories. It only serves to reinforce the wedge between the professional and the sufferer.

More recently, Derek Summerfield (1998), in his work with the Medical Foundation for Victims of Torture, has come to the conclusion that PTSD is based on 'assumptions, and this is all they are...'(p.30). He goes on to say that these assumptions also 'demonstrate the danger of looking at war with a gaze borrowed from a psychiatric clinic, and the application of a paradigm that transforms the social into the biopsychomedical. This is a serious distortion serving neither the interests of the survivors nor the funders.' He warns against labelling survivors through terminology such as PTSD, which he maintains is a 'pseudocondition...that not only pathologises but may dehumanise survivors by stripping them of the complexity of their living realities and associations' (p.31).

The naivety of the professional's responses to the complexity of trauma delayed the possibility of meaningful services being developed for the survivors. They continued to be left very much to cope on their own. The blame was often put on the survivors for not being able to use existing services, rather than the services being looked at in terms of their suitability to meet the needs of severely traumatised people. The complexity of trauma demands complex responses. How we develop these responses will be shown later on, when we have adapted further to this new situation in which we find ourselves.

Trauma delayed through difficulties in asking for help

For those who did want to speak, for those who did want to get some help, there were other obstacles to be overcome apart from the labelling and misunderstanding.

Jean Amery (1999), in writing on the subject of torture, draws from his personal experience when he says: 'At the first blow...trust in the world breaks down... It is like a rape, a sexual act without the consent of one of the two partners' (p.28).[3] Those who have been violated, dehumanised and victimised by an oppressor fear those who are in authority or who have power over them. Uniforms, institutions or any form of bureaucracy are an anathema.

To be a victim is to feel vulnerable and powerless. Asking for help, however innocuous, brings back feelings of helplessness. This is true despite the seemingly benevolent nature of the 'helping professions'. The other person, from whom help is being requested, then has the power to help or not to help. He/she is seen as an authority figure – can he/she be trusted or is he/she another Nazi/persecutor? For someone whose trust has been shattered, the fortifications which protect the professional therapist have to be broken down. I am convinced that if I had remained in my office waiting for survivors to come and see me to address the trauma they carried with them, I would still be waiting. Reaching out to survivors provides the avenue along which to meet this person who is fearful to trust. That trust has to be earned through repeated acts of accessibility and reliability by the professional worker.

Trauma delayed through the post-trauma climate

It is difficult to believe today, with television's constant reports on war and the effects of trauma, that, only a short while ago, such open coverage was very sparse. The war in Kosovo highlighted the plight of refugees and what displacement meant. Admittedly there were political reasons for this coverage – namely, Britain's personal involvement. When we are no longer bystanders to events in the world, our attention is more focused on the issues.

In contrast, the silence of the world towards the Holocaust survivors echoed throughout society when World War II ended. In schools, history lessons gave no attention to the Holocaust. Films, theatre, literature and the media all remained closed on the subject. The Nuremberg trials were possibly seen as a closure of these heinous crimes against humanity. The establishment of the State of Israel – a homeland for the Jews – was thought to move the process of forgetting on, leaving the past behind. Permission to talk only really arrived with the fiftieth anniversary of the ending of the war and the 'liberation' of the camps.

The lifting of this blanket of silence turned attention to others who had suffered. Japanese prisoners of war are also beginning to find a voice. The atrocities meted out to them reveal a similar long-term impact of the trauma.

Trauma delayed and its impact on health

The years of deprivation in World War II left long-term physical vulnerabilities for the survivors. Years and years of silence compounded these vulnerabilities due to the resultant stress being offered no conduit. The evidence of this was not seen immediately. Indeed, the survivors initially seemed to recover from the starvation and brutalisation they endured and became '"invulnerable" to "normal" threats, such as illness. Death was only imaginable as a result of force, by murder' (Brainin and Teicher 1997, p.89). More recent evidence, however, has indicated that a biological vulnerability was left by the trauma which predisposes the survivors to difficulties as they grow older.

Bas Schreuder (1997), a psychiatrist working with survivors in Holland, believes that it is this factor together with psychological ones which contributes to the re-emergence of trauma as people grow older, rather than 'age-specific changes' (pp.17–31). Floribel Kinsler (1998) draws attention to both cancer and heart disease being threats to survivors in later life. From my experience, evidence of this has been seen quite dramatically in the last year of our work. The onset of such life-threatening illnesses seems to be sudden and severe, and confronts the ageing survivor with his/her own mortality. Kinsler also notes early cases of osteoporosis as well as breast cancer in child survivors.

Despite this evidence, and despite our knowledge about the impact of prolonged stress on health, no compensation claims can be made by Holocaust survivors on the grounds of ill health if these were not submitted by the 1960s at the latest. The monetary implication of proving such causal connections has led to inconclusive lessons regarding more recent traumas such as the Gulf war. This is despite the fact that we know from the examination of people who have been traumatised in road accidents, for example, that their injuries often do not appear till many years after the accident. The often long-term time delay in the physical or psychological repercussions is not accepted as evidence for compensation from war.

The predisposition to health problems in later life due to earlier severe physical and emotional deprivation is not overt, and is therefore often overlooked. The survivors of death camps, for example, had learned that to look frail or unwell would have meant immediate extermination. Survivors have reported to me how some women prisoners would draw blood from a finger to put on their cheeks and lips to give them some colour in order to look healthier. Physical appearance and signs of strength were essential requirements for work and therefore survival. Past responses have been adapted to current times. If you were to walk into our centres for survivors today, you would see a group of people who take above-average care with their appearance and are, on the whole, meticulous in terms of the image they present to the outside world. Yet they may carry within them the horrific memories of being lice-ridden, with sores on their bodies, hardly able to stand due to weakness, suffering dysentery, tuberculosis and life-threatening illnesses. To be sent for treatment was also life-threatening. Medical expertise was used for evil purposes, such as the well-known experiments of Mengele.

Those who work in the health professions therefore have to be particularly alert to the background of survivors traumatised in this way. Entering a hospital for a survivor can bring back memories of the death camp. To enter a hospital, to see staff in uniform, to have a number put on your wrist may evoke memories of the prisoners entering a death camp. To feel helpless and dependent on staff, to feel vulnerable to medical procedures, to lose control under an anaesthetic sometimes produce powerful negative reactions as the trauma is re-experienced.

As our services have become better known, medical staff in some hospitals have become more aware of the patient's Holocaust background. They use our specialist knowledge to assist them either through direct contact with the patient or by supporting their staff. However, this educative process is slow. In the meantime, it may be necessary, as I have done, to accompany the survivor to a hospital appointment both to support him/her and explain to medical staff about sensitivities that may be experienced.

An example of this was a child survivor who had been given the diagnosis of breast cancer. Her own mother had been murdered in Auschwitz and she had no close family to support her in this current ordeal. In the process of meeting the consultant, it emerged that he was seeking her permission to involve her in trials for the use of a particular drug. Such experiments were abhorrent to her. She wanted to refuse, but feared that this might produce a negative response from the doctor. My presence there allowed me the opportunity to speak to the doctor and explain about this person's Holocaust background, and why she did not wish to be included in these trials. The response could therefore be understood rather than dismissed as an unco-operative gesture.

The sensitivity to medical examination and procedures of those who have been severely traumatised applies to a wide range of experiences. The Medical Foundation for Victims of Torture, as the name suggests, provides its own medical advice and care for those who have suffered the humiliation and pain of torture.

In contrast, Annemiek Richter (1998), who worked with women who had been raped during the war in the former Yugoslavia, was alarmed by the often inappropriate quick-fix responses by many of the medical and mental health professionals who were brought in. She compares this to some of the women's support programmes and other more enlightened initiatives. She questions the assumptions that Western medicine can be universally applied in other cultures, and emphasises the need to listen to those who have been victimised. She concludes that '"sexual violence and women" should be adapted to particular socio-cultural contexts' (p.125). It is this emphasis on context which will be looked at next.

The context of the trauma

> At 4.30, 'coffee' – a light mint infusion without nourishment and with a repulsive taste – was distributed. We often took a few swallows and used the rest for washing, but not all of us were able to do without this poor substitute for coffee and consequently many inmates ceased to wash. This was the first step to the grave. It was an almost iron law: those who failed to wash every day soon died. (Donat 1967, p.173)

That was a glimpse of life in extremity under the Nazis. 'We will not understand the survivor's behaviour apart from its context. That is the context' (Des Pres 1976, p.45).

Each context needs to be understood, for each differentiates it from the other. Those who were in hiding, often living in confined, sometimes suffocating spaces, lived every minute in fear of being betrayed and discovered. They shared the powerlessness and fear of the victim, but may or may not have been subject to the starvation and brutalisation of those in the death camps.

The impact of trauma will vary according to the context in which it takes place. The effect of civil war, in which neighbour turns against neighbour, will be different than if the enemy is external. There will be different responses if traumatised people have to move countries and adopt a different mother tongue. There will be different responses if people return to their familiar surroundings after the trauma, such as the British who had been Japanese prisoners of war, compared to those whose communities were wiped out.

Those exiled from their homeland face additional trauma to the horrors they may have encountered in wartime. If you were told to leave your homeland within the hour, what would you take with you in the small case you were permitted to take? What would you feel like to leave behind all that was familiar to you in your home, your neighbourhood, your community? Moving home in peacetime is high on the hierarchy of stress factors in our lives. To move home forcibly, to be in exile, is worse than an eviction. Jean Amery (1999) writes, 'If one has no home, however, one becomes subject to disorder, confusion, desultoriness' (p.47).[3]

For a newly arrived refugee, the situation converts from one in which there may no longer be a literal threat to life to one in which his/her emotional life and meaning are fundamentally altered. Arriving in 1939 from Nazi Germany, for example, being perceived as an 'enemy alien', without money, without possessions, without family, without language, without status either of nationality or work, threatened one's whole sense of being. The war that followed, plus having to negotiate one's way around London, say, without street signs and without lighting, only exacerbated the stresses brought with the refugee. The nostalgic longing never left these refugees as they tried to create 'café societies' in the areas in which they settled.

The label 'refugee', used as a blanket term, does not give recognition to the diverse contexts the refugees come from or the particular circumstances in which they find themselves in in the host country. My more recent work with Bosnian refugees highlighted the political and economic context of the society they had lived in. This needed to be incorporated into the way we responded to their situation in this country. Politically, some had experienced both fascist and communist regimes. The Sarajevo community contained assimilated Jews and Moslems, Serbs and Croats. As refugees they were thrown together in their need to leave a war-torn community and seek refuge here. Their basic needs for food and shelter took precedence over the differences which could have divided them. However, these differences had to be understood and worked with in the subsequent approaches we took in offering them meaningful help. The employment of a Bosnian community worker to act as a facilitator helped to overcome linguistic difficulties and to raise awareness of the diversity and multiplicity of this refugee population.

The importance of the political and economic context has emerged over and over again in the work I have undertaken in Hungary and Slovakia. I needed to take account of the post-communist context which contributed to a state of passivity in the population arising from the doctrine that the State provided for all people's needs. This meant that the idea of self-help and mutual support were alien ideas in those communities, which affected the type of service which would be meaningful.

The differences between Eastern and Western Europe are only part of the equation. Patrick Bracken's (1998) work looks at an even wider context and comments:

> ...what clearly emerges from work in a number of areas is the importance of contextual factors in shaping the experience of and response to trauma. Issues of context are not secondary factors that merely impinge on the progress of a universal psychological or biological process. Rather, issues of context in terms of social, political and cultural reality should be seen as central to this experience and response. (p.55)

This argument leads Bracken to question the usefulness of intra-psychic inter-pretations of trauma which are exported from Western to non-Western societies. He also believes that the 'technical solutions' offered are often without meaning for those on the receiving end. He concludes that the challenge for those offering help is to support people through times of suffering by 'listening and hearing their different voices in a way that does not impose an alien order' (p.58).

In a similar vein, Jean Giller's (1998, pp.128–46) work in helping victims of torture in Uganda also takes issue with professionals' responses to them by treating the 'inner individual'. She felt this to be at odds with what she experienced in Ugandan society. She learned more from her observations of how the tortured Ugandans coped with their trauma without the aid of counsellors and therapists. It was practical assistance they needed rather than psychological help. Being there, immersing herself in Ugandan society, expe-riencing the hardships in the aftermath of trauma seemed to sensitise her to perceive what really helped these survivors to cope. It dispelled for her the myth of the 'expert', and it is in her humility that the seeds are sown for a more humane and appropriate response to the trauma.

For those of us who cannot visit the context in which the trauma takes place, or when we are faced with a trauma that is long past, we have to use our creative imagination to help us to be more in tune with the survivors and what they have been through. We have first and foremost to listen to them, to read about their experiences, and to familiarise ourselves with the context of the trauma. We need to ask questions, to learn from the survivors, and then our assumptions will be quickly dispelled. The theme of survivors as our teachers will be looked at later in the book when we focus more closely on the relation-ship between the survivor and the professional worker in our therapeutic approaches.

The severity of the trauma

We hear today of comparisons between 'genuine' refugees, who are persecuted and flee their countries of origin to save their lives, and 'bogus' refugees, who arrive here for economic reasons and self-betterment. Are those who leave their homelands to make a political statement against a totalitarian regime, such as those who left South Africa under apartheid, to be treated as 'non-essential' refugees?

Any attempt to compare suffering is doomed to failure and misconception. My eyes were opened wide on this issue when I began meeting with the first self-help group of survivors in the 1980s. There were survivors in this group from the death camps, as well as refugees who arrived in the 1930s. Early on in the group process, the participants were asked by the chairperson of the group (a camp survivor) to indicate what their wartime experiences had been, and why they wished to join the group. In listening to their responses, a hierarchy of suffering seemed to emerge. Those who had been in death camps believed that there was no suffering which could be compared to that experience. However, there was no general acceptance among those who had been in the death camps that their suffering was the same. Under this scheme, refugees were seen as having been 'lucky', and their voices were silenced in this climate of overwhelming pain.

The hierarchy also distinguished child survivors from adult survivors. The older survivors expressed the view that those who were children were too young to remember, and consequently did not suffer.

Not surprisingly, therefore, when we came to set up our services, we had to cater for these different experiences of trauma through separate groups. The 'hidden children' need to talk about their own unique experiences of suffering without having to feel guilty that they were not in camps. Those who came on the Kindertransport are also given space to talk of their unique experiences even though they may not have lived in fear of their lives from one minute to the next, unlike the children who had remained in Europe during the war.

When dealing with the Bosnian community, we needed to be aware that the older refugees were also Holocaust survivors, and therefore even more vulnerable to the effects of this current uprooting and displacement.

From the experience of working with Holocaust survivors, it emerges that the severity of the trauma does not necessarily have a direct effect on the ways the trauma is responded to by the individual. For example, some Kindertransport survivors continue to remain locked in their childhood grief – in a time warp – waiting to be reunited with their parents. On the other hand, some survivors who have been touched by death in the camps are able to find strategies to live in the present, even though their scars remain. We therefore cannot assume the outcome.

To begin to understand the severity of trauma, we also have to acknowledge the multiplicity of trauma. Annemiek Richter's (1998) work on sexual violence in wartime underlines the fact that women who are raped in war may also have suffered other violent traumas, 'such as loss of husbands, children, parents, relatives, homes, etc.' (p.18). Similarly, direct physical torture often exists alongside solitary confinement, starvation, sensory deprivation. We have no measure to identify the respective severity of each of these component parts.

Every response to trauma is interdependent on the relationship between the traumatised individual with his/her unique experiences, the trauma itself, and the environment or context before, during and after the trauma. The severity of trauma is not encapsulated. Thus the tortured and beaten prisoner may have had some relief from his pain when cared for by fellow prisoners.

Nietzsche once wrote, 'He who has a why to live for can bear almost any how' (in Frankl 1987). The importance of human reciprocity, of human values in an inhuman environment, seemed to lessen the severity of the pain (Davidson 1984). The Greek Jews who were not herded into ghettos and who, in a sense, had no time to establish support networks and camaraderie before deportation were decimated in the concentration camps. Not being left alone and being with others who share the pain have important implications when we come to look at how we deal practically in our therapeutic services with what Nietzsche refers to as the 'why to live for'.

The victim and the perpetrator in relation to trauma

When I was a child, I used to tell the following story:

> There was a man and there was a dog. The dog bit the man. The end.

Those who heard my little story would laugh and pat me on the head, probably thinking that it had a childlike simplicity but seemed somewhat lacking in its creative potential! Why do I remember that story even now? Why does it come back to me as I am addressing this very difficult and complex subject of trauma?

If we look at the story again in the light of my work with Holocaust survivors, the man could be seen as the victim, the dog as the Nazi perpetrator who inflicted pain and suffering on him. Taken to its nth degree, that was the end – the annihilation, the genocide, the Holocaust. The process of writing this does not flow freely. There is a fear of being misunderstood, a fear of getting it wrong and so alienating those I have tried to understand. The somewhat naive split in the story between the man and the dog – the one passive and the other the aggressor – masks the complexity of life in extremity.

In the stories of the eye-witnesses, we get a much richer analysis of the victim and the perpetrator. One survivor described her ordeal of going through 'selections' in the camps. While she lived in fear and dread that she would be selected for death, and as she grew weaker from the hardship she had to endure, she also described her image of Mengele standing before her. She noticed the bright shiny buttons on his jacket and his highly polished boots. She remarked on his good looks. Her own lice-ridden body contrasted sharply with this Aryan image. Another survivor told me the following:

> I looked at those well-fed Germans who externally looked like prime examples of the human race and yet inside were empty shells, devoid of those values which made them human. I looked at myself, whose outer shell was a pathetic specimen of life, yet inside I kept the values which my parents had given me and which no-one could take away.

The contrast here between the pathetic victim and the Aryan perpetrator hides a much more complex and sinister mechanism. Underpinning this dichotomy are the negative associations related to victims, which reinforced the Nazi belief in the notion of the 'Untermenschen', and their justification for the annihilation process.

Bruno Bettelheim (1943) and Hilde Bluhm (1948) also emphasised the image of the pathetic victim. To this they added their observation of prisoners who identified with the Nazi aggressor. Bettelheim (1971) wrote, '...old prisoners were sometimes instrumental in getting rid of so-called unfit new prisoners, thus patterning their behaviour on Gestapo ideology' (pp.169–70). Such theory rests on the rather simplistic notion expressed by film director Liliana Cavani in *The Night Porter* when she maintains that in every environment, and every relationship, there is a victim–executioner dichotomy.

Primo Levi (1988a) on the other hand – who, unlike Bettelheim, experienced first-hand the horror of the death camps – rejects such analyses. He argues, 'I do know that I was a guiltless victim, and I was not a murderer; I know that murderers existed, not only in Germany and still exist...and to confuse them with the victims is a moral disease...' (p.xvi). Levi is at pains to try to understand the complexity of behaviour in the camps when he looks at the subject of collaboration in its varying degrees of severity, including the Sonderkommandos (groups of prisoners whose horrendous daily tasks included working in the crematoria) and the Kapos (prisoners who, as camp barrack leaders, assisted in the administration of the camp in return for better treatment). While the terminology evokes revulsion, there was no uniformity of response among these collaborators. Shamai Davidson (1992a) describes the Kapos as the mediators between the victims and the perpetrators – some of whom were indeed vicious and malevolent while others were more benign.

> In spite of the rigidity of his role and function, many Kapos saved their comrades by influencing the SS men and preserving and encouraging group solidarity. On the other hand, some Kapos behaved to their fellow victims solely in terms of increasing their own chances of survival, which meant readiness to exploit and to sacrifice the other inmates without hesitation, including active participation in cruel beatings and tortures in order to impress the SS. (p.60)

Such observations draw us towards an understanding that good and evil, victim and aggressor, passive and aggressive, are on a continuum and not split simply into an either/or configuration. It led Primo Levi (1988a, pp.22–52) to identify what he called the Grey Zone and the Zone of Ambiguity. Perhaps only someone like Primo Levi could differentiate the levels of collaboration in the camps: the complexity of moments of pity amid unrelenting bestiality; the paradoxical image of SS guards playing football with prisoners from the Sonderkommando; the bizarre nature of mass murderers going home at night to their wives and children and their physical comforts.

Rather than blame the prisoner for collaboration, Primo Levi blames the system and structure of the totalitarian state. Levi (1988a) concludes, '...I ask you to meditate on the story of the "crematorium ravens" (Sonderkommondos) with pity and vigour, but that a judgement of them is suspended'. Instead he suggests all who would judge should first imagine living with 'chronic hunger, fatigue, promiscuity and humiliation, that he has seen die around him one by one his beloved...that, finally, he is loaded on to a train, eighty or a hundred persons to a box car; that he travels towards the unknown, blindly, for sleepless days and nights, and that he is at last flung inside the walls of an indecipherable inferno' (pp.42–3).

Against this vivid landscape of death and destruction, we learn to be humble rather than judge. We learn to see the small gestures which enabled some prisoners to hold on to their humanity. Victor Frankl, himself a camp survivor, wrote in his book *Man's Search for Meaning* (1987):

> ...we who lived in concentration camps can remember the men who walked through the huts comforting others, giving away their last piece of bread. They may have been few in numbers, but they offer sufficient proof that everything can be taken away from a man but one thing. The last of human freedoms – to choose one's own way. (p.65)

Though ultimately only the Nazis decided the fate of life over death, Frankl believed there were situations of moral choice.

Shamai Davidson (1984), Terence Des Pres (1976) and others emphasise the importance of human reciprocity which could be seen in small acts of kindness from one prisoner to another. An illustration of this can be found in the following account of one of the survivors I was in contact with over a long period of time. This man was on a train towards the end of the war. The extreme conditions of starvation, filth and weakness were threatening to end the lives of many. This survivor, who in one breath had told me how he survived by putting himself first, in the next breath told me how he had talked to his friend and willed him to stay alive. His friend lived, and they kept in touch even though they were in different countries. This friend owed his life to this survivor, and yet the latter could not acknowledge what he had done to help him. Human values seemed to have no place in that world, and so his good deed was denied by him. His morality paled into insignificance against the cruelty and bestiality which were meted out against him. Listening to such accounts gives greater insight into human suffering.

The range of responses of the prisoners in the death camps alerts us to the complex mirroring in our current work with Holocaust survivors. In today's world, survivors have a special sense of who other survivors are. Their reactions to certain members in the HSC, whether positively or negatively, seem to be based on factors which link to their past. As a non-survivor I do not have access to the same senses. In a way, this also saves me from falling victim myself to any tendency to focus on what survivors may have had to do in order to survive. Among themselves, survivors acknowledge the range and complexity of camp behaviour, but they also wish to keep that knowledge contained within the survivor groups. Once it goes outside the survivor community, there is a justifiable fear that this survival behaviour will be misunderstood, and cast a negative light on the victim. There is therefore a code of conduct which has emerged and which arrests any tendency to 'tell all'.

If we look further at the complexity of trauma, we must also take account of those who were not subject to persecution, yet risked their lives to save others. While I will look at the subject of altruism in more detail in the closing of Part II, I believe it also has a place here on the continuum which we are now addressing. It raises for us issues that relate to our own grey zones, our own uncertainties when faced with life-threatening situations. How would we behave? On a day-to-day level, would we intervene if we saw someone being attacked? In more extreme form, would we risk our lives to hide someone whose life was under threat? Would we assist someone to flee the country and put ourselves in danger? In preparing ourselves to pass through the door to the other world of extreme trauma, we must ask ourselves these questions, even if we cannot imagine the answers.

The transmission of trauma

'The plague of destruction and violence that struck the first generation continues disturbing their descendants and their individual stories' (Wilgowicz 1995, p.423). Is it inevitable for the consequences of extreme trauma to persist in subsequent generations born after a trauma such as the Holocaust?

Yael Danieli (1985a) points out that as a result of the 'conspiracy of silence' following World War II, survivors were not able to communicate the horrendous ordeals they had been through, not to mention the massive losses. An effect of this was that 'the only option left to survivors, other than sharing their Holocaust experiences with each other, was to withdraw completely into their newly-established families' (p.299).

However, as with the survivors themselves, there are many variables which affect how the second generation are affected by their parent(s)' experience. Shamai Davidson (1992b) has noted that attempts to make causal connections between survivor parents and their children regarding the traumatisation is 'problematic because of the complexity and large numbers of interacting variables that are involved' (p.89). He then goes on to list some of these variables as: pre-trauma personality of the survivor parent and the nature of the Holocaust traumatisation; the age of the survivor of the trauma; the loss of previous spouse and children; whether both parents are survivors or only one; the personality of a non-survivor parent; additional trauma affecting the child in his/her early years (e.g. in displaced persons camps); and the psychosocial conditions in which the child grew up. Danieli (1985a, pp.304–13) identified four survivor family classifications which she found influenced the responses of the second generation – 'victim' or 'numb' families mostly emerged from concentration camp inmates whereas 'fighter' families were partisan or resistance fighters during the war. The fourth classification were families of 'those who made it'. She felt it was essential to concentrate on the individual survivor's war history in order to understand the issues that relate to his/her children, though none of those categories were 'pure' or mutually exclusive.

The continuum between the past, the 'rupture' of the Holocaust victimisation and the present helps to move the survivors and their families on from a fixed position lodged in the Holocaust trauma. However, rarely does that mean 'going back to normal' or returning to pre-victimisation ways of being and functioning. It is not my task to go into a detailed analysis of the impact of trauma on the second generation. However, to ignore it would deny the impact that trauma can have on subsequent generations.

In my work with survivors, I have been confronted with the overwhelming pain of a survivor having to deal with an adult child's drug addiction. This is not an isolated event in our survivor community. Nor is death by suicide of the children of survivors, or slower death through eating disorders. As we came into this work with survivors relatively late – long after the trauma – there were many complex processes which developed in certain families to cope with the aftermath of the trauma.

An enormous amount of literature has emerged which looks in detail at the effects on these adult children of their parents' Holocaust experiences. Shamai Davidson (1992a) noted that even when survivors seemed to be coping well with their trauma, they nevertheless carried vulnerabilities which affected many aspects of their lives, particularly their parenting abilities. Included in this is the ability of the parent to help the children achieve autonomy, separation and a full sense of self. Bergman and Jucovy (1982) also maintained that children of survivors do not get a chance to live their own lives. They feel compelled to undo the trauma experienced by their parents.

My experience of listening to the children of survivors has indicated that some of them have been flooded by their parents' experience while others speak of secrets in the family – of never quite knowing the detail of how their parent(s) survived. I also have the opportunity to speak to the first generation; they explain that many of them wanted to spare their children from the horrors they had been through and hence kept silent on the subject. Others felt that their children must carry the memories of those horrors for them when they are no longer alive to speak for themselves. They become what Dina Wardi (1992) calls 'memorial candles'. As whole families and communities were often annihilated during the Holocaust, the children then became the only means to link the past, present and future. This is a very heavy burden for them to bear on their own.

Those in the helping professions have to be aware of the difficulties which arise in families with a Holocaust experience. The difficulty in separating, the guilt involved in moving away and being independent, has to be understood rather than pathologised. Child survivors, for example, who may have lost their parental models, did their best to raise their children. They may have wanted to give them everything they could to make up for what they themselves lost in their childhood. However, there was no parent to guide them or advise them what to do when their baby cried, or how to react to a rebellious teenager. They did not want their children to starve, either literally or metaphorically, as they had done. Food, education, comfort were meant to counteract the deprivation they experienced. However, emotionally there remained, at times, gaps which could not be filled by these external means.

It is perhaps not surprising that many children of survivors went into the helping professions themselves, including work with Holocaust survivors. On the other hand, some reacted by trying to break the link with their parents' Holocaust past by marrying out of the faith and trying to form an independent identity from their parents. The issue of gay and lesbian children of Holocaust survivors was highlighted at a conference in 1995. The conflict raised by 'coming out' in a family with a Holocaust background was a repeated theme. Having a separate identity to their parents – parents who had witnessed the persecution and destruction of homosexuals under the Nazis – aroused fears for the children and exerted pressure on them to conform. There was an additional concern of the parents about the possibility that future generations would not be created through their children to replace those murdered in the Holocaust.

An awareness of the complex issues the children of survivors face was brought to light during the Gatherings of the Second Generation organised in the UK. Several hundreds of second generation came together. As with their parents' generation, they felt relief at sharing some of the trauma they carried. However, the need to continue to share their issues was not catered for. Our services increasingly received requests for therapeutic responses. An initial response to try to bring together first and second generation did not work, as the latter felt they wanted their own issues heard and understood as distinct from their parents'.

Dina Wardi's (1995) approach of using small groups as a 'corrective experience through dialogue' (p.338) with the second generation served as a useful model in our work. We have facilitated similar groups. They feel 'normalised' and less isolated as they listen and respond to others who have gone through similar experiences with their parents. The group also has the function of serving as what Wardi calls a 'matrix of mirrors' (p.338), helping to build up a new sense of familial identity.

We also have to be aware of the people for whom the impact of the parents' trauma does not cause such difficulties. It alerts us again to the individual differences and warns us against generalisations such as the 'second generation syndrome'. The arguments against such classifications are very similar in nature to those already mentioned relating to survivor syndrome. There may be other contributing factors apart from the Holocaust which affect relationships. It led Howard Cooper (1995), a psychoanalytical psychotherapist, to conclude that the conflicts attributed to second generation Holocaust survivors are not exclusive to them. However, he adds, 'Even if we steer clear of "syndromising" the second generation, we still recognise the toxic consequences of those born to parents who encountered (in David Grossman's words), "the Nazi Beast!"' (p.145).

There have been trends to subsequently link this phenomenon to the third and fourth generation of survivors, as though there is no end to the poison which emerged from the Holocaust. I personally have concerns about the commercial business that ensues from the promotion of generational victimisation resulting from trauma. At the same time, some process needs to be evolved to try to contain the effect of the trauma within the two generations so far mentioned. One of the ways would be in developing a better dialogue between the two generations before the older survivors all die. Second, the professionals involved in this work could relieve the burden on the second generation by helping in the process of memorialisation of the survivors' experiences, and for the silenced voices of those who were murdered.

Communication between the generations may be enhanced directly through facilitated group discussions where children can talk to the first generation, who are not necessarily their parents. This relieves some of the pain of the personal accounts of their parents' suffering. Such a group has been set up by Hedi Fried, a psychologist and an Auschwitz survivor, in her centre in Stockholm, Sweden, called Café 84. Alternatively, we are planning to bring the two generations together in a creative project involving art to develop a memorial for the future rather than focusing on the past traumas.

Another option would be to involve the second generation in volunteering or fund-raising, or bringing their expertise into our centres for survivors. We have a child of survivors working in our café, one offering manicures to members of the centre, another taking a poetry group, and some recording testimonies of the survivors' life histories. Feelings of helplessness, of not being able to repair their parents' tragic past, are thus converted into positive, practical ways of helping. Joint projects between the generations will continue in as many creative forms as possible.

Before our services began, the second generation felt isolated in their task of remembering for the future. We now work alongside them ensuring that museums, educational organisations, testimony recording services, research projects and memorial plaques all have a part to play in remembrance. Our own buildings and the staff contained within also take on the remembrances of the survivors as they grow older and frailer.

Working with the Bosnian refugees reminds us that we cannot become complacent in keeping the memory of the horrors of the Holocaust alive. Ethnic cleansing, concentration camps and the torture in former Yugoslavia bring back strong memories of the language of the Holocaust. Through our awareness of the impact of trauma in our work with the Holocaust survivors, we try to respond now rather than in the future with these Bosnian refugees, and, we hope, prevent some of the transmission from one generation to another. We have to create a new community. We have to allow integration while, at the same time, ensuring their identity remains through language, culture, food and so on. Helping the parents and grandparents to adjust to this new situation allows the children to get on with their lives, make new friends and achieve well at school, university and careers. We have to be aware of the stresses caused by lack of employment, low income and inadequate housing and how these affect family relationships, including the children. These children are, in fact, also first generation, as most of them also came as refugees – a few have been born since arrival. We need to create as stable an environment as possible or their children may also be affected by their displacement, as has been described in the second generation of Holocaust survivors. This is made even more challenging as most of the elderly members of this group are also Holocaust survivors as well as current refugees.

We are not, however, going into this current work with blind eyes. The timing of the interventions needs to be understood as well as the means by which we respond.

Is it ever too late to respond to trauma?

Focusing on the transmission of trauma highlights the problems that emerge if trauma is not responded to early enough. As we have seen, the trauma is then delayed and re-emerges in later life. In the process of the delay, the children of the survivors may become the receptacles into which this overspill of unresolved grief is poured.

Some survivors have said to me that they wish our services had been available when they came to this country, as they may not have had to face the difficulties they are experiencing in their later life. From our work with the Bosnian refugees, it would seem that early intervention can help both practically and emotionally in the adjustment to a new country. However, one of the survivors I have worked with has said it is never too late, and this is now a 'second opportunity' to help those who have been extremely traumatised many years ago.

It has always been my belief that issues can be addressed irrespective of someone's age. An example of this can be seen in the work I undertook with an eighty-three-year-old widow who was not a survivor. After her husband's death, she became agoraphobic, suicidal and felt her life was over. In my weekly work with her, what had initially appeared to be a warm and loving relationship with her husband began to change to one of resentment, particularly covering her husband's infidelities. She felt guilty about the negative thoughts she had about him which she felt may have contributed to his death. As she shared the reality of what had happened, she became more confident to go out again and came to see me at my office. She decided to move home and, for the first time, visited her daughter in Israel. She lived happily for many years more and made the last part of her life a positive one.

The motivation to address unfinished business in one's life does not end at the age of forty years. Those who have the courage and commitment to deal with unresolved issues do so irrespective of chronological age. This belief, based on my working experience with older people, has been crucial to the understanding of the more specialist work with ageing survivors of the Holocaust.

However, when opportunities arise to prevent future trauma emerging, we have to take action. It is the miracle of survival how well people cope with the aftermath of severe trauma. It could be argued that the work with the Bosnian refugees should now cease. They have settled in this country, the children are going to school and their basic needs have been met. Contrary to this, we are currently developing plans to open a new centre for the Bosnian refugees. We are doing this because we know that, according to Maslow's hierarchy of needs, the basic needs have to be met before others can be addressed. We know from our work with Holocaust survivors how important it is for people who have undergone war trauma to continue to be supported through social groups and to create a community in which they can try to repair what was broken in the war. This sense of continuity, of identity, of belonging, is crucial to the emotional adjustments of these traumatised people to their current situation.

There are therefore both shorter-term and longer-term interventions which need to be catered for. Therapeutic responses should be made available as soon as possible after the trauma. However, the method(s) of intervention opens up the debate again about the meaningfulness of the response to the traumatised person.

One hears over and over again in the media about the counselling services which are sent in following a disaster, such as the Paddington rail crash in 1999, both for victims and rescuers. It is true that following death, or dealing with the aftermath of horror, it can help to recount endlessly what has been experienced or witnessed as a cathartic process. However, such interventions are time limited. After a while, one is expected to resume a 'normal' life. Yet, for some, this is not possible. What help should be offered on a longer-term basis?

It is interesting to note how survivors of disasters continue to support each other, sometimes focusing on a collective action such as compensation – the *Marchioness* boat disaster, for example. The importance of consulting the traumatised sufferers, rather than any assumptions being made about what we as professionals think is best for them, must be the basis for the facilitated responses which follow. Jean Giller (1998), working with torture victims in Uganda, writes:

> The lessons are clear: the perceived need which is being addressed should always be carefully investigated, with the full involvement of the people who are meant to benefit from it. This demands a respect for local priorities, which should extend to respect for local forms of healing if some 'treatment' is required. (p.144)

This brings us into the realm of how we work with the effects of extreme trauma, having now had an overview of how complex a subject it is. We have to know how to reach out to those who have been traumatised; how to respond in a way that engages the survivor rather than alienating him/her further. Having internalised some of the issues raised under the complexity of trauma, the reader may wish to explore new ways of working with severely traumatised people based on listening, absorbing and creating responses which meet their needs.

Endnotes

1. Excerpts from *At the Mind's Limits* by Jean Amery (1999). Copyright © Indiana University Press. Permission to reprint is also granted by Granta Publications for the author.

2. *The Forgotten*, by Elie Wiesel. Copyright © 1992 by Elirion Associates, Inc. Reprinted by permission of Georges Borchardt, Inc., for the author. Permission to reprint is also granted by Sheil Land Associates Ltd, London.

3. Excerpts from *At the Mind's Limits* by Jean Amery (1999). Copyright © Indiana University Press. Permission to reprint is also granted by Granta Publications for the author.

PART II

Learning from Survivors How to Respond to Atrocity

Introduction

In preparation for our journey towards the world of extreme trauma, we bring with us remnants of the world with which we are familiar. Forced to travel into unknown territory, we pack in our small suitcase those valuables which we think will help us, comfort us and give us strength when we arrive at our destination.

Those about to embark on their deportation to Auschwitz, as described in Elie Wiesel's book *Night* (1981, first published 1958), prepared in the only way they knew how: 'The women were cooking eggs, roasting meat, baking cakes, and making knapsacks' (p.26). No-one could imagine the scale and magnitude of the inhumanity and brutality which would be inflicted on these same people. From the moment the journey began, the familiar world changed. 'It began in the trains, in the locked boxcars – eighty to a hundred people per car' (Des Pres 1976, p.53).

> The temperature started to rise as the freight car was enclosed and body heat had no outlet... When dawn finally rose...we were quite ill and shattered, crushed not only by the weight of fatigue but by the stifling moist atmosphere and the foul odour of excrement...we were to live for days on end breathing these foul smells, and soon we lived in the foulness itself. (Kessel 1973, pp.50–1)

Elie Wiesel (1981) contrasted the hell of the conditions in the cattle wagons to the 'blossoming countryside' (p.34) rolling by as glimpsed by those who could see out of the train. This contrast marked the boundary between the two worlds. Many died on the way as the familiar world was left behind, and they were engulfed by the pain, shock and fear which confronted them.

The same railway lines which had carried holidaymakers in other types of trains to their destinations were now taking people to their death. The same railway companies which planned the timetables, which sold the tickets to their customers, were arranging these transports to the death camps. The familiar sound of the train moving along the track would never have the same meaning again. These trains became conduits for destruction rather than a means of communication. Their link with the outside world was severed as the doors of the cattle trains were flung open:

> ...we saw this time that flames were gushing out of a tall chimney into the black sky... There was an abominable odour floating in the air...that smell of burning flesh...we had arrived at Birkenau, reception centre for Auschwitz. (Wiesel 1981, p.39)[1]

That was only the beginning. As families were torn apart, as valuable possessions brought on the journey were forcibly taken away, as people were stripped of clothing, hair and all manner of dignity, as vicious blows rained down on them, as a number branded on the arm replaced a name and personal identity, nothing external remained from the world of the living and life.

For those wishing to work with people who have undergone such extreme trauma, it is essential to recognise the necessary transition from a situation which was familiar and known to one which was incomprehensible. To enter into the world of extreme trauma as witnessed by the survivors, to get closer to their suffering, we have to adapt our familiar practices by learning from them what needed to be discarded and what could be kept during the incarceration. For example, Elie Wiesel survived his initial selection in Auschwitz by declaring he was eighteen years old instead of fifteen, and that he was a farmer, not a student. This meant he would be used for work rather than murdered immediately.

In this part of the book we will reassess our practices in the light of the reality of that trauma. When we look again inside our small suitcase which we have brought on our journey, we will need to review the usefulness of the contents. Will our theories and practices, which we have carefully wrapped up inside, be of help to us when we confront horror of such enormity? Will we find that what we value so much, which gives us our professional identity and purpose in our work, will have to be reassessed in terms of its usefulness? Will we find, like the prisoners in Auschwitz, that the only usefulness for the once-valued bank notes was as toilet paper, in a world in which there was no paper to wipe away the excrement (Des Pres 1976, p.54)?

When we enter a world in which trauma is severe and prolonged, we need to question what we know, to unlearn our familiar approaches and relearn new ways which have meaning for those who have been traumatised. We may find that some things from the past may help to sustain us on this journey. We will see as this journey unfolds how some of the incarcerated held on to memories of home, and to possibilities of keeping some sense of humanity. As we develop in this specialist area of work, we may also be nurtured by the strengths which allow us to move into that 'other world', while at the same time maintaining a link with this world, so as not to lose hope.

While not all trauma is as severe as that illustrated through the Nazi death camps, the same principle holds true. When dealing with traumatised people, we must never forget the reality of what they have actually experienced. In the comfort of our working environments, in the peace of our therapeutic space, it is easy to forget the detail of the horror. By forgetting it, we are not challenged to adapt the way we work. At the forefront of our minds must be the trauma, for it is that trauma which must form the bedrock of our therapeutic responses.

Endnote

1. Excerpts from *Night* by Elie Wiesel, translated by Stella Rodway. Copyright © 1960 by MacGibbon & Kee. Copyright renewed © 1988 by The Collins Publishing Group. Reprinted by permission of Hill and Wang, a division of Farrar, Straus and Giroux, LLC. Permission to reprint is also granted by Sheil Land Associates Ltd, London.

Chapter 4

Working with the Effects of Extreme Trauma

Trying to find the right approach to reach out and work with the effects of extreme trauma is, as Primo Levi (1988a) wrote, like trying 'to apply the theorems of plain geometry to the solution of spherical triangles' (p.65). How we shift our thinking away from traditional therapeutic concepts towards more creative responses that are more meaningful for those who have suffered severe trauma will now be addressed.

We have already briefly observed how psychoanalytic and psycho-dynamic approaches have proved inadequate and often inappropriate in working with the effects of severe trauma. Those specialising in trying to understand, rather than diagnose, people who have survived repeat this concern over and over again. Brainin and Teicher (1997) – the former a psychologist and training analyst, the latter a psychoanalyst – have commented: 'Our psychoanalytical vocabulary is not adequate. The psychoanalytical theory of trauma was developed before Auschwitz, and must be reappraised in the light of this experience' (p.92).

Similarly, Hedi Fried (1997), a psychologist and an Auschwitz survivor, concludes from her work with survivors that 'therapy in its classical form is not always appropriate for survivors... We can see how much strength someone gets from the unorthodox methods used... It also shows that no healing is possible, but that survivors can learn to live with their trauma' (p.111).

Perhaps the contrast between understanding the impact of extreme experience, rather than diagnosing and explaining post-trauma behaviour, is highlighted in an interview between psychoanalyst Anna Ornstein and Marcus and Rosenberg (1989b). She compares Terence Des Pres's work, as detailed in his book *The Survivor* (1976), with Bruno Bettelheim's writings (e.g. 1943, 1971). She feels that Des Pres 'heard' the survivors' description of what it was like to defecate into one's pants and live with the stench of one's own excrement, while Bettelheim reduced these experiences to 'anal regression'. Des Pres gave a description of the sense of humiliation as this was being experienced by people whose overall level of psychological maturity was not reduced to the lowest common denominator. Bettelheim, on the other hand, by 'explaining the same situation with the concept of "anal regression", created the impression that survivors had become children or savages in this process. Should the latter have been the case, their actual suffering might have been greatly reduced' (p.105). Ornstein goes on to emphasise that Des Pres had the advantage of not being a psychoanalyst and did not feel compelled to 'explain' the survivors' experiences before he understood them.

George Kren comments in 'The Holocaust Survivor and Psychoanalysis' (1989) that 'Des Pres's implicit argument is that Freudian Theory presupposes a level of civilised conduct, and that it is only in that context that Freud's conclusions are valid' (p.10). Robert Krell (1989) also attacks traditional therapeutic approaches in a similar vein, saying that 'psychologic therapy represented a series of accusations, a continuation of victimisation'. Survivors were 'accused of denial if they resisted describing the concentration camp experience; of guilt or guilt feelings, perhaps having done something "shady", or worse, in order to survive; of exhibiting Nazi-like behaviour if aggressive and angry...' (p.219).

While much of this backlash is focused on psychoanalytic and psycholog-ical therapy, I believe that the problem is much more widespread. Each emerging therapy carries with it its own set of dictates which gives it its identity and following. I am often asked to accept counselling students on placement in our centres, yet I am unable to do so. Those wishing to train in this field first need to absorb the principles and theories of what they are taught. Only when this is internalised, and practised, is it possible to deviate from what they have learned. However convincing the theory, however humanistic and client-centred the approach, it is only of any value if the person we are working with feels helped.

To analyse some of the difficulties of traditional therapeutic work, I would like to examine some key principles which may serve to illustrate the gulf between the therapist and the traumatised person.

The therapeutic relationship

The starting point for a therapeutic relationship depends on one person asking for help from another person, the helper. My own psychodynamic training taught me the importance of the structure of time, of place, of assessment of the person-in-situation gestalt, of contract, of trust and of empathy. A professional relationship was built up with the client. Skill, training and experience were needed by the professional in order to offer help, hence putting the helper in the position of an authority or expert. Indeed, that may have been exactly what the 'client' was seeking by asking for help. It could be this very inequality in the relationship which differentiated it from other relationships and which allowed the therapy to develop.

For someone who had been victimised, however, being vulnerable in the eyes of an authority figure would be an anathema. In my work with survivors of the Holocaust, I do not see them as patients, or even clients, but individuals whom we engage in a process which may assist them in living out the latter part of their lives more peacefully, even if we cannot heal their wounds.

In our work with the severely traumatised, there is a shift in the relationship to a more equal partnership. The survivor acts more as a teacher and a guide for the professional worker, as we learn from the survivor which approaches may help.

Therapeutic boundaries

The therapeutic relationship brings with it codes of conduct regarding the disclosure of personal information by the professional. The boundary is there to protect the professional, and also to reinforce the special nature of this therapeutic relationship.

Such boundaries present great obstacles to those who have survived severe trauma. In contrast to the traditional approach, Robert Krell (1989) maintains that, in working with survivors, 'I opt to offer much more of myself than I do with other patients' (p.224). He believes that survivors seek out therapists with whom they feel some degree of intimacy is possible.

Working with survivors of the Holocaust often necessitates informal as well as more formal relationships. It may mean having tea together, participating in social events, using touch as a way of bridging the gap between survivor and non-survivor, and sharing personal information about oneself.

I would like to illustrate the importance of touch for people who have been severely traumatised, as this may be seen as treading on dangerous ground professionally. One survivor from Auschwitz asked me if I would touch her on her back where she had recurring pain from having been beaten with a rifle in the camp. I felt privileged as a non-survivor to share the pain she carried with her; that she trusted me enough to allow this contact to happen. A kiss on the cheek, a hug, a gift are common features of our work. They emerge over time as natural phenomena. They are earned demonstrations of the bond of commitment the survivors see daily in their contact with us. I have never felt threatened or uncomfortable when this happens.

Talking as a focus for therapy

Though today there is an acknowledgement of creative therapies such as art, dance, drama and music, there is nevertheless a heavy emphasis in psychotherapy and counselling on talking as the primary medium of the therapy. For those who are able to talk, this can bring effective relief. This would include traumatised people who wish to bear witness.

For some, however, talking does not bring relief. Problems with language, if English is not the mother tongue, make it difficult to express experiences. Counselling is often seen as the panacea for those who have undergone trauma. Words can often not describe horrific events, and yet therapists often remain intransigently bound to this familiar way of working. Robert Krell (1989) emphasises that when dealing with survivors of the Holocaust, nothing normal can be found. He advises, therefore, that, 'In light of that reality, we must depart from the notions that traditional uncovering psychotherapy, with free association and a reliance on insight and dream interpretation can help. They seldom can' (p.221).

My work with Bosnian refugees similarly confirms that they do not, on the whole, wish to talk about what has happened to them. We therefore have to develop therapeutic alternatives which acknowledge the trauma without necessarily reliving it.

In my view there is no magic in going back to the past for those who have suffered severe trauma. For those who wish to, we have to offer that option, and journey with them as they retell their story. However, Donald Meichenbaum (2000b) advises that 'great caution is required before therapists impose this therapeutic dictum to self-disclose on all traumatised clients. Some clients do not wish to "stir up" old memories. Some clients do *not* wish to self-disclose' (p.106). He quotes a client's reaction to reinforce this point. '"It seems like it's a benefit for the therapist to have the story told. I am not sure how much it does for me"' (p.107). He goes on to point out that there are also cultural differences, and he gives the example of South East Asia, where traumatised people prefer to focus on their 'here and now' problems, rather than consider the past.

In my experience of working with refugees and survivors, the traditional notion of asking for counselling and therapy as a first option has been very rare. If people did come to the organisation, it was most often for some practical problem they may be experiencing, particularly as they were growing older. For example, there may have been financial or housing issues which needed to be addressed. In my early work with refugees, their hidden agendas from the Holocaust could only be heard in whispers, and were not overt manifestations of their unfinished business and unresolved grief.

Those who survived in Europe during World War II were not able to come forward in the same way. They remained unreachable. Therapy and counselling in a social-work office did not allow me to reach out in any meaningful way. I became aware that survivors were suffering but could not be reached. The community was dying without being heard. A wasteland had developed between the professional and the survivor. There was an urgency to adapt my way of working. How this shift took place – moving me beyond the familiar approaches – will be looked at next.

Chapter 5

Rethinking our Therapeutic Approaches

I would like you to imagine for a moment the following scenarios:

A man is walking down the street and he falls down a deep hole in the ground. He struggles to get out and goes on his way. The same man, on another day, walks down the same street and falls down the same deep hole. He again struggles to free himself, and goes on his way. This event is repeated many times until the man learns to walk around the hole to avoid falling in. He finally decides to walk down a different street.

The second scenario is found in the well-known story of the difference between heaven and hell.

In hell we see a group of people standing around a pot of food, using spoons which are so long that the food can not reach their hungry mouths. The people starve and die.

In heaven, we see a similar scene of people standing around a pot of food, also using long spoons but, this time, they use them to feed each other, and so are nourished and live.

As I immersed myself in the world of the survivor, I came to realise that my tools (training and experience) were often ineffective in reaching severely traumatised people. Although the spoon (tool) I was using was beautifully made and well constructed, if it could not 'feed' the empty mouths, it was of little value. The spoon was straight and did not bend. It could only be used in a certain way. Just as the survivors themselves had to adapt very quickly to the chaotic world of the camp in order to have a chance of survival, so I had to make substantial changes if I were to be able to enter this incomprehensible world I was beginning to encounter. I had to find a way of not falling down the same hole like the man in the first scenario, and thereby repeating the mistake of returning to the familiar. I had to find new and creative ways of reshaping the 'spoon' so that it could be used more effectively.

The creative process

What was the key which helped to unlock this intransigent situation? The answer seemed to lie in the creative process itself – in those parts of the brain which liberate us from convergent logical ways of thinking towards a more diverse, multidimensional perception of the world. When faced with war and other extreme situations, old habits, routines, rules and norms may become dysfunctional for those who confront the trauma. Working with the effect of these situations challenges us, the professional workers, to find within ourselves as yet untapped and uncharted realms. These then form the link between the traumatised survivor and the non-survivor.

If you turn a picture or even handwriting upside down, the image you see looks strange and often unrecognisable. Some people may give up looking at the unfamiliar and pass on to something more familiar. For others, however, a transition is made from the left- to the right-hand side of the brain, and an image emerges from this unusual position.

Making these shifts is the focus of Betty Edwards's (1981) book *Drawing on the Right Hand Side of the Brain – How to Unlock Your Hidden Artistic Talent.* Practising these shifts, opening up the mind to explore alternative ways of 'seeing', is essential in moving from a fixed, traditional way of working towards creating more meaningful approaches for people who have been traumatised.

Many professionals I have encountered have been fearful of using images, stories, music, art or other creative responses in their work. To illustrate how this can be done, I would like to focus on two vignettes.

Vignette I

A SURVIVOR

> Jack came to see me at the point in his life when his son had committed suicide. He felt numb and powerless, having been unable to save his son from death. Jack was used for slave labour in Auschwitz – he was then

fifteen years old. He experienced the most extreme suffering during that time and later in Bergen-Belsen. His losses were massive. He was currently facing his past again – his vulnerability and lack of control over events in his life had reactivated a deep sense of loss about his family who were murdered in the Holocaust. It seemed there was little comfort I could offer in the face of such enormous tragedy. I felt deskilled. At the same time I remembered that despite the tragic events of his life, Jack had managed to marry, have children and run a business. There were strengths in him which had helped him to cope. In addition to this, he told me about his love of writing, literature and the theatre. It was that aspect which I focused on.

Initially, art therapy was offered to create images to express his tragedy. However, these images were too overwhelming, and he terminated the therapy.

Some of the child survivors were attending group analytic therapy sessions outside Shalvata and Jack joined. However, the discomfort which he felt again led him to stop his involvement. He said he felt threatened rather than supported in that environment.

Once again a victim in relation to his son's death, Jack started to write. This creative medium empowered him. He began to study for a degree, which he obtained. He went on to gain a distinction in his Master's, and is currently finishing his doctorate. He continues to write plays, some of which have been performed. He achieved this despite having missed out on formal education during the war, and despite all the horror and deprivation he had experienced in the death camps.

What lessons emerge from this brief illustration? In the face of overwhelming suffering and pain, there are demands made on the person offering help to be as open to creative approaches as possible. Jack himself has often told me, subsequently, how my belief in his ability to write saved him from being overwhelmed by his grief and despair. Traditional therapeutic approaches – counselling, art therapy and the group analytical therapy – could not reach out to engage him. Returning to the past and focusing on his trauma would not have allowed him to move on. However, the creative approaches in his writing allowed him to feel more in control of himself again and reconnected to his own strengths. He was then able to use supportive sessions with one of the specialist workers in Shalvata.

Vignette II
A SURVIVOR

> Anna was a child survivor in Auschwitz. She came to see me with the request that she would like to produce a book for schoolchildren. She wanted the children to understand the Holocaust through the eyes of a child, as she had been. She wanted the children to identify with her.
>
> During our meeting together, Anna became tearful, and I commented that she seemed to be carrying much of what she had been through. She was relieved that I suggested she should meet one of the staff at Shalvata. She met with him to write the text for her book. In the event, she did not feel that he could help her to express her story accurately. However, she did not want to give up her urgent task. I then suggested that the art therapist could help her with the illustrations. She agreed to this, and one of the survivors helped her to write the text.
>
> During the sessions with the art therapist, Anna used the artist's skill to illustrate her book. The accuracy of his drawings gave her a sense that her experiences were at last being documented, and this brought her great relief. The medium of art helped her to find some meaning in her survival. The rapport and trust she built up with the art therapist reduced her sense of isolation and strengthened her resolve to complete her project. She has now had her book published.
>
> Anna still lives with her trauma, but does not carry this alone. The fragments of her memory as a child have been documented into a meaningful whole which can be seen by others.

Survivors as our teachers: listening in a special kind of way to survivors of extreme trauma

This creative shift – from traditional therapeutic responses to those in which there are a range of therapeutic options – develops from listening to survivors about what seems to help them. It moves us on, from thinking that therapy only concerns the client talking to the therapist who is there to help him/her towards seeing the therapy as an opportunity for the therapist to listen and learn as he/she works alongside the survivor. This is a significant and fundamental understanding when working with traumatised people. The role of the therapist becomes much more that of facilitator, rather than expert. It involves a process of unlearning, to free us to learn new approaches.

Elie Wiesel (1982), when talking to medical staff, advised them, 'Listen to survivors, listen to them very well; they have more to teach you, than you them.'[1] The importance of listening to survivors is the focus of an interview between Donald Meichenbaum and Michael Hoyt (Hoyt 2000). Meichenbaum comments, 'I usually listen very attentively to how clients tell their stories... I help clients to become better observers and become their own therapists' (p.63); '...clients come up with suggestions themselves' (p.60). He cautions therapists 'not to be a "surrogate frontal lobe" for their clients': 'They should not do the thinking for them, nor put words in their mouths; they should be respectful, collaborative and remember that most people evidence the potential for a great deal of resilience and courage' (p.61).

When we listen to survivors, we are less likely to categorise them collectively, and we begin to see the individual emerging. This individual is not only a traumatised person, but one who lived during a time when there may have still been order and hope. We need to know people's origins, who they were, what family they came from, what life they had before the Holocaust. One child survivor I have worked with could vividly remember dancing on the table in her parents' home, her small feet enclosed in black patent leather shoes. Yet this same person could not remember the faces of her parents, who were taken away from her by the Nazis and murdered.

Listening to survivors, we hear accounts of how they tried to cope in the hell that they were in. We hear their stories of how they used their own creative imagination to help lift them in moments of despair. One survivor told me how the women in her barracks would talk about food and remember tastes of home. Another told me that when he became tired from the slave labour he had to endure, he would imagine being asleep. When we listen closely, we hear how storytelling, humour or songs were used to sustain prisoners suffering in these brutal environments. We hear accounts of how sabotage was used by some slave labourers in munitions factories as an act of defiance in a hostile, punishing world.

When we listen to survivors, we become aware of the strengths within them which have helped them to reach this moment in time. 'There is a need for the therapist not to hold a pathological bias, but instead to be sensitive to the client's strengths and resources, and to listen actively to how the client changes his or her narrative in an adaptive fashion' (Meichenbaum 2000b, p.107).

When listening to survivors, we begin to understand how we need to learn more about the nature of extreme suffering and the paradoxical interface survivors encountered. What helped them to cope then will help us to understand how we can reactivate these mechanisms when trauma reappears even long after the event. Aspects of surviving are revealed as the witnesses to these heinous events tell their own story.

Patrick Bracken (1998) describes this metaphorically: 'It is only at night when the bright light of the sun has diminished that we can see the stars in our sky. However, these stars are also present, but invisible, during the day. The point is that bright sunlight can serve to conceal as well as reveal the nature of reality' (p.42). Bracken has worked with a range of traumatic war experiences in the world, and makes a strong case for professionals not to be naive nor arrogant when responding to survivors of war trauma. He maintains that 'the challenge to western NGOs [non-governmental organisations] and other agencies dealing with refugees and other victims of violence around the world is to establish ways of supporting people through times of suffering by listening and hearing their different voices in a way that does not impose an alien order' (p.58).

To avoid alien responses to traumatised people, the meaningfulness of the therapeutic responses needs to emerge from them. For those who have been victims, for those who have suffered under totalitarian regimes, therapeutic responses need to have at their core the concept of liberation and empowerment to move the traumatised person on from victim to survivor.

'Liberation' and 'empowerment' as a focus for therapeutic responses

If we imagine ourselves incarcerated in a hostile environment where death is a daily companion; if we imagine the suffocation of the overcrowded barracks and stench from the crematoria; if we imagine having to stifle our voices in the cramped spaces in which we are hidden; if we imagine the overwhelming fear that accompanies severe trauma, how we would long to breathe in the fresh air, to see the trees and the clear blue sky.

Reclaiming this world, which, in peacetime, we take for granted, proved to be elusive. Writing about his liberation from Buchenwald, on 11 April 1945, Elie Wiesel (1996) comments, 'Strangely we did not "feel" the victory. There were no joyous embraces, no shouts or songs to mark our happiness, for that word was meaningless for us. We were not happy. We wondered whether we ever would be… We mourned too many dead to speak of victory' (p.96). [2]

Re-entering this other world – the world of the living and life – also took major adjustments. The experiences of extreme trauma seemed to render those who were touched by this suffering as 'outsiders', and somehow different from those who have not suffered similarly. These 'outsiders' were scattered throughout the world trying, as Elie Wiesel (1996) puts it, to 'learn – or relearn – to live' (p.98).

Relearning to live would involve strategies which would serve as an antidote to the death, destruction, powerlessness and dehumanisation encountered by the victim during his/her incarceration. To be truly liberated is to no longer feel a victim at the mercy of another's brutality. To no longer be a victim is to have an identity, to have dignity, to have control over one's own destiny. To no longer be a victim is to feel healthy, strong and 'nourished'. To no longer feel a victim is to find meaning in one's life again, and to have a sense of belonging and peace.

In our therapeutic work we have to address these issues. We also have to relearn what we have been taught in the past, and be challenged by the deskilling process which may accompany these new approaches. We have to be committed to a sense of liberation for ourselves as we struggle to reach out to the person who has been traumatised. When we focus on what was denied or taken away during the trauma, we begin to see how certain approaches can begin to rebalance the negative effects of these experiences. As we have already noted, there can be no cure for the deep wounds which exist. However, each time a survivor feels empowered and in control over events in his/her life; each time he/she can laugh and enjoy some event in his/her life; each time he/she shows care and concern for another human being; each time he/she finds a voice to express himself/herself; each time he/she can feel free to weep and mourn, this freedom brings with it some sense of victory over the Nazis.

While I have focused here on Holocaust survivors, the concept of empowerment is fundamental to our understanding of how to work with the effects of severe trauma in a variety of situations. It puts emphasis on how people coped, not only during the trauma, but subsequently. It underlines the importance of how people who have been traumatised are able to help each other and find further strength from a sense of belonging and sharing with others who have gone through the trauma. It focuses our attention on how to minimise dependency and vulnerability by offering survivors different choices and options in the therapeutic work.

When we see survivors of trauma as people rather than patients, clients or victims, we become interested in who they are. Jean Giller (1998), in her work with victims of torture in Uganda, commented that while they had read extensively about Uganda before they went to work there, 'we knew so little about Ugandan people and how they appeared to be coping in the aftermath of tragedy without the aid of therapist or counsellor' (p.134). She also notes the importance of the shared experience in helping survivors of trauma to cope with what had happened to them.

Our therapeutic task becomes one of preventing the patterns of the past repeating themselves in the present. In facing the dark shadow with the survivors, we test out new ways of working which correspond more directly to the needs of the survivors. The use of informal social approaches, of mutual support, then comes into the domain of the therapist's repertoire. Leaving behind the 'purity' of the traditional therapeutic responses to traumatised people helps to build the bridge between the professional and the survivor. It is the importance of this concept which will be focused on now as it is crucial to our understanding of how we can reach out to people who might otherwise remain unreachable.

Mutual support groups as a focus for working with severely traumatised people

Moving from 'outsiders' to 'insiders'

'We are all brothers, and we are all suffering from the same fate. The same smoke floats over all our heads. Help one another. It is the only way to survive' (Wiesel 1981, p.53, first published 1958).[3]

I will begin by looking at a change which happened in my work and taught me about the essential importance of developing opportunities for traumatised people to meet and support each other – people who, until that point, had not come forward to ask for help.

This turning point, as I call it, happened in the early 1980s when a camp survivor came to see me, having heard of my name through an organisation in Israel. She asked me to help her set up a self-help group. The participants wished to come together to meet socially. They did not want therapy but, instead, they wanted to help each other. My role was defined as finding them a place to meet. The venue needed to be away from Jewish Care's premises, as many of them still held on to the residue of their animosity towards Anglo-Jewry for not having done enough to help them when they came to the UK from war-torn Europe. I was also in danger of being seen as part of that negative response, as I was also a non-survivor and part of Anglo-Jewry.

I found that my usual professional role was not functional in this mutual-help type of group. As they shared their experiences with each other, in this informal social setting, in a venue of their choice, I could hear their hidden agendas, but had no authorisation to deal with them.

I observed, I listened, I learned – survivors came to know me personally. Not only was I individualised to them, but I began to see each one as having gone into the Holocaust, experienced the Holocaust and adapted after liberation to what had happened in a unique way. This was not a homogeneous group; they came from different countries, had different mother tongues, and very different experiences in the Holocaust. My willingness to cross the professional boundary and act as facilitator in this group, in which I was made an 'honorary member', played a major part in all the subsequent work which followed.

What I realised in that experience, which lasted over two years, was how the mutual support approach was much more meaningful for survivors because it mirrored the camp experience. In the non-clinical, informal atmosphere of this group, where we shared refreshments together, and shared in parties, there was a more acceptable environment for the therapeutic work to take place. They felt not only that they belonged, but they were also 'normalised' in that group.

They named the group the SOS group (Survivors of Shoah). There was music; there was laughter and enjoyment. They celebrated being together but, at the same time, the Auschwitz numbers were clearly marked on some of their arms. What it taught me was how, amid horror and adversity, it was possible to sing, and to share a joke, and this helped to pass one more minute in that hell that they had been through. What worked in the past experience in the camp seemed to have relevance today. The past was acknowledged, particularly in the first two meetings, but, subsequently, the focus shifted to being actively involved in the current agenda of this group. They began to gain strength from each other, to have an identity and to find a collective voice.

These survivors taught me how to engage with the coping side of their lives. I was learning how to 'feed' them and how they could thrive. They were in fact 'feeding' each other and I was facilitating that process. We can now see how the story mentioned earlier in this chapter about heaven and hell has direct relevance to our therapeutic work. I was learning how to free both myself and these former victims from the incarceration in psychopathology.

The Holocaust destroyed the individual's support network. Bringing survivors together in groups of this kind allows them to re-create a community for themselves, which many have said was their greatest loss in the Holocaust. In addition the members collectively serve to act as replacement family for those who were murdered in the Holocaust. As they grow older and feel more isolated, such an opportunity can be life-saving.

Mutual support groups are gaining importance in working with victimised people. Yael Danieli's (1985b) project emphasised that mutual support groups help to overcome 'Survivors' resistance to institutions…their fear of being stigmatized, labelled crazy (stemming from the Nazi practice of gassing the sick or mentally ill), or considered psychologically damaged by their victimization' (p.4). She concluded that sensitivity to these wishes precluded making her project part of a mental health facility. This mirrors the SOS group's choice of a neutral venue. Indeed, the SOS members became incensed when the funding agency included them under its mental health services in its annual report. The positive aspect of this was that the members felt sufficiently empowered to express their views to the funding agency, thus reinforcing their image as survivors rather than sick victims.

Those who have the courage to facilitate such groups have to be prepared for the fact that there are no clear-cut methods or frameworks. Danieli (1985b) writes of her work, 'No a priori design existed for the Project. Format, methods of treatment, and more ambitious goals developed gradually through trial and error, flexibility of approach and especially through feedback from survivors and their offspring on what they needed and found most helpful' (p.3).

Danieli emphasises that the reasons why group and community approaches are so successful with Holocaust survivors 'reflect the fact that the Holocaust was a group phenomenon and affirm the central role of the "we-ness" in the identity of its survivors… These modalities acknowledge that perhaps only collectively can they find a meaningful response to their horrific history of victimisation' (Danieli 1985b, p.7).

Evidence of the importance of mutual support in the concentration camps can be found in a range of literature. Survivor Kitty Hart, in her book *I am Alive* (1962), confirms that she could not have survived alone. Eugene Heimler, an Auschwitz survivor, wrote in his book *Resistance Against Tyranny* (1966), 'None of us who have survived would be here unless there had been others who helped us in our survival' (p.161). Eugene Heimler went on to establish his own unique method of helping people after the war, known as 'social functioning', and created the Heimler Foundation in Britain. I had the privilege to work with him and learn from him when he joined our Steering Committee prior to the establishment of the Holocaust Survivors' Centre.

What was referred to in Part I as Nietzsche's 'The why to live for' was enhanced by being part of a pair or a group. Elmer Luchterand (1967) maintained: 'The pair was thus the basic unit of survival…one could not exist in the camp without participating somehow in a sharing relationship' (pp.245–64). When these interpersonal bonds were severed, as in the case when someone was murdered, this often undermined the sustaining factors which affected coping under extreme conditions.

Edward Bond, in his poem 'Soup' (1991), very movingly reflects on how a mutually supportive relationship sustained a mother and daughter in a death camp.

> I will tell you the greatest story in the world
> It is set in a death-camp
> Where else could the greatest story in this world be set?
> A mother and daughter were prisoners
> I will not tell you what the neglect of the gods
>   and the attention of men had done to them
> After three years they were freed by friendly soldiers
>   (soldiers are friendly on the day of freedom)
> One of them gave the mother a bowl of soup

She went aside with her daughter and said
    I am old and ill
    I cannot live long when we return to the world
    The soup would be wasted on me – sooner pour it on this earth
    trodden to stone by prisoners
    Drink
    The world will need the young who have endured and learned
The daughter said
    You are old and suffering has made you weak
    Your need is greater
    Drink
    Without you I could not be happy when we returned to the world
    and perhaps I would not survive
The starving do not debate long over a bowl of soup
They agreed that each in turn would drink one spoonful of soup till
    the bowl was empty
The mother began
She dipped the spoon into the top where the soup was thinnest
And even then – as if accidentally – she spilt half of it back into the
    bowl
And drank only what was left in the spoon
Then she gave the spoon to her daughter
She too dipped it into the top of the soup and did not even pretend
    to fill it
She drank and gave the spoon back to her mother
So there began a contest between the two women each to drink less
    than the other
When they put the spoon into their mouths it was hardly worth
    licking
They might as well still have been drinking the rations served in the
    camp
And then the mother dipped the spoon into the pieces of solid food
    deep in the bowl and filled it to overflowing
When the daughter saw that at last her mother was taking the good
    food to eat – her mouth opened in a weak smile
And the mother put the spoon into her daughter's mouth
So turn and turn about the two women fed each other spoonfuls of
    soup till the bowl was empty

If there were a judgement day
And a God dared to show his face at it
The story of these two women would exonerate many
Who otherwise would be condemned by their deeds
The race that can find two people to eat soup in this way is not
    wholly lost.

(Edward Bond's poem 'Soup'[4])

In a similar vein, Shamai Davidson's (1984) contribution to our understanding of social bonding and human reciprocity in the camps highlights the importance of these mechanisms acting as a mitigating factor against the traumatic processes. One survivor said her survival was linked to remaining with her sisters throughout her time in Auschwitz-Birkenau. Others may have 'found' a protector among the older inmates, who may have acted as a substitute for a lost loved one. The groups, Davidson notes, were well integrated and were characterised by mutual aid and sharing of everything. Loyalty and mutual concern were features within the group, with little concern for those outside. There was often a commonality of language, culture, previous ghetto or national background which united them. This enabled a joke, a reminiscence, a familiar phrase to lift an apathetic, despairing inmate to a level in which this humaneness, this sense of caring and belonging, gave a flicker of hope and some will to live.

Group activities included storytelling, playing, singing and 'joking' as well as stealing food or sharing information and advice. Each group had its own identity and culture and helped to maintain links with the destroyed cultural past. Shamai Davidson (1984) maintained that 'this bonding capacity continued to be evident during the recovery period and throughout their life cycle' (pp.570–571). An understanding of these human relationships in a paradoxical world of evil and inhumanity helps us to give meaning and importance to the social groups which form the foundation of our therapeutic work. It is in these detailed studies of camp life that we begin to appreciate how important it is to create opportunities for such social bonding in the present re-experiencing of the trauma in these ageing survivors. I have summarised the key features which are present in mutual support groups for those who have undergone trauma (Table 5.1). I have indicated how the

Table 5.1 The importance of mutual support groups for those who have undergone severe trauma

KEY FEATURES			
Gives a sense of *identity* which may have been lost in the trauma	Gives an experience of *sharing* with those who have undergone trauma	Opens up possibilities for *enjoyment* to lighten the darkness of the traumatic past	Helps to *reinforce the strength and coping* of the survivor
Produces a sense of *belonging* and reduces isolation	Allows members to *care* for each other	Creates possibilities for *socialising* in the recreational aspects of the group	*Reinforces health* of the survivor
Gives a feeling of being *insiders* rather than outsiders	The caring preserves a *sense of humanity*	Releases *creativity* in the nurturing environment of the group	Feels strengthened to *find a collective voice*
Allows for a *sense of family* to replace those lost in the trauma	The human aspect restores *personal dignity and trust*	Helps to look at ways of *celebrating survival* together	Feels more *control* over events in one's life
Helps to build a *new community* which may have been annihilated		The triumph of celebration gives some sense of *victory over Nazis*	*Empowerment –* emerge as survivors rather than as victims
Helps to give *meaning* to survival		*Sense of liberation and hope* generated	

OUTCOMES

impact these groups have on current coping can be observed in a range of 'outcomes'.

Though the primary focus has been on camp survivors, and the link between past coping behaviour and current adaptation to the trauma, the same principle of mutual support would seem to hold true for other traumatised people. Shamai Davidson (1984) himself generalises his findings by pointing out that when conditions of life are particularly harsh, and survival is difficult, there is often an increase in reciprocal relationships. He illustrates this through Bent Jensen's (1973) article on 'Human Reciprocity – An Arctic Exemplification', which focuses on socio-cultural patterns of villages in the Arctic.

The long hours of discussion I had with Shamai Davidson during his sabbatical in England strengthened me to see the coping capacity which was present and could be built on in the survivors. The lessons I learned from him have enabled me to respond not only to the way we develop our services for Holocaust survivors, but also the Bosnian refugees with whom we work.

The application of the concept of mutual support to a current experience of war trauma: work with a group of Bosnian refugees

Having seen how mutual support groups could benefit severely traumatised survivors even long after the war, we then needed to see whether such approaches could assist people more recently traumatised by war, and perhaps even prevent some of the long-term impact of their trauma.

From 1992 onwards, about 350 refugees who came to the UK from Bosnia were assisted to settle in this country through the work of the Jewish Refugee Committee of World Jewish Relief. Details of their reception and integration into the UK will be developed in more detail in Part V.

Following their reception and settlement in this country, one could argue, and, indeed, it has often been forcibly maintained, especially for economic reasons, that the refugees should be encouraged to integrate into the host community, rather than keeping a separate identity. The refugees themselves sometimes react against the notion of forever being seen as refugees and outsiders, and want to make a new life in this country. However, our long-term experience of working with the delayed effects of trauma has shown us how, initially, traumatised people seem to cope and get on with their lives. Just like the refugees and survivors of the Holocaust, these refugees were not coming forward to ask for help with the emotional repercussions of their trauma and uprooting. One could easily assume that all was well, and that further involvement could cease.

We have learned that when trauma is not addressed, when the losses have not been recognised, then the effects are carried inside the individual and may affect health and adjustment to this new environment. In isolation from each other, the sense of alienation exacerbates the trauma.

With this knowledge, gleaned from the Holocaust work, it became crucial to offer an opportunity to recreate a community in microcosm in which these refugees could support each other in adapting to this new situation. A group, which calls itself The Friends of 'La Benevolencija' (the name 'La Bene-volencija' links these refugees to the Jewish community in Sarajevo), was established, and gave the members a sense of identity and belonging. This need for an identity in an alien country argued against a process of assimilation. Attempts at integration did continue, details of which will be described later on. In the process of integration, many more left with time on their hands. The void to be filled affected morale. Financial restrictions did not allow for recreational diversion from the stresses the refugees expressed.

The way through this potential minefield of festering emotion was realised in the establishment of the club. In a similar vein to the first SOS group for survivors, this very mixed group of refugees required a neutral venue in which they could share tastes of 'home' in the food they cooked; where they could speak in their mother tongue; where they could produce a newsletter which would link them with other Bosnian refugees worldwide. The group is comprised of Jews and Moslems, Serbs and Croats, young and old, all of whom had to be accommodated under one roof. The life-force for this club evolved through an elected committee from the membership who work with the facilitator/community worker in developing a meaningful programme. The emphasis in this club, like the SOS group, is on empowerment, using the skills, strengths and coping capacities of the refugees. It strives to minimise the potential conflict of transferred differences from Bosnia, through its focus on task and survival rather than recreating political tensions. Art work, book launches and music allow memories of a life before the trauma to be treasured and celebrated. These creative approaches are also used as media to convey to the host community the richness of their culture, who they are and what they bring in as their unique contribution. Dignity and self-respect are important by-products of this collective identity.

Within this social, informal setting, practical problems can also be addressed. The refugees assist each other at times of illness and bereavement, as well as sharing pleasurable events such as births and marriages. The outings to the English countryside, as well as London's attractions, help to orientate the refugees to their new 'home'. The Friends of 'La Benevolencija' club has been an invaluable resource in helping the refugees to adapt and integrate, and to buffer them from some of the harsh realities which their dislocation to another country brings in its wake.

Mutual support or self-help

We have seen how mutual support among traumatised refugees and survivors reinforces the strong and healthy features of those who have suffered, and empowers them to cope better with their present lives.

However, both the SOS group and the Bosnian club had at their core a dedicated facilitator to guide the often divergent and potentially conflicting interests of the members. In the Bosnian group, the facilitator was also a member of the community and shared the experience of being a refugee. This had the advantage of him understanding the cultural and linguistic character-istics of the group. The disadvantage, however, meant that his own political and religious background served at times to act as an impediment in reaching out to some members of the group.

As a non-survivor in the SOS group, I had not experienced the trauma that the members had undergone in the Holocaust. On the other hand, for this very reason, I did not bring my own experience of suffering to compete with the pain which the members of the group were carrying. My continued presence in the group was seen as helpful by the majority and essential to its ongoing development.

The facilitator ensures the protection of the individual in the group and the survival of the group as a whole. The facilitator is not necessarily the designated leader. The role of the facilitator is to contain the chaos and raw experiences which can emerge when a group of severely traumatised people come together, even when their aim is to promote mutual support. When the threat to survival is no longer an external force, issues of power and control within the group may become more prominent.

The presence of a facilitator may diminish the concept of self-help but, at the same time, augment the therapeutic possibility of mutual support. The sensitivity of the facilitator is, of course, crucial in obtaining the delicate balance which allows the group to feel it is in control of its own destiny.

The SOS group and The Friends of 'La Benevolencija' club emphasise the fundamental importance of mutual support groups both as a first step in reaching out to vulnerable and severely traumatised people, and also as a basis for an ongoing, meaningful approach to help people to live with the effects of their trauma. Mutual support forms the foundation from which other therapeutic approaches may then radiate. The strengthening which results from the sense of belonging and identity, the relief of being with others who have similar experiences, may allow the dark shadow to be faced. The increasing number of survivors from the Holocaust who are now bearing witness to these heinous events in their past, the increasing role of survivors as educators to young children in schools and the increasing emphasis on the need to memorialise what happened for future generations have emerged as a consequence of this support.

Mutual support acts as a catalyst for memory, remembering and remembrance of the traumatic past to be linked to the present and the future. In parallel with the development of this collective response to the trauma, through the establishment of these groups, is the collective response of bearing witness. Though each story is individual, there is a collective need for the past to be remembered. The recording of testimony will be looked at next as a meaningful therapeutic option for those who have suffered severe trauma.

The scream: hearing the stories of survivors

'If nothing else is left one must scream. Silence is the real crime against humanity' (Mandelstam 1970, pp.42–3).

I witnessed a confrontation at a conference in November 1999 on the subject of 'Taking Testimonies Forward', in which survivors were challenged by historians on the subject of the accuracy of their eye-witness accounts. The argument concerning the unreliability of the witness in reproducing facts, especially when a long period of time has elapsed, gave the survivors a sense that the validity of their accounts was being questioned. A huge gulf emerged between the recorder of the atrocity (the historian) and the witness of these heinous crimes (the survivor). In the dynamic which emerged, the essence of the complexity of the testaments to human suffering is contained.

The reaction is not only a personal one for the living survivor, but this 'scream' is for the dead who cannot now speak for themselves. In his chapter entitled 'The Will to Bear Witness', Terence Des Pres (1976) writes of survivors that, when 'facing man-made horror, their need becomes strong to remember and record – to ensure, through one's own survival, or the survival of one's word, that out of horror's very midst (from where else can it come?) the truth shall emerge' (p.35).

Only those who were there, amid the horror, know what really happened. How to tell it, how to find the words that the listener could make sense of, produced a tapestry into which the varied perceptions were interwoven. No two survivors experienced what they went through in the same way. No two survivors would recount their story in the same way. Did this invalidate their accounts? This question begins to border on revisionist viewpoints, and ultimately lead to conclusions that the gas chambers did not exist. The difficulty in recounting horror of such magnitude as existed in the Holocaust led Elie Wiesel (1970) to express that silence is the only adequate response. Nevertheless he concedes that the scream cannot be silenced and has to find an outlet. It has to be heard because the living have a debt to the dead. 'In the survivor's voice the dead's own scream is active... The survivor allows the dead their voice. He makes the silence heard' (Des Pres 1976, p.36).

The vehemence of the survivors' response at the conference is therefore understandable. Now, as these survivors grow older, they have a great need to entrust this remembrance to others. In this way they, and those murdered in the Holocaust, will live on. Des Pres (1976) emphasises how those who face extinction make a pledge that death should not be absolute. The sense that suffering has not been in vain can help to release the witnesses. However, when they hear their experiences distorted, they fear what will happen when they no longer have a voice to correct their reality.

To unlock this potentially damaging dynamic, we need to create a space for a dialogue of understanding. The survivor's story is not history for him/her but part of his/her life and death. It is his/her truth, which time has shaped to accommodate the horrific memory into the present with which he/she has to co-exist. Historians who use oral testimony only have access to what is told, rather than what is untellable. This is only part of the whole, and yet is assumed to be the whole. In his/her quest for fact and truth, the historian often confuses the diversity of eye-witness accounts with their unreliability. They do not take account of the role of the listener, and how this also shapes the story that is told.

Henry Greenspan (1998b), a psychologist who has been listening to survivors retelling their stories for twenty years, has observed, 'Survivors do not recount in a vacuum but always to an imagined audience of readers or listeners; and what survivors say, how they say it, whether they say it at all, will depend in part on their perceptions of who is listening' (p.65). In an attempt to make the telling hearable, Greenspan argues that some of the essence of the story may be lost or missed. The survivors are trying to make a story out of what is not a story. In trying to convey this otherness of the experience, the survivor may use frames of reference which have meaning to the listener, such as survivor guilt, rather than the extremity of terror or loss. 'For certainly it is easier for us to accommodate the guilty survivor than the utterly abandoned survivor… The pain that the guilty survivor directs inside is kept outside for us' (p.70).

In the urgent task of gathering in testimonies before the eye-witnesses have died, the quantity and speed of the operation may result in incomplete records. The survivors themselves have a sense of the danger of this happening, and often record many times with different testimony projects. Trying to make sense of something which does not make sense, trying to portray events which are incomprehensible, cannot be done quickly. Memories which have remained dormant for so long do not necessarily spring into consciousness. Support after the retelling gives courage to pursue further memories, an essential feature often ignored by testimony-taking projects.

This leads us to look at the role of the therapeutic facilitator as an instrument for the untold story – 'what remains unasked, unheard, unsaid and unknown' (Greenspan 1998b, p.71). Many testimony projects use trained volunteers to record testimony, while some organisations, such as AMCHA in Israel (a psychosocial service for Holocaust survivors and their families), prefer to use trained therapists for this purpose. As issues emerge during the course of the testimony, the therapist can then support and follow up the aftermath of reliving past trauma. Working with a survivor over time, when there is no pressure to end the process of telling, allows a relationship to build up. It allows the witness to be at the centre of the process.

When we focus on the survivor, we emphasise what Greenspan (1998a) refers to as the question of how we, as listeners, can enter *in* to what survivors have to convey (p.57) and how they can retell their memories at all. After the conference, one of the historians asked me what I wanted from the survivor. My answer was that there was nothing that *I* wanted – I was not searching for facts or truth. I was listening and responding to an individual survivor's account of his/her unique experience and his/her wish to convey this to me – a non-survivor. In the diversity of these accounts we begin to grapple with the trauma.

Moving the stories on: survivors as educators

Recording the past as testimonies for the future creates what Maria Rosenbloom (1983) calls 'paper monuments'. The tapes and the videos are the tombstones for those who were murdered. The survivor's role in this process is central and crucial. The intense drive to remember the past blurs our vision concerning other remembrances for the future. The miracle of survival also needs to be documented, and this would include images of survivors today. We must in the future remember their resilience and their strength. We must record how they have managed to find their collective and individual voices. We must record them as survivors and not only as victims.

The danger of this being misinterpreted by revisionists is a reality. At the same time, not to record their health and how they cope, despite their past, would only be showing half the picture. Videoing times of enjoyment in the centre, documenting the creative material produced in the centre and keeping the records of issues of concern discussed in the Advisory Committee (an elected consultation group of survivors which will be detailed in Part III) can be powerful evidence of the triumph of the human spirit.

The present takes on prominence in the process of remembrance. It is the evidence needed to give hope to others who have undergone severe trauma that there can be some light which emerges from the darkness. For the survivors, that 'light', that way forward to the future, is embodied in the children who want to listen and learn from them. 'Education as remembrance brought relief no sleeping pill or insightful analysis could match' (Krell 1989, p.222). The Holocaust is now part of the national curriculum. Our therapeutic task is to help survivors to speak publicly about their experiences, to individualise it to these children and students – to help them to identify with the survivors as people, whose childhood was very different from theirs. It is no longer the faceless statistics of six million corpses, but they are the living witnesses of unimaginable horror.

Many of the survivors often feel anxious about speaking to these children, but the positive responses in their questions and in their letters reflect the effectiveness of their work. Supporting the survivors is our therapeutic task. Regulating how much they can expose their emotions needs careful handling. At its best, this two-way experience gives some meaning to survival in the eagerness of these children and students to learn from the survivors. It opens up opportunities for issues such as racism to be addressed, and thereby brings the lessons of the Holocaust into our everyday lives.

The task of the therapeutic facilitator as a witness

'You didn't go through the horrors of the Holocaust, you didn't suffer, so why should you be affected.' This statement was made by survivors to the professional staff who attended the conference on 'Taking Testimonies Forward'. The survivors were incensed by a professional worker's claim of needing support after listening to the survivor's accounts of atrocity. The survivors felt that the reality of their own suffering bore no significant relationship to the professional worker's experience of merely listening to the horror.

While no comparison can be made between the survivors' reality and the impact on the facilitator, some clarification is needed to enable both truths to co-exist.

In my experience of working alongside survivors, I have witnessed the 'screams'. I would like to give a few examples of this phenomenon both from my individual contact with survivors as well as in my role as manager of the centres.

1. I was sitting with a child survivor as she was struggling to remember the detail of what happened to her when she was left behind by her family who were taken by the Nazis. I suddenly found it difficult to breathe and experienced a suffocating feeling in the silence of her forgotten memory. What transpired was her experience of having been buried in order to hide her from being caught and deported. The fragments of her memory were not all open to recollection. However, this reconnection to a memory which had been buried deep inside her for fear of remembering it

resurfaced for air and was faced in our encounter. I witnessed the fear that she had carried with her from the time of the trauma. This acknowledgement released other memories both about her trauma and also about her home before the trauma began.

2. The second example relates to an incident in which a survivor phoned me in great distress to report an event which had happened in our social centre. This survivor had taken a piece of bread, which she had found in the centre, to eat with her tea, without realising that it had already been claimed by another survivor who had wanted to eat it at a later point in the afternoon. This other survivor accused her of stealing her bread, became enraged and called her a thief. The 'accused' said she was so overwhelmed by this reaction that she thought she could not return to the centre. In our subsequent discussion, the incident was put into perspective. It seemed to have ricocheted from the past into the present. It related to a real trauma in which a piece of bread meant the difference between life and death. With a full stomach we have great difficulty in imagining the pain of starvation. Yet this experience never really leaves those who have been starved, as this incident underlines. Remembering this with the survivor reduced the pain of the accusation, and she continues to attend the centre.

Echoes of these gnawing pains are glimpsed in the refusal of survivors to queue for food at lunchtime at our centre. It is evidenced in the abundance of food in our centres, for 'the Holocaust was a thousand days of hunger, a thousand daydreams of food' (Haas 1996, p.60). 'I'm afraid of hunger,' one survivor commented. As therapeutic facilitators we become witnesses to these re-experienced nightmares which find their way into our daytime reality.

3. A peaceful card afternoon in the centre broke out into confused turbulence over the transport arrangements for some of the members. Taxis that had been ordered did not arrive. Taxis that did arrive were turned away by those who had decided to take lifts with other members. Logistically this did not present an overwhelming challenge, but the chaos that ensued and generated throughout the centre seemed to come from another time and

place. Just the word 'transport' takes on a very different significance for those who were transported to the camps. The chaos of being herded into cattle trucks, the uncertainty, the fear and the confusion remain as memories waiting to be unleashed. As facilitators, we have to be constantly vigilant and sensitive to what it means if current events trigger these powerful memories from the past.

4.   One survivor expressed her fear that there were now too many people coming into the centre at certain times, and she did not think she could continue to attend. The Yiddish group is an example. Its very success and popularity has brought more and more people into the group. As it has grown larger, it brings another dynamic which threatens its equilibrium. Space to talk and space to breathe become more restricted, and intimacy can easily convert into hostility. Overcrowding is linked to the inhumane environment of the camps or the cramped conditions of those who were hidden. A recent incident related to a new member being bullied by an older member into sitting at the back of the room. It seemed to demonstrate an underlying dynamic which emerges in the fight for space. Being together is the aspect to be encouraged, while overcrowding is the aspect to be avoided. The same issue is repeated when new members join the centre. Are they bona fide members? Could they go to some other centre? Are they just using the centre as a cheap option? Who are the insiders and who are the outsiders? The careful introduction of new members, by the staff, allows the above questions, posed by the survivors, to be acknowledged.

We are daily reminded of the presence of the Holocaust in the lives of survivors, even if they do not talk about it: '…thousands of stimuli have the potential for eliciting strong feelings in survivors. Sights, smells, sounds, items, situations, strong feelings evoke sadness or anger as they remind him of a fuller time which has evaporated' (Haas 1996, p.63). Haas talks of these as the survivor's vulnerabilities. He cites an example of a survivor when he comments, '…many times I would come home from work upset. My children would ask, "Why is Daddy angry?" I wasn't angry, but something hit me that day. Maybe I heard German spoken…' (p.63).

In the setting of a Holocaust Survivors' Centre these vulnerabilities need to be understood and allowed to find an outlet. Anticipating these triggers and being aware of how they may present themselves is essential to understanding how these manifestations from the past are managed. The freedom to bring the 'bestiality' of the Holocaust experience, as one survivor put it to me, allows for the repercussions from the past to be addressed without necessarily repeating this experience in the present. We also have to remind ourselves that this *is* another time, and this is not a death camp.

In a general day centre for the elderly, these voices from the past may never be heard or witnessed. A professional colleague once commented to me that, by bringing a group of survivors together, all we were doing was recreating a camp experience in which they were once again imprisoned. The question challenged me and demanded an answer. It is true that by bringing a group of severely traumatised survivors together, the dynamics of their suffering are brought into focus. The dark shadow is faced as events from the past are recreated in the present. In a non-specialised day centre, this dynamic would be absent, and so the past would have to remain locked in the past, returning at night in the solitude of nightmares. If it did ever surface, the resulting behaviour may be seen as difficult to contain without reference to its context. The freedom to be a survivor and to express the rage is more likely, in my experience, to liberate the survivor from his/her past so that he/she can begin to look at the future.

Those who specialise in working with the long-term effects of severe trauma witness the aftermath on a daily basis. Even though we can never know what it was really like to undergo unrelenting torture and inhumanity, we do get glimpses of this 'other world'. We do witness suffering, and it has the power to touch us.

Learning to respond: the shift between the 'other' and ourselves

Having passed through the door into the world of extreme trauma, having seen the impact of that trauma on the lives of those who have experienced the suffering, how do we respond therapeutically to what we have learned and witnessed from the survivors? The powerlessness generated through the re-experiencing of trauma can limit our role to one of passive observer. We may witness suffering, we may be empathetic to the pain, we may create a 'culture of belief' (Harris 2002) to facilitate trust, but we may nevertheless remain inactive in our responses. Can we witness suffering and not be drawn into issues about justice and social change?

Kate Harris, working as a counselling psychologist with asylum seekers, argues that much counselling tends to be focused on accepting the status quo and coming to terms with the imperfections of life and accepting limitations. She sees political action as part of the therapeutic work with those who have been exiled and traumatised. She contrasts this to the more traditional understanding of therapy in which political activity has an uneasy relationship to the therapeutic task.

This last section of Part II focuses on the thinking behind the shift between the 'other' and ourselves, and prepares us for the more detailed look at how we implement these ideas in our practice. Identifying with and internalising experiences of suffering makes a bridge between the 'I' and the 'Thou' (Buber 1958). We are no longer just observers and bystanders to suffering, but are touched by it, and need to respond.

As I write this section of the book, the festival of Passover is fast approaching – the story of slavery, cruelty, persecution and, finally, liberation. What is so special about this story is not only its direct link to the suffering in the Holocaust, but also its message. Each Jew is asked to take on the mantle of slavery – to imagine that we ourselves were slaves in Egypt, and thus directly connected to that experience.

> Today flowing back into yesterday,
> Like a river enclosed at its mouth.
> Each one of us has been a slave in Egypt,
> Soaked straw and clay with sweat,
> And crossed the sea dry-footed.
> 'You too, stranger.'
>
> *(Primo Levi's poem 'Passover'[5])*

Fundamental to this thinking is the basic Jewish ethic of helping the stranger. What does this ethic mean in practice? The floods in Mozambique prompted a rapid and generous response from the community – both Jews and non-Jews. Media coverage reinforced the plight of those suffering people. In contrast, the stranger on our own doorstep has met with quite another response – namely, in the treatment of asylum seekers. Somehow the distance and the difference of the sufferer are safety factors which shape the humanitarian nature of our response. The closer the proximity of the stranger, paradoxically, the more indifferent or even hostile the response.

Indifference is the root of inactivity. In the 1930s, those who wished to escape the Nazi regime and find a safe haven in Britain helplessly waited for their quota number to be called. Those who had to wait too long never made it. Parents were desperate for their children to be sent to safety, but the heart of the community only partially softened to accept a proportion of these children into its midst. These were Jewish children. Some found their way into non-Jewish homes, and their lives were thereby saved.

It is not my aim to condemn, but to try to understand how this could have happened. Some have argued that the impending world war and the worsening economic climate were mitigating factors in this closure to humanity. However, today, the group of Bosnian refugees we work with remain largely 'outsiders' to the community. Organisations involved in their care – both the Jewish Refugee Committee and Jewish Care – ease the conscience for the rest of the community. My appeal to certain members of the community – those with the resources to help individual refugees obtain work – met with very little success. Yet this is the soul of our own existence. Our future depends on this connection between these 'outsiders' and ourselves. The dictum 'there but for the grace of G-d go I' means that we may see others suffering, but do not want to be contaminated by it. The word 'refugee' evokes a certain response. In the Jewish community it reminds us of our exile and of our own insecurity. In times of peace, such thoughts are often avoided, and in these circumstances, there is a blurring of boundaries between Jew and non-Jew in their attitudes to the newcomers.

As a result of my work with displaced and traumatised people, I cannot remain silent in the uncomfortable climate of xenophobic outpouring that relates to current asylum seekers. The very words resonate with an emptiness of meaning. Instead of asylum being equated with a place of safety and refuge, the propaganda machine ensures the opposite becomes a reality. Violent attacks, humiliations and racist hatred become 'normal' responses to those who are seen as threatening our equilibrium.

In a series of articles in the *Guardian* (March 2000) on the 'Asylum Debate', four days of prominent coverage exposed the dynamic in the 'Garden of England' around the port of Dover. In this quintessential British domain of fair play and tolerance lurks a monster demanding to be unleashed. The rationale for 'sending them back and closing the door' is argued with frightening clarity.

Those who manage to avoid the effects of the brainwashing see the danger in their midst, and challenge both the racist and the bystander. One such person mentioned in the first *Guardian* article by Vikram Dodd, on 28 March 2000, is the Reverend Norman Setchell, who runs English classes for the refugees in a church hall. Setchell is quoted as saying, 'I don't want to look back in five years' time and hang our heads in shame because we haven't done enough... What bothers me is the fundamental lack of compassion coupled with the lack of knowledge and awareness of where these people came from...'

The article ends with a local resident in Dover making the following statement: 'People will tell you the refugees are all thieves, it's unbelievable what you hear. It makes me ashamed to be British. I think Dover has something to be ashamed of. I don't know what kind of noose we're making for ourselves.'

This last sentence is about mankind's future. For the world to be saved from destruction, each one of us has to take responsibility for ensuring that enough goodness remains. I have always been fascinated by the Jewish principle of the 'Lamed Vov' (Montefiore and Loewe 1974). The idea behind this is the necessity of maintaining thirty-six people of good deeds for the whole of humanity to continue. However, the principle rests on the idea that we never know who these thirty-six people are. They are not identifiable and, hence, we cannot be lulled into a state of complacency about our own future. To ensure the world continues, we have to act as if each one of us could be one of the Lamed Vov. This sense of collective responsibility would guide our actions as individuals. In this sense we cannot be bystanders. We cannot watch and not react when we see people attacked and abused. We cannot leave it to the few to speak out when our society's morality is being threatened.

This is the legacy of the past for the future. Eventually we may all be in danger, as illustrated in Pastor Martin Niemöller's (1995) closing words of his poem: 'And finally they came for me and there was no-one left to speak for me' (p.9). Gays, blacks, Jews, intellectuals: any group can become the target of scapegoating and persecution.

How we respond to these inherent destructive forces can be enacted through small deeds rather than some grand unachievable designs. I believe people can be influenced by good as well as by evil, as evidenced in those people who risked their lives to save others.

Let me begin with a personal account. My mother would recount stories of her life in the 1930s in rural Germany. In the small village she knew everyone. She went to school with the other children in the village. At Christmas time they would join their Catholic neighbours on their sleigh ride to the church for Mass. My grandfather's shop selling textiles, as well as the wine produced in his vineyards, was well patronised by local people. With the rise of Hitler and the Nazis, that idyllic life began to change. Families were split apart as younger members joined the Hitler Youth. One such family were neighbours of my mother. The three sons became ardent Nazi supporters and forbade their mother to visit my mother's home. She defied them and continued to be friendly with my mother's family. By doing so, she took a risk that she would be denounced by her sons.

At Kristallnacht, my mother's home was brutally vandalised by the Nazis. My grandfather was arrested and my mother and grandmother hid under a bridge in the water until the next day. However, despite these vicious scenes, my mother also told me how the daughter of the gaoler was a friend of hers, and had comforted her with the reassurance that my grandfather would be looked after and receive medication for his heart. These were just two instances of personal human kindness in the face of persecution and violence.

Studies of altruism by Douglas Huneke (1988), P.M. Oliner and S.P. Oliner (1988), and Mordecai Paldiel (1988) emphasise that altruism is in all of us. Those who rescued Jews during the war, for example, were not special in the sense that their exemplary behaviour, which earned them the title of the 'Righteous among Nations', was something beyond our reach. As Paldiel writes, altruism is 'a basic human trait which needs to be aroused from its enforced slumber and cultivated – by tolerating its soothing presence in our lives, instead of repressing it'.

The search to understand the rescuer points to certain traits being identified which predispose the individual towards an altruistic response. Huneke (1988) lists these as: 'a spirit of adventurousness; parental model of moral conduct; socially marginal (religiously inspired non-conformity); empathetic imaginations; theatrical skills; spirit of hospitality; personal experience of suffering; containment of prejudice; group intervention (communal)' (p.489). However, the Oliners' (1988) study did not seem to be able to draw significant conclusions, but instead underlines the statement of those interviewed that they could not have acted differently under the circumstances – they knew they had to do something and could not just stand by and watch.

Thinking about the rescuers at this point in the book underlines the theme of hope, that there is something which can be done to offer, as Douglas Huneke (1988) puts it, 'Glimpses of light in a vast darkness' (p.486). If we see ourselves, the therapeutic facilitators, as having these strengths within us to become the instruments of remembrance, it will motivate us to devote our energies to ensuring that the suffering which has happened will not have been in vain. Our work is much more complex in that it must include some vision of a future. 'The task,' as Mordecai Paldiel (1988) states, 'is not so much to meticulously search out and select the few Righteous persons, so as to be able to praise, honour and salute them...from a distance, but the rather no-less arduous charge of looking into our own souls in order to widen the channels through which the altruistic archetype, buried in the deep recesses of our fathomless mind, may flow unimpeded...' (p.524).

The thrust of this statement moves us out of the passive bystander position into a position in which we must respond. In my fight to ensure that the services which will be described in Part III became a reality, I had to find within myself uncharted realms which would guide me. To move what was in effect a collection of ideas into a concrete project made personal demands on me which earned me a reputation of being forthright and assertive.

I have learned from survivors not to be a victim; I have challenged decisions, I have asked questions that I was sometimes frightened to ask; I have spoken in front of large audiences of professionals; I have talked to the media to ensure the voice of the survivors is heard; I have travelled alone to many countries, developing a network to strengthen our work.

There is much which we have already left behind in our journey towards finding the right approach in our therapeutic work with survivors of extreme trauma. However, there is much we still have to learn in applying this to practical responses. We are not, as some have said, 'all survivors', but we may be closer to understanding what we can never know; we may be closer to responding to what we cannot share; we may be closer to a future which we cannot imagine.

Endnotes

1. 'The Holocaust Patient,' by Elie Wiesel. Copyright © 1982 by Elie Wiesel. Reprinted by permission of Georges Borchardt, Inc., for the author. Permission to reprint is also granted by Sheil Land Associates Ltd, London.

2. *All Rivers Run to the Sea* © 1996 Elie Wiesel is reprinted by permission of HarperCollins Publishers, London. Permission is also granted by Random House Inc. (Alfred A. Knopf), New York.

3. Excerpts from *Night* by Elie Wiesel, translated by Stella Rodway. Copyright © 1960 by MacGibbon & Kee. Copyright renewed © 1988 by The Collins Publishing Group. Reprinted by permission of Hill and Wang, a division of Farrar, Straus and Giroux, LLC. Permission to reprint is also granted by Sheil Land Associates Ltd, London.

4. 'Soup' (1991) by Edward Bond is reprinted by kind permission of Methuen Publishing Limited. © Edward Bond (1991).

5. Excerpt from 'Passover' from *Collected Poems* by Primo Levi, translated by Ruth Feldman and Brian Swann. English translation copyright © 1988 by Ruth Feldman and Brian Swann. Reprinted by permission of Faber & Faber, Inc. an affiliate of Farrar, Straus and Giroux, LLC.

PART III

A Therapeutic Model for Working with the Aftermath of Atrocity

Introduction

I focused in Part II on the importance of listening to survivors about how to respond to atrocity. In Part III, I will be applying the lessons I have learned from them which have helped me to translate their trauma into a more meaningful therapeutic language. I will show how the survivors guided me to develop services which have helped them to live differently with the aftermath of atrocity. Contained in the following pages is a detailed account of a therapeutic model – Shalvata (a therapy centre) and the Holocaust Survivors' Centre (a social centre) – which has evolved during my journey with survivors.

Shalvata opened in 1990, initially as a general mental health centre for the Jewish Community, as well as for continuing the work I had already started with Holocaust survivors. In 1993 the Holocaust Survivors' Centre opened next door to Shalvata. As a result, more and more survivors began to use the service. The inappropriateness of trying to offer a therapeutic service to Holocaust survivors within a mental health facility clarified itself, and by 1995 Shalvata became a specialist service, and the general mental health work returned to Jewish Care. This significantly augmented the therapeutic development of the work with survivors.

This part of the book should be the easiest to write because I am very familiar with it. Yet it challenges me the most, because my heart and soul are bound up with it. The richness and texture must be experienced by those who read it. It needs to be imbued with life and vitality to perhaps encourage others to take something from it which they can use. Merely describing how the model functions and works would not do justice to those who have helped to make it – for the survivors were not put into these services which developed, but they themselves helped to shape and design the form which we now see.

When I started writing, I began with the model, but soon found it too distant – too remote. It begged me to find a different route. This led me to the survivors themselves. They pressed me to speak about our encounters together. In their voices, the essence and truth of what needs to be understood is contained. The anecdotes scattered throughout the text give glimpses of the varied and colourful possibilities in meeting those who have been traumatised. If I were not writing, perhaps I would not even notice the importance of these interactions. I have become much more alert, much more sensitive to the nuances that exist around me, in my daily contact with survivors. They are there waiting to be noticed, waiting to be recorded, as evidence of the different ways of hearing and working with the aftermath of trauma. They allow me to personalise how I work, what it says about me and who I am, for there is something particular in how I relate to the survivors. Others may do it differently, and there are no universal conclusions drawn which would guide all responses to severe trauma. These anecdotes are like a diary of everyday happenings, which I now wish I had started much earlier.

The following more detailed accounts of the journeys undertaken with survivors over many years introduce the reader to people whose stories tell of unique events. It is important for the reader to meet these survivors, to get to know them a little and to observe what seems to help them in these encounters with me.

Chapter 6

Encounters with Survivors

Let me tell you about how I have worked alongside survivors as they journeyed into the realms of the dark shadow. These stories are not really case studies, although some theoretical books would call them so. They are encounters, whose dynamic is as revealing as the content of what is spoken about. They move forward and backward in time. At their core is the severe trauma, the rupture, which dislocated the survivors from this world, and then placed them back in an altered state in which no resting place could be found.

Irena

Background

Irena was born in Lvov in Poland in 1933. Lvov was a thriving town full of culture and interest. Her father was a businessman in the leather trade. Her parents created a comfortable home life for Irena and her sister. Irena has one photograph of her father, her sister and herself, but no memory of her mother. She remembers very little about her home except for an image of their kitchen with its oven range and a chimney which went up through the ceiling.

Irena's life was shattered in 1941, when her parents were deported to Auschwitz. She never saw them again. Her sister was also separated from her the same night. Irena does not know what really happened to her, as she never wanted to talk about it after the war. Her sister went to live in Israel, and they kept in touch until she died a few years ago.

Aged eight years old, Irena was sent to the Warsaw Ghetto and was later hidden in a sewer and then in a convent. Memories of those times are very fragmented and she is troubled by their lack of clarity. The compensation she now receives for her years of suffering is a concrete acknowledgement of that trauma.

Aged twelve years old, in 1945, she came to England, where she has lived ever since. She married and has a son and daughter, and several grandchildren. Irena worked as a teacher. In adulthood, she began to enjoy her life. Together with her husband she led a very full social life. Her world once more fell apart when her husband left her and the children. The sense of abandonment acted as the trigger for the unresolved trauma in her childhood during the Holocaust.

Irena requested that her parents' names, Zigmund and Basia, are recorded here in their memory.

The encounter

Irena is not her real name, but the name she calls herself. The question is, who is she? No name, no identity, a child lost in time. The first contact we had was through the SOS group in the mid-1980s (see Part II) – we got to know each other through that informal, social group. I picked up fragments from her past – memories of the Warsaw Ghetto, experiences of hiding in a sewer and later in a convent, gave glimpses of her traumatised childhood. It was difficult for her to remember the details. As a young child of eight years, hidden in a cupboard, she had watched her parents being taken away by the Nazis, and never saw them again. Silhouettes of her parents' faces revealed little detail of what they looked like. Alone, all alone. This is the overwhelming remnant of a trauma too devastating to recall. Only memories of hunger, overcrowding and abandonment remain with her. No mother, no father, no protective shield around her, she felt vulnerable, powerless and helpless. Time did not stand still, and the little girl began to develop. There was no-one to guide her through the turbulent changes of growing up. Her adopted home after the war in a remote part of Wales reverberated the isolation she had carried with her. Second-hand clothes passed on from the other children in the family reinforced her sense of worthlessness.

The longed-for connection to another human being was realised in her marriage to a handsome, vibrant man who symbolised the hope of 'liberation', freeing her from all she had suffered. The parties, the journeys into new places, the dancing, the fun and zest for life seemed to reconnect her to the essence of herself as a child and, for a while, she felt whole again and glad to be alive. Her two children, a boy and girl, replaced some lost murdered souls that had depleted her family. The Holocaust became more of a memory that belonged to the past. Yet it also remained. It robbed her of the support she needed as she took on her role of a mother. How did mothers behave? What did mothers have to do? How should she comfort her child who was crying? She coped and found the strengths to deal with these unknown events.

This is not a story with a happy ending. The happiness she found was a respite, an interlude, until the trauma erupted again with such ferocity that death lurked nearby, and she came close to taking her own life. The excitement and thrill that had united her and her husband transformed to despair when she again experienced the pain of abandonment and loss as the marriage fell apart. Her husband had also survived the Holocaust. Irena still feels that the absence of help at that point in their lives contributed to an irreversible change from which she has never recovered. The subsequent divorce reinstated the dark reaches of her earlier trauma. She hung between life and death.

In her continuing despair after the divorce, Irena found me many years ago. We struggled together to hold on long enough for death not to take away any other options. There was still something she needed to do, and that gave us a breathing space. She wanted her children to know what had happened to her and her family in the Holocaust, and that she was not a neurotic, mad woman, but someone who had suffered. She felt the emotional repercussions of her traumatic marital breakdown had in some way damaged her children. She especially wanted to reconnect to her daughter. She hoped that her daughter would understand her mother's reactions in the light of her Holocaust background, rather than judging her apparent irrationality.

First of all, *I* had to understand. The past gained access to the present as the trauma was relived. Her silent, hidden voice began to find the words to grapple with this re-emerging trauma. Images emerged as newly created 'photographs' gave the undocumented past a reality. We imagined her mother's face, how she would have liked it to be, if she could remember it. Phone calls, visits, her centrality to the development of the Holocaust Survivors' Centre, gave nourishment to her empty stomach. Tears flowed, anger thundered, sobbing despair drowned the space we sat in.

The safety, the accessibility, the trust which developed between us, the cups of tea we drank together, the hug, the touch, seemed to strengthen this vulnerable, hurt person. There was no rush to crowd this experience into a short episode in time. Irena regulated, within the space of an hour or so, what needed to be addressed that day. She needed my commitment to be there for her – not to leave her as she had been left before.

And so it was that, time after time, she would return. When she felt strong enough, her ex-husband also participated, as well as her daughter and, at times, her son. She conveyed what she wanted to say to them. In that space, they needed to listen to her. The dignity, the respect which our relationship conveyed, painted another picture of this 'out of control', jealous, punishing figure seen by her family. Our dialogue, which reflected who Irena was, why she was, and what she would like to be, opened the door for another dialogue, this time with her daughter.

The recurring themes in our encounters – of revenge on her ex-husband; of the unfinished business related to the 'burial' of her parents; of her sense of aloneness; of her deteriorating physical health; of her ageing; of her concerns for the survival of the centre; of her ongoing depression – appear with ritualistic regularity in our meetings as the associated emotions are confronted. These repercussions of the dark shadow are faced on a continuum from extreme despair to laughter and hope. Present strategies, which Irena has developed, help to contain the amorphous, engulfing and chaotic threats from a traumatic past. Planned holidays, soothing cruises, shopping with her daughter, playing bridge, give meaning to her often meaningless life. These moments of relief help another day to be lived. They have become the focus in our encounters, both through Shalvata and the Holocaust Survivors' Centre.

Let us take one of those days, and detail one of the meetings Irena and I have shared.

Irena is waiting for me, with a cup of tea made for her by the receptionist in Shalvata. Irena had told me that she likes to be offered a drink, as her everyday life of living alone does not provide this service. I accompany her to my room.

Irena is small in stature, as many of the survivors whom I encounter are. Her well-groomed blonde hair and immaculate style of dress conceal the sadness and weariness she carries inside her. Irena always sits opposite me, and places her cup nearby. Each time we meet, the mood is different, and I quickly sense the expression on her face.

She often comes to see me having played bridge in the HSC. By osmosis, she mops up the mood of the centre. She feels passionately about the centre, and I have come to rely on her to gauge the grass-roots feeling there, and to suggest ways of addressing the needs. This particular day she is angry about the issue of the HSC providing taxis for some members to come to the centre. She begins with something concrete, something which can convey the emotion she is carrying. We deal with the issue on the presenting level. She often consults her watch, regulating the time she has available to her. She takes control over this aspect of the meeting and times the ending.

She is ambivalent about getting on to the subject of herself and her personal life. The anger felt in the centre becomes focused on her ex-husband. She looks at me as this repeated theme once more springs forth. Accounts of his holidays, of his erratic contacts with her, of his social life, of his relationship with their children, remain as unresolved wounds – sometimes overwhelmingly painful, while at other times accommodated in her desire not to be alone. Resolving the conflict between them, Irena feels, would be giving her ex-husband a victory. She believes that this current wound, which can never be healed, is a constant reminder of the earlier hurt inflicted on her when she was torn apart from her parents.

The unending pain cannot be relieved, only contained. In the repetition, a scabbing occurs on the wound, as the impact of what bothers her remains behind in my room after she has left. She fears that she will bore me, as she recounts her ongoing anxieties. Balanced against the depressing recurrence of hurt and suffering are healing glimpses in her relationship with her daughter and her involvement with her grandchildren. The grandchildren seem to offer Irena a second chance to be the mother she could not always be to her own children because she had no model to base this on.

She tells me of the clothes she has bought for her next holiday. She went with her daughter to buy new outfits. She tells me she had remembered an earlier discussion we had about treating herself well, and she felt good about it. We talk about clothes and about fashion. She watches what I wear, and comments on it. She talks animatedly on such subjects. The link between her daughter and myself are obvious; we even have the same name. More particularly, she feels I am the solid, stabilising anchor in her world. In the middle of our meeting, she comes over to me and says that she wants to give me a hug. For a child without its mother, this is a powerful moment.

'I'm not OK' is interspersed with coping. The depression which Irena says never leaves her is lifted temporarily during moments of enjoyment and connectedness. Her fears about her ageing and health problems are balanced in the times I see her dancing during the celebrations of Israel Independence Day in the HSC, and watch her having her hands massaged by her daughter who volunteers as a manicurist in the HSC. My encounters with her, and her active participation in the HSC, seem to strengthen her ability to cope, and act as an antidote to the continuing moments of sadness and despair. Our encounters alone would not be enough to channel the rage of her grief at what she has lost. The HSC offers her other avenues. The recreational aspects help to lighten the darkness. Outings to art exhibitions, operas and concerts reawaken life-enhancing passions which tended to become buried in the aftermath of her re-experienced trauma relating to her divorce.

Her participation in the committees of the HSC gives her a voice, dignity, an identity and status. She regards the HSC as her second home in which she belongs and to which she contributes. The HSC gives her back a community which she lost when the Holocaust started. Irena has become the person to whom other members turn when they want their views expressed. She is often the spokesperson, ensuring that the more silent voices are heard. She is seen as strong and forthright – a far cry from the terrified child left on her own. Yet, in the space of our encounters together, she expresses her need for me to be there for her, most particularly during the years that lie ahead. She is more aware of what she cannot change, and clearer about aspects of her life which she can do something about.

The fragmented world of her memories of the past is repeated in the disconnected process of this meeting. Her improved self-esteem, her self-respect and dignity allow these fragments of her lost childhood to be brought together. What I offer Irena is not insightful interpretation to link her past to her present, but my willingness to move with her in this labyrinth of half-remembered memories that invade her daily life, and help her to find strategies to live differently with her trauma. I began with no notion of the end. That does not mean there is no structure, nor plan, but the 'nourishment' needed for this child who had been left hungry takes longer.

Chava

Background

Chava was born in Antwerp, Belgium, in 1938. Her parents were from Poland. They married in Belgium. Her father worked as a couturier in men's and women's fashion. Her grandparents had a factory manufacturing fur, and her mother worked for them.

Chava was three years old when she was sent to a convent to be hidden from the Nazis. She remembers very little of her early childhood, except for glimpses of her home, the chickens that ran around in the garden, and her grandmother singing.

Chava does not remember her mother. She cannot remember her face, as though she did not exist. Her mother was deported to Auschwitz and did not survive. Chava spent the war years till 1946 hidden in the convent, first with her sister and then separated from her. After the war, the children came to England to live with their father who had left Belgium prior to the war.

Chava went to school in England. Though her mother tongue was French, Chava has no trace of an accent. Indeed, there are no overt signs to link her to her traumatic past. They are as hidden as the experience she went through.

Her post-Holocaust childhood was also traumatic and she left home as soon as she could. Her failed marriage and her daughter's health problems compounded her difficulties and her coping strategy broke down at the point when she came to see me. Chava wanted her parents' names Frania Iglinski and Leon Luftman to be recorded here.

The encounter

When Chava first came to see me, her long, flowing hair and small stature evoked an image of someone much younger than her (mid-fifties) years – reminiscent more of adolescence than adulthood.

A chance meeting near her home brought us together. I was rushing along the street, late for an appointment, when a familiar face stopped me to say hello. I had seen Chava at the child survivor support group which had been meeting at Shalvata, but knew very little about her. She seemed distressed that day, and briefly told me that the reason for her upset was the deteriorating health of her daughter, and how helpless she felt, watching her daughter grow weaker. I encouraged Chava to come and see me at Shalvata, yet sensed that it would not be an easy decision for her to make.

What helped her to make the decision to come to Shalvata is not clear, but she decided to do so. This informal encounter outside my office may have played a significant part in freeing her to seek help. There were also others in the self-help child survivor group who knew me, and I was therefore not a stranger to her.

Those early meetings were a testing time. Uncertainty, mistrust and fear lurked closely to her overwhelming wish to share the burden she carried. Time and patience set the rhythm to contain the anxiety and distress. There was no pressure to reveal more than she felt comfortable with. It became clear that Chava had coped with life until this present moment in time, and I needed to remember this as her emotions began to crumble.

She slowly revealed how her daughter's illness had led the daughter to abandon her three young children, and this event had triggered memories of her own from a past she thought had been long forgotten.

Chava soon began to talk about her wartime experiences. In the convent, life took on another meaning. The darkness, the grey stone walls of the cellar in which these two young girls were kept, gave no warmth or comfort to counteract their abandonment and loss. The primitive sanitation and inadequate food gave them no sense of nurturing or caring. Too young to even register the reality of what was happening, Chava clung to her older sister as some ray of normality and sustenance. Though they were kept alive physically, no-one came close to 'hold' them or reassure them. Chava's older sister suffered from the responsibility she carried in the departing words of her mother to take care of her little sister.

This one source of warmth departed when Chava's sister was separated from her in the last year before the war ended. A little older by this time, she experienced her isolation. No toys, no playthings to ease her sense of being alone – she struggled to recall this void in the dark hole. Only reflections of that 'other place' still haunt her.

These tragic years were brought to me not only through Chava's words, but through a painting of the cellar which she had kept hidden in a cupboard at home. The painting showed in matchstick form these two abandoned children, waiting for their mother to return. In contrast to Chava's other art work, the childlike quality of the painting recaptured the time it was meant to represent. She painted it as a child, not as an adult. The pain it contained forced it to remain hidden, until she came to see me and could share this moment of bringing it out of hiding. The naivety of form in the painting spoke more than words could describe of her 'missing years' – her lost childhood.

Little by little, more of the truth of Chava's trauma was revealed. It was not a smooth progression of a structured testimony, but took its own momentum in bites which could gradually be digested. Intermingled with these snapshots from the past were present concerns for her grandchildren, who had also been tragically abandoned by their mother. The youngest grandchild became the focus for Chava's attention. As she cared for him, she seemed to begin to care for herself.

Many practical problems also presented themselves in our meetings. They offered an opportunity for an oasis to be created in which trust could be established through repeated evidence of my concern about her day-to-day reality. Chava had found it necessary to give up work because of the emotional resurfacing of her past trauma in her current anxieties about her daughter. To ignore her financial and material circumstances at that point would have increased the stress she was already having to bear on an emotional level. Focusing on issues for which there were solutions counterbalanced the often overwhelming feelings of powerlessness accompanying this 'child' who had been so deprived.

An example of this can be seen when Chava asked for my help in obtaining an increase in her German 'health' pension, awarded to her for emotional damage received during the Holocaust. The reassessment necessitated a visit to a German psychiatrist, on whose recommendation the money would either be increased or decreased. The power invested in this German authority figure was, needless to say, like rubbing salt into a wound. Reliving her traumatic memories with this psychiatrist who spoke with a German accent was a cruel necessity. I accompanied Chava, with my own issues having been firmly addressed beforehand, so that our combined energy could be concentrated on this matter in hand. The small increase was in fact granted.

Creating a solid, dependable figure in Chava's unsettled life seemed a basic requirement to work with her. Being the link for her in the complex world of 'helping' organisations ensures that her basic needs continue to be addressed.

As the pressures in her current life subsided a fraction, more tragedy emerged from the dark shadows of her past. Post-Holocaust trauma added to an already fractured foundation. She told me that her father, who had claimed Chava and her sister after the war, then brought them back with him to England. The realisation of her mother's death was soon revealed. Her father's new wife, Chava's stepmother, offered the children no haven for their sadness. Her father's abuse of Chava compounded a surfeit of tragedy. The children were sent away to a boarding school. Chava was relieved to be away from home, but soon faced another loss. Her sister met a sudden death from a brain tumour reactivated through a blow to her head by an irate teacher at the boarding school. Her sister, who carried so much of the pain of loss for their mother, now left Chava once more on her own. Chava coped by making herself liked by the other children, by concentrating her energy on enjoying life, and not thinking too much about what had befallen her. As a child, she wanted to be like the other children. She felt that this short time of her life, away from the horrors of home, were the best years.

Happiness was short-lived and elusive. Her father reclaimed this good time from her when he brought her home again. Her threshold of tolerance was finally reached. Escape seemed the only option. The route was into an unsatisfactory marriage, out of which her one daughter was born. Her 'absent' mother seemed to leave unfilled hollows. There was no model to draw on in her own task of motherhood. Hedonistic longings to ward off the despair of her suffering focused her attention on her own life. Her child, though cared for by Chava, was difficult to accommodate. The child's demands competed with her own need to survive. The years she lost in the Holocaust needed to be recaptured now she was 'free'.

Relationships brought excitement as well as the danger of abandonment. Security seemed out of reach, as Chava tried to control the endings of these affairs. Trust seemed to pass her by. Chava lived well and made enough money while working. However, signs that things were not progressing satisfactorily showed up symptomatically in her daughter. This necessitated professional help, but it was terminated early in the process.

Without Chava's daughter's permission, I cannot venture deeper into how the trauma manifested itself in her life. Suffice it to say that Chava regards her daughter's problems as Hitler's legacy, and yet the one area that eludes her. Her daughter is the reminder of the 'unfinished business' of her tragic past.

What Chava *could* do was address these remnants of a shattered life left incomplete in the struggle to survive. Chava began to write about her time in the cellar. She found the words and means of expression as part of a sharing experience with other members of the creative writing group in the Holocaust Survivors' Centre. Some mastery over a language which was not her mother tongue gave her a sense of both achievement and control. Having written a short story in *Out of the Dark* (1996), a collection of vignettes published by the HSC, she went on to write a book.

In this process of writing, she began her mourning. Strengthened by her increasing belief in my ability to help her, she opened up to the possibility of 'burying' her mother. During the months she had been coming to see me, Chava seemed to be reconnecting to other aspects of her past – namely, her Jewish roots. She said to me one day, 'You know, whenever I come and see you, I buy a kosher chicken.' Amused by the association, I also understood that her Jewish identity was becoming more central to her life.

In marked contrast to her early appearance in our work, Chava changed her hairstyle by cutting off her long tresses and adopting a much shorter, sophisticated style. She dressed smartly and with care and seemed to be moving out of adolescence into adulthood. Chava was passing along a continuum. Though still young in comparison with some of the other survivors, age was the uncontrollable reality snapping at the heels of all. My presence in her life, though I was a little younger than her, gave her another model to copy and identify with. Her good looks, which had been the outward sign of her wish to overcome the horror, now seemed less significant, as she turned the 'mirror' inwards to what lay inside her.

Inside were held the unshed tears for the mother who had never come back. She had vividly described this incomplete ending as 'carrying her mother on her back, without a resting place to put her down'. We talked about the ritual of Jewish burial, so that her mother could be at peace. This was something concrete Chava could do for her mother, and perhaps would give some meaning to why she herself had survived.

Unable to perform this ritual myself, I involved my colleague, Sonny Herman, a rabbi as well as a psychotherapist. Chava had mentioned that her sister was buried in London. The possibility of her sister's grave offering sanctuary for her mother's unburied soul seemed to have resonance for Chava.

In this act she would not only be helping her mother, but would also be ensuring her sister could at last be reunited with their mother.

The three of us – Chava, Sonny and myself – travelled to the far side of East London to seek out her sister's grave. In this disused wasteland of a cemetery, we searched for her sister's name. A small slab of concrete, eroded over the years by the weather, was all that remained of this tragic life. Sonny's first task was to have Sylvia's name printed out clearly so that her grave could be identified again. Chava stood between Sonny and myself, and Sonny recited Kaddish (prayer for the dead) for Sylvia. Chava later described this event, and the subsequent 'burial' of her mother, as one of the most meaningful for her in her therapeutic journey. She felt this was something only 'a mother and father would do for you', and that Sonny and I symbolised those people in her life.

Over the next few months Chava and I focused on mourning her mother and discussing the consecration of the stone. 'Burying' her mother was also paradoxically bringing her mother to life. To Chava, my response to her unvoiced wish to address this aspect of her past seemed to give her a sense that she was not alone, and that she could perhaps get close enough to 'touch' another human being.

We returned to the cemetery once the headstone had been set, and Sonny once more recited Kaddish – this time for Chava's mother. Chava invited another survivor from the centre, as well as a cousin of hers. This Auschwitz survivor, who had returned from that hell, participated in the 'burial' for those who were murdered from his own family, as well as for Chava's mother.

The ritual brought a release that discussion at Shalvata could never have achieved. There was a sense of closure – yet the complexity of what this meant should perhaps be reflected on. The 'burial' of Chava's mother also underlined the finality of death. There was no more hoping that her mother would return. Did this set Chava free, having herself freed her mother? Could Chava now get on with her life with the knowledge that her own survival had enabled her mother to be remembered? Did her action help to overcome her sense of powerlessness that she had felt in not being able to save her mother?

We can only observe, in the events which followed, that the effects of severe trauma are not overcome simply or straightforwardly. Having coura- geously confronted the painful reality of death, Chava became immersed in writing her book. She once more hid herself away from the world, writing furiously about those years of isolation and solitude. Emerging into daylight to come and see me, and to attend the creative writing group in the HSC, she seemed to have an urgent mission to record this trauma in her life. She described to me how she would creep around her flat on tiptoe, so as not to be heard, as the memories of her incarceration returned.

From time to time, problems with her daughter would dominate our meetings. Chava would draw on her own strength and mine to manage these events in a different way. The focus was increasingly on herself. She would always arrive in plenty of time. She needed time, plenty of time, to unfold her story. One-and-a-half hours we would sit together, sometimes more, sometimes less. She would regulate what she needed. She always sat opposite me. We would drink tea together. Sometimes, she would read me extracts from her book. At other times, she needed my help to write a letter. All manner of emotions came and lodged in the space of our meeting room. Each time as she left, she would arrange for the next meeting and turn and kiss me on the cheek. The bond which was being cemented at that time would prove to be of crucial importance in the events which followed.

Chava's often punishing regime of concentrated energy, which she put into her writing, led her to feel very fatigued and drained. One afternoon, when she allowed herself time to break away from this task, she met up with one of her fellow survivors from the centre. During that encounter, she suddenly experienced severe pain. On examination some while later, she was diagnosed with breast cancer. Chava had experienced very few physical health problems until that time, so this diagnosis came as a great shock to her.

In the trauma of her illness, Chava faced perhaps the biggest challenge – whether to go ahead with an operation and treatment and have a chance to live, or refuse medical help, with the knowledge that the cancer would advance and could lead to her death. She felt as though a curse had been put on her, and she felt powerless again against this overwhelming event. She felt she had lost the fight to stay alive – if she did live, what was there to live for? She asked the question, why? Was it not enough what she had endured during the Holocaust, and afterwards? Was it not enough that she had such a volatile and insecure lifestyle? Was it not enough that her daughter was ill, and that her grandchildren suffered as a result? She felt there was no future for her, and this diagnosis of cancer offered her a way out of her misery.

The realisation of that reality haunted me and pained me. How could I best help Chava to find a pathway through this maze of emotions? I also had to deal with my own inner turmoil at the thought of 'losing' Chava. I remember one particular Friday in the grave moments of despair. It was a warm summer's afternoon. I joined Chava in the park. Together with the survivor who had attended her mother's 'burial', I sat with Chava. Her justified anger poured out of her. There were no answers to her questions, only a belief in the worthwhileness of this terrified person.

Subsequent meetings between Chava and myself drew a demarcation line between her past trauma and the current one. As a child, helpless and alone, she had no choice about what happened to her. In the dark cellar where she was hidden, she was dependent on food given to her by the nuns. Imprisoned without the means to escape, her fate was sealed. Her life was again under threat, only this time she did have a choice and could take action which could save her life. The decision rested in her hands. In the space of our meetings she weighed up her life. My energy was focused on remembering the strength she had found in herself which had enabled her to live until that moment in time. I encouraged Chava to contact me whenever she needed to. I strengthened myself during those weeks through Sonny Herman's support, as well as my own inner beliefs which had served me well in crises that had arisen during my personal and professional life. In my years of working with Chava I had witnessed her love of life and her ability to convert negative experiences into positive ones in a quite remarkable way. This was not someone who gave up easily and so, by fragile threads, she clung on to her life.

She decided to have the operation. I went with her to see the consultant at the hospital. A suggestion of using trial medication for Chava brought fears and anxiety. I was there not only to support Chava, but to explain to the consultant why this 'experimental' treatment was anathema to someone who had been traumatised in the way Chava had been in her young life. Chava was relieved that I asked questions she did not feel able to ask, because the whole experience was overwhelming for her. The operation and subsequent radio-therapy were endured courageously by Chava. Slowly she came closer to the realisation that death had been averted and there was still more she needed to do with her life.

She returned to her writing and, this time, the title of her book changed from *Y* (why) to *For Love of Life*. She connected to family in Israel and in

Australia, and she visited both in those far-flung corners of the world. She made a promotional video for Jewish Care in which she spoke about the services she was using.

Chava's recovery was not fast nor miraculous. She felt tired, she got depressed, she struggled, but she did not give up. Recurring themes related to family, relationships and practical problems often dominated our meetings. What became apparent was that Chava was changing in how she dealt with them. Increasingly she took control of these events. We would talk about strategies, and she was learning how to reflect more before she acted. Her own creativity helped her to find new solutions to long-term problems. Her sense of herself, her identity, her dignity were emerging as strong features in her relationship to her world. The video testimony she made for the Shoah Foundation reflects a sophisticated, articulate woman speaking with powerful simplicity about a tragic life which she had managed to survive.

It became apparent through Chava's use of words that my years of being with her, learning from her, providing her with a solid and secure base, helped her to no longer be a victim of her past. In one of our meetings she said, 'I realise that I have the key to changing my life... I have a choice... I am not a victim.' In the same meeting, she commented, 'I know I was loved by my mother – I can't prove it, but it is what I feel.' The internal image of her mother (*in loco parentis* – myself) seemed to help her to be the 'mother' to her grandchildren in a way she could never be to her daughter, because she did not know how. Living without judgement, without criticism of what Chava may not have been able to do for her daughter, allowed her the possibility to make good the lost years of her motherhood. In her sixties, she is now ready to be the mother she could never really be – it is, in this sense, never too late.

Repairing some of the damage of Hitler's legacy, bringing some sense of peace in the closing chapter of this tragic story, is the best that can be hoped for. When Chava is able to say, as she has done recently, 'I love my home... I never thought I could be so comfortable with myself... I feel I am a decent person', there is some sense of victory and meaningfulness in the hours of pain. Ensuring the publication of her book, searching for new projects which will structure her life, helps to contain the vulnerability which will always remain. For, as Chava put it, 'I feel bruised inside, and when I speak about it, I want to cry.' Chava metaphorically describes how she tries to take control over the negative thoughts that endanger her equilibrium and swing the balance towards depression and powerlessness. 'I tell myself I am like a video machine – I can turn the sound down, I can fast-forward the film, or I can turn off the video. When I realise that there are thoughts in my head which will not help me to cope with my life, I tell myself to turn them off – I don't need them in my life.' If we remember the story of the man falling down the hole in the street until he finds a way around the hole, or walks down a different street (see Part II), we can see how an apparently intransigent problem can be looked at differently and a more creative solution found. Chava embodies this process and uses her released creative energy to engage in other ways of responding to familiar situations. Chava has travelled a long way on her journey out of the dark shadow.

In Chava, we see that the patterns of the past do not have to repeat themselves in the present. Her father's words that she will never be any good are not a self-fulfilling prophecy. The earlier hedonism has been shaped by her maturity. Pleasures from music, laughter, writing, her home and people she cares about lift her beyond more transient pastimes and relationships. Her inner world is connected to her external environment. There is a life beyond the bounds of the therapy room, and this is as much a part of the therapeutic encounter as the interaction between us. Chava and I have moved on together. By observing and experiencing what seems to help her, I have the confidence to pass this on to others.

Felix

Background

Felix[1] was born in Germany in 1930. His father worked as an accountant and his mother stayed home to care for her two children – Felix and his sister Greta. They had a comfortable home life and Felix had good memories of his early childhood.

However, after the Nazis came to power in 1933, life became much harder. Felix was later forced to attend a Jewish school. The rising persecution increased the family's anxieties. They went into hiding where they remained until 1944 when they were deported to Bergen-Belsen.

By 1944 the conditions in Belsen had deteriorated dramatically. Though the family remained together, the lack of food, appalling sanitary conditions and violence of the SS resulted in Felix suffering malnutrition, dysentery, fever and an infestation of lice. His childhood years were suspended in Belsen.

After the war, the family went to South Africa where other members of their family had escaped to in 1939. In the post-war years, Felix continued to suffer from anxiety and depression and pain in his lower limbs, for which he sought professional help. The medical opinion pointed to the impact of his camp experience and his insecure childhood. Despite the difficulties, he excelled academically. He gained a doctorate in law and remained teaching in a university setting.

He always wished to return to Europe, as he never felt he belonged in South Africa. He came to England. He met his wife and they had one daughter. He continued to teach at university, but the remnants of his turbulent childhood did not go away. When he was forced to take early retirement, his earlier trauma resurfaced. It was at that point that our encounter began.

The encounter

Felix came to see me on the recommendation of one of the child survivors from the self-help group which met at Shalvata. That was about nine years ago. Felix participated in that group, having survived Bergen-Belsen during his childhood years. His mother, father and sister all survived together in the same camp. Felix always maintained he did not suffer like other survivors from the camps like Auschwitz, and played down his trauma. His mother and father formed a protective shield around him and seemed to lessen the impact of dislocation, uprooting and loss.

School and the usual childhood pursuits had an unwelcome absence in Bergen-Belsen. To make up for lost time, after liberation, Felix became an industrious student. In South Africa where the family eventually settled, Felix's determination and ability resulted in him being awarded a doctorate in law.

Felix remained close to his parents and continued to live with them. In their home, the shattered community of his European origins was held together through language, familiar food, customs and traditions. In South Africa he felt like an outsider, and increasingly longed to return to Europe. Felix continued to have difficulties in finding his roots and being able to settle in one place. He came to England and began teaching at university. He met Eva, who became his wife, they set up home and their daughter was born. All seemed to be going well until changes at work started to threaten his equilibrium. Pressure on older staff to take early retirement brought Felix face to face with a void which he could not fill. Memories of the Holocaust, of that endless time in the camp, seemed to emerge as he began to talk in the child survivors group about his past. Felix sought out medical help, but also realised he needed to talk more about what had happened to him and what was happening now.

It was not easy for either of us. Felix both wanted help and resented it. His academic status and professional achievements led him to question my ability to help him. He was angry about finding himself in this vulnerable position. Despite my willingness to give relevant personal information about my background, he resented the fact that he did not know enough about me, and would have preferred me to be his 'friend'.

The warning signs at work became a reality, and he was forced to retire. He retreated into the cocoon of his home. As he was unable to venture out, even into daylight, I visited him at home. Sometimes he remembered moments of retreat in Bergen-Belsen when he would hide in the bunk hoping the trauma would pass. Now incarcerated indoors, he also spent long hours in bed, unable to emerge to face the reality of what had happened. He would have liked my health, my strength, my job, my life. I came in from that world outside, in which there was life and vitality, into his world, in which there was darkness and deadness.

Often he would cancel our meetings, saying he was too unwell to see me. Dependent on Eva, he would shut himself away. He was fed and taken care of, but his life had been suspended. Despite the depths of his despair, he did not wish to take his own life, and this was an important factor to hold on to.

As time went by, he came to see me at Shalvata. The physical activity of a journey, even though Eva drove him, was part of the therapeutic process. A cup of tea and biscuits were always the start of what became like a ritual. Occasionally, Eva would join us, as we struggled with the pain of Felix's current trauma. Without work Felix felt he was nothing – no identity, no status, no security. There was no structure in his life and, like many other survivors, having no work was seen as life-threatening. Once more Felix felt like a victim, powerless to do anything to change his situation.

Let me give you an image of Felix. In the darkest days, Felix would come in wrapped in layers of clothes. Often he would wear a cap as he felt the cold so much. He would join me in my room, sometimes still wearing his outside jacket. He maintained a certain look of former times – a shirt and tie as well as a jacket speaking silently about a wish to return to work and 'normality'. His wavy hair showed signs of greyness emerging from colour that belonged to his youth. The incongruity of his life seemed reflected in the paradoxical attire of trainers on his feet contrasting with what was otherwise a formal appearance.

His good looks were overshadowed by a heaviness of step and expression. Silence predominated the early moments of our meetings, but as he began to talk, so his demeanour relaxed. He would then peel off the outer layers of clothing, but would wrap his arms around himself as a response to the discomfort which he felt.

He spoke in a soft voice still echoing his South African accent. The voice which had once given lectures to hundreds of students was lost in the depths of his despair. He would focus on the pain in his legs, rubbing them to try to bring them to life. The more anxious he felt, the greater the pain he experienced. He said this pain reminded him of the 'paralysis' he felt as a child in Bergen-Belsen and in the years which followed. Hunched in his chair, his breathing often became more difficult. Sometimes we would focus on that aspect as a tangible way to bring some relief.

I noticed how Felix became more 'alive' by the end of our meetings. However, I could not see him often enough to maintain the momentum. An opportune meeting with someone who volunteered to help in our work seemed to offer another option. He agreed for us to visit, though he was somewhat dismissive. The goal was to encourage Felix to go out for short walks, as his muscles seemed to be seizing up from sitting all day, and also to build up Felix's confidence after his reclusive life. It was hoped that Eva would also feel supported and have some time for herself.

Eva was Felix's twenty-four-hours-a-day carer. His total reliance on her, plus the fact that she had to work to bring in an income, was a great strain on both of them. Felix's loss of income and position as breadwinner compounded his loss of self-esteem. These practical issues were also addressed with Felix and Eva and some solutions were found through specific funds. Eva came once to the group for spouses of survivors which meets at Shalvata. However, Felix felt uncomfortable about her sharing personal issues with the others in the group.

Felix seemed to be walking through a mire. Each session began with the horrific pains he felt; his fears about his future; his hopelessness at not being able to work; his anger at other people's good fortune, including my own; his fears about his mother's ageing and health issues, and his daughter's academic achievements and social life. He reported on the uselessness of the antidepressant medication prescribed by the psychiatrist he was seeing, his problems sleeping and the tension which was lodged inside him.

In this mire, I also began to sink. Nothing seemed to change. I felt useless, and exhausted, in this seemingly intransigent situation. The deadness was powerful in its destructiveness. Despite this, there was a warmth that co-existed under the cloud that covered us. He continued to return to my room, maybe not every week, but with the intention to do so. I listened when he spoke about Bergen-Belsen. I asked questions about things I did not know. He gave me papers to read about the horror of that camp. I offered no interpretations but allowed him to make connections between his current trauma and his past. Following discussions with Sonny Herman, my consultant, I realised that I should not try to change anything; I should accept the repetition and focus on my own survival of Felix's pain. This liberated me from any sense of my own omnipotence, and made it possible for me to continue on this journey with him. Instead of goal-setting, or focusing on the past, as a way of moving forward, I worked on a more primitive level in trying to build a bridge between the living and the dead. I needed to remain in the world of the living if I was to help Felix to hold on to his life in this sea of deadness.

Nothing seemed to please Felix. His excellent academic career paled into insignificance against what he saw as his current suffering. His love of opera and music, his enjoyment of writing and intellectual discourse were all out of reach to him.

Reluctantly at first, as always, Felix joined the T'ai Chi class in the HSC. The proximity of the social centre next to Shalvata made it easier for him to combine these classes with his sessions with me. I arranged for another volunteer to visit him at home to help him start to use his computer again. He joined a men's group at Shalvata, which, although short-lived, reconnected Felix to some other survivors he knew. One of these survivors was a man who had also gone through a very deep depression from which he had emerged. Short separations from Eva, when her mother was dying, were both threatening and yet coped with. A holiday with Eva in Italy brought relief from the suffering. Though this too was short-lived, he seemed to be beginning to make reconnections to the outside world.

We journeyed on through these intervals of time in which some light began to flicker. Felix became a more regular attendee at our meetings, and a bond was formed between us. I felt lighter, even though the content of what was spoken about remained as a constant.

Felix began to talk more about his mother's ageing and his fears about her death. More than a mother, she had been his means of survival in Bergen-Belsen. She remained his protector, even in her late years, and he could not imagine life without her. He continued to depend on her as a source of strength. In preparation for her inevitable end, we spoke about her more often, and what he could do to make the last years of her life more peaceful. Most times he would fall back on old habits from childhood, talking about his need of his mother. His anxiety about her increased as he described a medical condition she was suffering from, which had resulted in pain and weight loss. In her late eighties, the strenuous journeys to England became more and more arduous.

Despite his fears and fatigue, I noticed almost imperceptible changes during my meetings with Felix. He spoke more openly to me, compared with the reluctance that marked the beginning of our earlier encounters. He spoke about another planned visit to Italy where he and Eva would meet his mother. He doubted whether he would make the journey, as he still had problems with the residues of the cocktail of medication which remained inside him until the end of the day. In preparation for this journey, Felix's psychiatrist agreed for him to reduce some of the intake of tranquillisers at night – a major change in this seemingly downward spiral. Felix was walking more strongly, his eye contact was more direct, his voice was more powerful. I felt confident that he would be able to cope with his trip and, like a mirror, I reflected back to him this changing image of himself. He told me that his psychiatrist had also noticed differences in his mood and response. I also spoke with Felix about what it would mean to his mother to see him functioning better – it would be a 'gift' to her which would be so important at this time of her own frailty.

In the absence of Felix, I wondered about him and hoped. A postcard from Italy read, 'Gorgeous weather, superb food, good company, nice continental atmosphere, no pains.' The same day that the card arrived, Felix phoned me to say he had just got back. He felt full of energy and full of life –

pain seemed to have left him as swiftly and unaccountably as it had come upon him. The suddenness of the reversal shocked him. He wanted to come and meet me as soon as possible.

Not seeing himself as ill any more, Felix asserted himself. Tea and biscuits were no longer a necessary part of an already forgotten ritual. In the reception area, the staff at Shalvata were presented with a different person in the same external form.

Despite the elation Felix felt at being alive, he was also fearful that he could swing back. He was aware that a current trigger could result in the 'depression' reclaiming him. Having encountered mood swings in others I have worked with, I was not naive about the potential transitory nature of these changes. However, Felix's awareness of the precariousness of his current sense of well-being made it possible to talk about strategies to achieve further equilibrium. I also ensured that he kept his psychiatrist fully informed. He singled out his mother's deteriorating health as a possible cause of future relapse in his own functioning. To avoid this, he needed to use this energy to ensure he was more in control over events in his life.

In the weeks that followed, Felix spoke much more about his wartime experience. While in Italy, in an environment in which he felt at home and familiar, he told his story about his time in the camp to people he met in the hotel. Having regained his life, he acknowledged publicly what he had witnessed of death. Being released from the death-like experience of the depression was like liberation once more. He acknowledged his roots; he reconnected to his Jewishness and spirituality; he believed once more in himself.

Felix now started his day at 6.30am rather than 1.30pm. He regularly went back to synagogue. He contacted former colleagues at university. He was invited to a reception to meet the president of the university. He arranged to visit his mother in South Africa. He reconnected with old friends – he was reunited with himself.

In this time of transformation, Felix remained in close contact with me. He was much more open and generous in his recognition of the part he felt I had played in his 'recovery' through my relationship with him. Through patience, through understanding of his wartime experiences, through my own Jewishness, through the person he saw in me, he had managed to survive what he called 'a more tragic time' than his experience in Bergen-Belsen. Without my being there for him, he maintained that he would have been 'six feet under the ground'.

Felix returned from South Africa with the news that his mother had cancer. He spoke those words with strength and fortitude. He was also able to say that the trip had been a positive one for him.

Nine years of being there for him. Nine years of fighting with him not to give up. Nine years of journeying with him in a world of pain and darkness. Nine years of building the foundation from which new life could grow was an extraordinary experience in which I have learned much about myself as well as about the depths of human suffering. With these wounds which do not heal, we searched to find a way through. There is no cure, but there can be some relief. Going to hell and back with Felix as he re-experienced his wartime trauma in his current life, and surviving with him to see some light at the end of the tunnel, has helped me to move forward in my learning about suffering and how to respond to it.

A diagnosis of anxiety and depression seemed far removed from the reality of Felix's world. Though the symptoms may be similar, I felt that Felix's difficulties needed to be understood through reference to their context. This focus helped me to think differently about how to respond. Without work, without structure, the chaotic world of the Holocaust came back into focus. As a child with his mother, he had managed to cope with the anxiety and fear which surrounded him. As an adult, whose mother was now reaching the end of her life, he felt there was no buffer to take the impact of his once more shattered life. All he had lost – his childhood, his education, his security, his comforts, his community – sought an outlet. When this major loss (his work) was experienced in the latter part of his life, the grief was almost overwhelming. On the other hand, his enforced retirement was also an opportunity to express the inexpressible, and a chance to return to his unfinished childhood. During the nine years, Eva and I became the supports for him as his mother had been in the past, and he clung to both of us in his need to be cared for.

His mother died. He grieved for her and again feared being unable to manage. However, his now-practised episodes of coping steered him out of a bereavement without end and into a new life. Having once more mastered his skill at the computer, Felix started researching and writing an academic book related to the Holocaust. He visited South Africa again to deal with his mother's estate, and reconnected to friends who encouraged him to take on further studies. Being accepted on a training course in a subject of his choice has given his life meaning again and he feels he has a future. He has now returned to live in South Africa with Eva, while their daughter, now in her twenties, remains in their house in England. Felix and Eva will return for the summer, and said they will contact me at that time.

Whether Felix ever lapses into depression again is an unknown. However, what we hold on to is this positive experience that enabled him to emerge from the dark shadow. For him, there is no longer darkness without end. He feels there is still much more he can do with the remainder of his life, rather than just waiting to die. His family have to adjust with him to these vast changes in his life. He has to take care not to overstretch himself or his family in his attempts to catch up on the time he lost in his illness.

Like the other encounters I have mentioned, my meetings with Felix were only part of a whole. Indeed, Felix's own addendum to this record is to emphasise the 'snapshot' aspect which it captures. We both recognised that without the support of Eva, and her efforts to maintain a sense of home life for all of them, including their daughter, the outcome may have been very different. Felix also insisted that outside of our meetings there were times of respite from the darkness. Visitors to their home, dinner guests at their table, helped to counterbalance the isolation felt in Felix's world which he brought to Shalvata. The positive relationship of the dedicated volunteer did much to strengthen Felix outside of our meetings. Long-term friendships persisted during the difficult times. Contact with the psychiatrist allowed medication to be monitored. The connection to the HSC, however peripheral, offered a means of marking a change in Felix's journey back to 'life'.

Marsha

Background

Marsha was born in Bonyhád in Hungary. It was a German-speaking community in which Jews had lived since the seventeenth century. It was a prosperous, middle-class, sophisticated town. Marsha's father had a textile shop. Her mother stayed at home to look after her six children. Marsha was the eldest. The family were orthodox Jews. Marsha had a very protected home life. She went to a Jewish school, and was unaware of events going on in Europe in the early 1940s. Marsha went to stay with an aunt and continued private studies.

In 1944, Marsha was deported with her whole family to Auschwitz. She was sixteen years old. She and her two sisters were separated from the rest of the family. Her brother also survived, but the rest of her family were murdered. After the war, she was sent from Auschwitz to Buchenwald. In the chaotic aftermath after liberation, she searched for members of her family. She managed to trace her brother through the Red Cross. Marsha went to Switzerland. In 1946 she went to Israel and fought for the establishment of the State of Israel. In 1948 she married and had two daughters and one son. Her husband worked in the import/export business. In 1967 he suffered a heart attack. They left Israel for Switzerland during the 1967 war. They decided not to go back to Israel and brought their children with them to England in 1967.

Marsha's two daughters work in the helping professions and her son is an accountant. In 1985 Marsha's husband died. It was at that point I met Marsha. This encounter with Marsha differs from the others presented in that the focus of our work is on the recording of her testimony.

The encounter

Marsha found it difficult to cope when her husband died. Counselling could not reach her in the depths of her unhappiness. We became acquainted through the Survivors of Shoah (SOS) group, chatting informally over cups of tea and social interactions. Marsha got to know me and trusted me enough to tell me that there was something she needed to do, and she needed my assistance.

She came to see me at my workplace even before Shalvata had started. Marsha told me she needed to write down what had happened to her in Auschwitz-Birkenau as she wanted her children to know. I became her scribe and she became my teacher. So fundamental was this learning experience for me that it has remained etched in my mind, and has helped to shape the way I listen to trauma. Whenever I speak of my work, these memories of my encounters with Marsha become conscious again.

In my early discussions with Marsha, she began to talk about her incarceration in Auschwitz-Birkenau. Her soft Hungarian accent evoked powerful images of horror. In the ordinary words, extraordinary events unfolded. Marsha felt her command of English was not good enough to convey what she wanted to say, and yet she had the imagination to tell a story that could be transmitted to others.

Week after week, Marsha and I would meet and we agreed that she would speak to me and I would then write it up for her in the first person. Let me give you a flavour of what she described.

> One day, I was ordered to search through some clothing and chanced to find a diamond hidden away in a shoulder pad. Yet I could so easily discard it: it had no usefulness to me; it could not get me what I needed – the food which would sustain me. The diamond had no value in that world. The beauty of the diamond only reflected me as I really was – dirty and full of lice.

After each session I would write up what Marsha had told me, and at the next session she would read the contents. The accuracy of my writing seemed to convey a sense that something had been understood, and we moved on.

This was not an historical document. Marsha herself maintained that these were only glimpses of a world that defied expression. They were like a collection of vignettes, powerful in their simplicity.

> The summer was very hot inside the overcrowded barracks – the air smelled fetid and rotten, the atmosphere was suffocating – it was a nightmare...

In the quiet of my room, as I searched for the words that would reflect these inner tortures, I was no longer just a listener or observer. Writing in the first person, as though I was Marsha, I came closer to what she had been telling me. I was not her therapist, nor she my client. I had been set a much harder task in which I was far from expert. With her upright posture and her head held high, she patiently allowed me to journey with her.

The importance of her good childhood experiences; her memories of home; her belief in G-d; being together with her sister in Auschwitz; her marriage and children; her life in Israel after the war were all essential ingredients to her survival. Her caring became extended to me – she advised me; she counselled me; she guided me through often turbulent and muddy waters in those early days of trial and error. A bond was established between us, which I believe still exists today.

A year and a half later, a document was typed and ready. That was only the beginning of other journeys which followed for Marsha. Having completed this task, Marsha's next task was to return to Auschwitz-Birkenau – the scene of her nightmares. She travelled with a group of young people, of which she was the only survivor. She described the experiences as follows:

...as we passed through to Birkenau, the horror of the place struck me once more. I went up into the watchtower from which the Germans had looked down on us. The emptiness of the place struck me and the absolute silence. It appeared like a timeless place – time does not exist. I had expected the earth to be red with the blood of those murdered there, but only greyness could be seen – the greyness of ashes. It seemed like a huge cemetery but without gravestones – so quiet and still. I tried to visualise again the seething bodies in that hell of forty years ago. I could see nothing, yet the smell of death still hangs in the air.

The questions she was asked, in the presence of her daughter in this revisiting of the camp, gave Marsha some meaning in her survival. The group members wanted to know what had happened to her, and she was there to teach them. The letters she received afterwards, and on a subsequent trip which included her granddaughter, were very therapeutic outcomes for her.

In the Holocaust Survivors' Centre her art work developed, and she found within herself untapped creative talents. Marsha agreed to speak at a conference I facilitated on the subject of 'Survivors as our Teachers'. The audience of professionals listened carefully as Marsha advised how professionals could help. She emphasised that it was never too late, and coined the phrase, which I have used frequently, that there is now a 'second opportunity' to address the unfinished business of the traumatic past that survivors have been through.

While quietly playing bridge in the HSC, she feels the mood of the centre. From time to time she asks to see me when issues emerge which she thinks need my attention. She underlines the importance of the HSC to the survivors. I have come to depend on her watchful gaze and sharp ears to alert me to any disquiet, and take her advice about how to handle these delicate situations.

Marsha has a life outside of the centre. Her home, her family and her work take her time and her attention. Marsha has moved on and I have moved on with her. I am not the same as when I first met her, and I am eternally grateful to her, as I am to all the survivors who have taught me what I know.

Endnote

1. At Felix's request, some of the factual details have been altered in order to conceal his identity.

Chapter 7

Translating Trauma into a Meaningful Therapeutic Language

The four encounters detailed in Chapter 6 took place in my room in the Shalvata part of the building. The word Shalvata has special meaning for me, linked as it is with the late Shamai Davidson's centre in Israel, in which he developed his work with Holocaust survivors. The name Shalvata (peace of mind or tranquillity) was meant as a memorial to him, and to embody the essence of his teaching. The foundation stone of the work was laid in Shalvata. Then layer upon layer has been built on through the lessons learned from listening to survivors. Much of the thinking about the adaptations to my work with the aftermath of atrocity has been crystallised in my room in Shalvata. It therefore seems appropriate to begin this account by looking at some of the therapeutic issues which emerge from these encounters, and the impact they make within the Shalvata context. In the process of change and adaptation which translates trauma into a meaningful therapeutic language, the limitations of a stand-alone therapy centre will be revealed. The latter section of Part III will widen the scope of the therapeutic interventions, by focusing on the work of the Holocaust Survivors' Centre, as well as its interconnectedness to Shalvata.

What do these survivors teach us about our therapeutic work?

We learn from the survivors about the importance of informal social groups as a first step to reaching out to people who have undergone trauma

Before we can begin to think about how we adapt our way of working with survivors, we have to overcome the immense challenge of reaching out and making contact with them.

I have already noted earlier in the book how vulnerability and helplessness are an anathema for those who have been at the mercy of totalitarian regimes. This was a major reason why survivors did not appear at the doors of social service organisations. For those whose trust has been shattered in the Holocaust, it was safer to keep a low profile and carry on functioning as best one could without any help.

Many of the descriptions of the treatment of PTSD assume that someone has agreed to be referred to a professional for help. This tends to ignore this most essential first step, which all the survivors described have mentioned – namely, the importance of the social support groups through which the therapeutic encounter ensues. The SOS and the child survivor groups have already been focused on as non-threatening, non-clinical ways of reaching out to traumatised people who would otherwise not have come forward for therapeutic help. The likelihood is that some would have physically or mentally suffered further trauma as they tried to cope on their own. Some of them may well not have been alive today without these interventions.

Building up trust through personalised, face-to-face meetings in an informal setting allowed me to establish the necessary bridge for the journey to begin, and for the stories to be told. We need to seek out opportunities to reach survivors who may not have identified themselves in any way to our organisations. Individual survivors and small groups became scattered all over the UK after World War II. Many were clearly not wishing to ask for help from organisations predominantly set up to help ageing, vulnerable people. Any sense of neediness or impoverishment was associated with charity. In contrast, as we began to administer the Swiss humanitarian fund for survivors, many who had undergone trauma began to identify themselves. There was a sense that claiming from this fund was their right as survivors, and thereby it became more associated with justice in terms of what they had lost. Claims for the Swiss fund revealed that there were many survivors living close to each other without any awareness that their neighbours may have shared similar wartime experiences. Out of this awareness, local social support groups developed, and this paved the way forward.

There is now an urgency to reach out to ageing survivors all around the UK, not only in London where our service exists. Joint projects with other organisations involved in working with survivors and refugees from the Nazi Holocaust have resulted in the appointment of outreach workers and local facilitators to bring survivors together to support each other. The sophistication of our service would be very costly to duplicate elsewhere, but these social, informal groups provide an important option to strengthen survivors and give them some sense of belonging and identity. Feelings of loneliness, of being outsiders, render the already vulnerable more vulnerable. If, as Elie Wiesel (1990c) observed, 'Loneliness is the key word that evokes, that describes the Jewish experience during World War II' (p.108),[1] then ageing compounds this already painful experience. Reaching out and gathering in these dispersed survivors gives recognition and acknowledgement to a long-overlooked and marginalised group of people. Efforts to reach them, efforts to listen and respond to them, lay a stronger foundation for further therapeutic work to take place. The focus of the therapuetic work needs to reinforce the strength and health of the survivor, rather than repeating the experience of being a victim.

The survivors teach us about the importance of creating a non-clinical, welcoming environment in a non-institutionalised setting as a means of drawing them into a therapeutic process

Perhaps the most courageous step these four survivors took in terms of the therapeutic encounters was in crossing the threshold that brought them into my room. That small physical step symbolised a huge leap across an unknown and uncharted space, and I never fail to admire their decision to do so. Chava thought long and hard about her commitment to come and see me. Felix never really resolved his ambivalence about sitting there in my room with his pain and suffering. Marsha found the head office setting, in which I was formerly based, incompatible to the vulnerability she carried. The formal offices, the strict security system, inhibited the therapeutic process. In contrast, Shalvata's relaxed environment, its light and airy decor, its friendly reception facilities, all seemed to ease the tension associated with entering this unfamiliar place.

Attention to detail in the therapeutic environment allows the process of listening and journeying with the individual survivor to begin, as evidenced in my work with Chava, Irena, Felix and Marsha. The rooms in which these encounters take place have the desks pushed to one side, while comfortable chairs are positioned around small coffee tables on which the cups of tea or coffee can be placed. The setting is an issue which will be looked at again in the latter section of Part III when I will focus on the development of the HSC next door to Shalvata.

In these encounters, as the dark shadow is faced, the environment concerns more than the physical appearance of the building. To differentiate this space from a medical setting, a more traditional therapy clinic or a social work office, other aspects of our sensitivity to the survivors' trauma needed to be implemented. Being accessible for crisis phone calls, being available for non-scheduled meetings, allowing the blinds on the door of our meeting room to be left open to avoid repeating a sense of suffocation from their traumatic past gives unspoken messages about our awareness of the past in the present. A sense of security is not easily created, but evolves through repeated evidence of caring and commitment. For people who have been starved and humiliated, feeding is slow, and trust has to be learned. The sitting area outside the meeting rooms allows survivors to stay for a while either before or after our encounter. Felix would arrive early for his tea and biscuits, while Chava would sometimes remain afterwards. For all these survivors the environment plays a key role in creating the possibility of using the service of Shalvata.

We learn from these survivors how the 'non-purity of the therapeutic encounter' is more meaningful for them when they re-experience trauma in the latter part of their lives

Visiting the refugee camps in Kosovo, Elie Wiesel listened to the stories of those traumatised by the war. He commented, '...and not a single man could finish his story. They all would break down in tears. We have to finish their stories for them, by helping to rebuild their lives' (2000, p.13).[2]

Wiesel links this therapeutic task to his own life and others traumatised through the Holocaust, only, for them, there were few hands reaching out to help them – few sympathetic ears to listen to the atrocity they had been through.

In each of the encounters I have described, years of silence deadened these stories. The rebuilding of survivors' lives was, for some, only a façade which cracked and fell apart, unable to sustain itself under renewed attack from current traumatic experiences. The depth of despair and hopelessness which resurfaced brought death's countenance sharply into focus. The will to live and survive as natural death drew nearer seemed to fade in the overwhelming darkness that overshadowed their lives.

What do these four survivors teach us about how we – the outsiders, the non-survivors – can help to maintain hope long enough for the conclusion of these stories to be told? By examining these encounters we see reflections of a world which facilitates a dialogue between the experience of extreme trauma and the therapeutic response.

In its most simple form, I would state that the only therapy which is of any use to a severely traumatised person is the one in which the person asking for help feels helped. However sophisticated, however skilful the approach may be, however insightful the analysis offered, it is meaningless to the sufferer if it speaks to him/her in a language that cannot be understood.

If we look closely at the encounter with Chava, for example, we begin to see the essence of a changing dynamic in the adaptation of the therapy to the specific needs of the survivor. While my psychodynamic training provides a backdrop for the encounter, the approach is not 'pure'. It allows survivors to meet socially, and for child survivors in particular to have a peer group which they may not have experienced before as their childhood and adolescence was taken away from them. It is not 'pure' as the practical needs of the survivor are dealt with simultaneously to the emotional issues. It is not 'pure' in the sense that professional boundaries may need to be crossed in order to convey trust and a sense of immersion and commitment to the unique experiences of the survivor – personal details from the helper as well as informal approaches need to be incorporated as well as more traditional skills of the professional relationship. It is not 'pure' in the sense that the therapist does not work in an isolated way with the survivor – spiritual, social, recreational and creative approaches can all be part of the therapeutic process. It is not 'pure' in its deviation from the sanctity of the 'therapeutic' hour. It is not 'pure' in its sanction of touch as a therapeutic phenomenon. It is not 'pure', because its very purity would foster a sense of 'Aryanisation', which is not in keeping with the needs of survivors.

Listening to the voices of these four survivors who have journeyed with me over many years, we hear a different story as they recount their versions of therapy. Therapy for them is as much about memorialising for the future as it is about acknowledging the past. It is as much about their capacity to be creative as it is about verbalising their experiences of trauma. It is about seeing the survivor as a whole person and not an amalgam of symptoms to be treated. These four survivors will remain with us as we continue our progress throughout the book. They will guide us in how we adapt our therapeutic work and we will continue to learn from them and reshape our responses.

As has already been stated, survivors are as individual and varied as the population at large. The responses therefore must be tailor-made for the individual. I am thus concerned that I do not make universal statements or evolve all-embracing models, which are by their very nature set up to be knocked down. My aim is to provide some pointers that I have learned along the way and, I hope, redefine and reshape these approaches through feedback from you, the readers.

Survivors are neither patients nor clients but people who have been on a journey, and may wish us to journey with them as they re-experience trauma in the latter part of their lives.

We learn from the survivors how to adapt the language of therapy to incorporate the vocabulary of their trauma

In translating trauma into a meaningful therapeutic language, I am at pains to avoid the use of jargon. Jargon serves to separate us from those with whom we work. Jargon gives power to the person using it. It is an 'insider' language which excludes those who find it unintelligible. Consequently, I have tried to steer myself away from shorthand diagnostic vocabulary in my search for a language which links better to those who have experienced atrocity. This exercise has helped me to review the terms 'clients', 'patients' and even the word 'therapy' itself. Terminology such as 'transference' and 'counter-transference' is therefore missing in this text (except for one reference by Danieli). In its place, I have found a way of translating this terminology through the detail of the human encounters. I will continue this theme as I address in more depth some of the processes that are used in our everyday therapeutic work.

Redefining assessment: looking for clues

It is common parlance in the early stages of therapeutic work to talk about an assessment process. Michael J. Scott (2000, p.16) maintains that the therapeutic process can be summarised using the image of an hourglass when describing PTSD:

- open-ended conversation – telling the story
- structured interview – diagnostic symptoms
- conceptualisation of the client's difficulty
- treatment programme implemented
- impact of programme assessed.

Assessment, treatment and evaluation guide us to diagnose and formulate responses for the individual's difficulties. We have seen earlier in the book the limitations of such medical terminology when working with the effects of severe trauma. Those referred with PTSD are assessed for symptomology and such assessments may include psychometric tests as well as structured interviews. The effort to make such assessments scientific and quantifiable helps us to think logically and convergently – to make some kind of order out of the chaos the sufferer may be experiencing as a result of the trauma. Such approaches draw us both into the trauma and round the trauma, taking account of other variables which could influence the behavioural reaction. For example, events which happened prior to the trauma also need to be considered as well as the trauma itself. We have already seen how early childhood experiences – earlier confrontations with other traumatic events and how these were dealt with – need to be included in this assessment. So far so good, but that is only part of the total picture.

Searching among the ashes

When we work with the effects of severe, prolonged trauma, such as that of the Holocaust, we have to search further for the clues which will help us. We have to search among the ashes, for that is where the trauma lies buried. In the greyness of the rubble, we may not easily hear the whimpers or be able to decipher the shape of the suffering. Assessment in this sense is not neat and precise, and we have to be prepared to allow another story to unfold which mirrors more accurately the complexity of suffering.

When survivors come to see me, I want to know who these people are, what journey they have been on, and what has brought them to me at that moment in time. Layer upon layer of coping can mask the deep wounds which have been inflicted. Too much structure, too much science, brings memories of totalitarianism. Instead of pathology and weakness, the story of those who survived has more to do with resilience and courage. The trauma is only one chapter in people's lives.

Searching among the ashes means listening and asking the right questions – asking for clarification at times of uncertainty; searching for signs of life in a sea of deadness. Those signs of life may be witnessed in the creative potential that can co-exist with depression and helplessness in the re-experiencing of trauma. Even in her darkest moments, Chava found the will to write her book. Irena's drive to ensure the Holocaust Survivors' Centre came to life gave her the energy to use her aesthetic talents in the creation of a new 'home' for survivors. Marsha's artistic abilities surfaced through the art class. In the imagination of these three survivors, a balance is created for the trauma to be contained.

In the ashes we find clues as to what helped them cope with the trauma. Paradoxically, in the ashes we also find the clues for the experiences of not coping as trauma resurfaces many years later. These clues help us to re-evaluate overt behaviours and make sense of them within the context of the trauma. Understanding Irena's rage at her ex-husband, in the context of her childhood abandonment and powerlessness, throws a different light on her behaviour. Her difficulty in letting go of this rage is not, as it initially seems, destructive, but it allows her to work through years of pent-up grief which could not find expression until she was again left to cope on her own at the time of her divorce.

Felix's life was suspended for a second time when he no longer had the structure of work. Long-repressed memories of a life without form or future in Bergen-Belsen brought deadliness and subsequent depression as overt expressions of unresolved trauma. When trauma resurfaces, both the survivors and helper can feel a 'madness' which lurks when that which cannot be explained is experienced. In these moments, those of us who work with the aftermath of trauma need to think of Victor Frankl's (1987) essential statement about the normality of the response in relation to the abnormality of the situation survivors have been through. We have to remember, as Donald

Meichenbaum (Hoyt 2000) says, that 'even in the worst scenarios, people evidence remarkable strengths. As a therapist, I need clients to attend to that part of their stories…' (p.54). We are challenged to hold on to these strengths, and not to lose hope.

At this point in my writing, as I search among the ashes, another survivor surfaces in my mind – an, as yet, untold story of an already buried tragedy. Sonia died, unable to tell her own story of a nightmare which remained with her to the end. She needed to be believed, but did not know how to express her pain. Long and arduous incarceration in death camps separated her from the world of the living. 'Trust' no longer had meaning in her vocabulary. Practical demands brought her to me, but reaching out to her was met with suspicion and contempt. A highly intelligent mind imprisoned her away from warmth and social contact. A one-off attendance at the SOS group was ridiculed and rebuffed by her. Despite the brief early contact I had with her, the depth and severity of her suffering impressed itself upon me. Her level of anxiety was extremely high, and she complained of physical pain in different parts of her body.

Despite her mistrust, she kept in contact with me, though made it clear that I could not help her. She repeatedly admitted herself to hospital as the pain increased. Short stays and tests revealed no physical reason for her described symptoms. An inability to find a cause for the pain she was experiencing brought anger which she directed at medical staff. Regular phone calls from the hospital pleaded with me to help them to deal with this apparently abusive person. On one such occasion, a heart consultant phoned me. He was sympathetic to Sonia's suffering in the Holocaust, but did not know how to help her. Each time Sonia was in the hospital, she also asked that I visit her. Interspersed with the rage about the incompetence of the doctors and nurses, Sonia allowed me to get a little closer. In a moment of quietness as we sat in the hospital, I conveyed a sense that she was once again imprisoned, with a barbed wire fence around her. Alone and separated as she was, it was difficult to reach her, but I would remain with her, even if that meant being outside the fence. She listened at that moment and she never totally lost contact with me. Buried deep in the ashes, Sonia was still breathing, but she could not find her way out from under the weight of deadness which had hidden her.

Her rage did not diminish. She decided to see the gastro-enterologist, and asked me to attend the meeting. Her pain, now focused on her stomach area, was becoming more and more severe. Admissions to different hospitals did not bring the needed diagnosis. Tragically, too late, Sonia was found to have stomach cancer.

It is difficult to know if there is blame to be apportioned. The gulf which remained between Sonia and this world impeded communication. Sonia became a nuisance to the hospitals and, in turn, their treatment of her increased her level of stress. The emotional pain which could not be reached, except fleetingly, needed an outlet physically. Life was so hard for Sonia that perhaps she needed the cancer, and needed to be believed. There is no certainty, and it is hard to know what the final diagnosis meant to Sonia.

What Sonia teaches those of us who are reaching out to help someone this traumatised is that pain is real and needs to be believed. Listening closely to what she had to say, and what she thought would help her, are the lessons she leaves. Sonia lived in a very nice flat and managed her day-to-day life. Those strengths, as well as her intellectual capacity, have to be brought into focus as we look at who this person really is behind the angry outbursts. I believe Sonia wanted to get close but did not know how.

Sonia poses more questions than there are answers. She exemplifies the complexity with which we are faced in our search among the ashes as we work with those who have suffered severe trauma. She speaks to us of the wide gulf between survivors and non-survivors. She speaks to us of Hitler's victory in her pain and suffering. She speaks to us of our inadequacies in dealing with her trauma. As we continue to search, she reminds us not to be complacent, but to endeavour to find a more meaningful approach. She remains with me as unfinished business in my journey of learning about what may help someone who has suffered this much. She needed a place in our quest to reach out and help. I hope she is now resting peacefully.

Redefining assessment using the metaphor of a reflecting mirror

We all use mechanisms of defence as a way of coping with stresses and traumas which affect our lives. However, transferred to a therapeutic environment, these same responses of denial, projection, repression and so on often have a negative connotation. Sonia, for example, may be described by some as a 'manipulative' client. In my vocabulary in relating to the aftermath of severe trauma, such terminology loses its meaning and importance. Sonia needed to be heard and understood in the context of her suffering. Far from being manipulative and controlling those around her, Sonia felt out of control in the trauma she relived daily. Her 'truth' was too painful to live with, and needed to be encapsulated and hidden deep inside her. The projected rage was not something that could be confronted, but only acknowledged in the images that reflected between the past and the present. In the chaos which often surrounds us as trauma resurfaces in the present, we again search for answers. Mechanisms of defence become equated with avoidance techniques by the client, as the therapist struggles to regain direction and control.

If we stay with the chaos, if we allow the traumatised person to guide us, we can stay with the present as we search together for ways to move on in the journey. The past does not have to be relived to deal with the present, as has already been mentioned earlier in this book. We do though have to take account of the past, which can be witnessed as reflections through this metaphorical mirror. Chava tended to ignore the horror of what happened to her as a way of coping. The unfinished business from the Holocaust could not be looked at directly at first, but it found expression in the grief and powerlessness she felt in relation to her daughter. In the tangible and the concrete of her current world, the hidden world of her lost childhood could be mirrored and acknowledged. The therapeutic task is to perceive these reflections, holding them in one's mind until the moment develops for the survivor to decide what they wish to do with them.

If we turn the mirror round slightly, we see our own reflection – how we look, who we are and how we respond play a part in the responses that emerge from those with whom we are journeying. We are not only looking for clues which help us to help them, but they are looking at us and evaluating whether we can offer them anything which may help them. Can they trust us? Do we care enough? Are we trying to understand them? Dealing with this pain on a daily basis can weaken us and threaten our confidence in coping. We have to look into the mirror and see how we respond. We have to look into the mirror to see how our personal issues resurface in the current encounter with the survivor. We have to look into the mirror to see how we sit with the survivors as we journey with them; how we learn from them; how we share with them as we move on to look at the therapeutic options that can be offered to them. The mirror helps us to see the 'otherness' of the world the survivor has witnessed – we may see it, but we are never part of it. Always keep the mirror close by you. Never forget to look into it and be guided by it.

Redefining the goals of therapy: looking anew at the language of empowerment

The goal of our therapeutic work is to make the survivor central to the therapeutic process, to put the survivor into the driving seat, to help the survivor to make choices about which therapuetic options are most meaningful.

Traditional assessment involves not only defining the problems, but also looking at goals and the suitability of the clients for the therapeutic work. Do they have the ego, strength and/or intellectual capacity to make use of counselling and talking through their difficulties? Should they be referred elsewhere for practical help, for example? Over what period of time should the clients be seen? Should brief or long-term work be offered?

Who makes these decisions? What choices are offered to the person being seen? If he/she does not return for treatment, how is that judged?

What does it feel like for someone who has gone through severe trauma to sit in a room and be assessed? What does it feel like to have his/her over-whelming feelings categorised and 'made sense of' by someone who has not shared these experiences of suffering? To facilitate a process of engagement, the traumatised person must be central to the decision-making. The decisions are not made about that person, but with the person. If he/she is not satisfied with what is offered, we have to look again. We must be challenged to find a pathway along which we can walk with the traumatised person.

'Empowerment' has been used as an important word throughout this book. It is a key concept in shifting the balance away from the weak, pathetic victim towards the strength of the survivor. However, like so many words, its overuse detracts from its original meaning. Working in the mental health field for many years brought me into contact with changing attitudes towards the vulnerable, voiceless members of society. Nevertheless, fundamental to the idea of empowering former victims to speak is the mechanism of one person having the authority to give power to the other person. It may be seen as a benevolent and worthy gesture. However, as we look more closely at the vocabulary and language we use to describe the therapeutic processes developed to work with severely traumatised people, we again find that the image we see may be an illusion. Is it really the helper who is empowering the traumatised person, or is it the survivor who has empowered the helper to work with him/her? As assistants to the survivor, our arrogance and expertness dissipate. In alliance with the survivor we search for freedom – the freedom to choose which way to go, which way to proceed. For those incarcerated and imprisoned, freedom becomes the ultimate goal. We have already seen how liberation from the death camps, for example, was a false liberation in the sense that the physical release did not also bring emotional freedom. Our therapeutic task is to address this elusive quest for emotional freedom with survivors. Through the centrality of the survivor in the therapeutic encounter and the choices he/she makes, we can together open up unexplored possibilities that relate to the concept of freedom. Freedom has meaning in the vocabulary of the oppressed. We must remember it and use it when we focus on choice as an essential ingredient in the food of those who have been starved, literally and metaphorically.

What choices can be offered in the therapeutic encounters?

In a climate of 'no cure' for the deep wounds which exist for those who have gone through extreme suffering, 'no hope' could easily be the corollary. The four detailed illustrations of the encounters I have had with survivors underline how hope is maintained against overwhelming despair.

The question to be asked focuses on: what can still be done, even at this late hour? The following are some of the choices which need to be addressed by those seeking a therapeutic encounter.

- Do I want to proceed with this encounter?
- Do I want this person to help me? Can this person help me?
- Do I want to talk about what is bothering me?
- Do I want to go back to the past to confront the impact of my trauma, or do I want to develop strategies for coping with the present?
- Do I want to find alternative ways of addressing the impact of my traumatic past on the present? Do I want to create visual images through art, or stories through writing?
- Do I want practical help, for example, with financial problems, housing or health issues?
- Do I want advice, for example, on how to make claims for compensation? Do I want to record my testimony?
- Do I want a ritual to 'bury' those of my family murdered in the Holocaust?

- Do I want to learn to speak publicly to help educate children and adults about the Holocaust?

- Do I want to increase my social skills and reduce my sense of isolation?

- Do I want to join some groups?

- Do I want to focus on my identity?

- Do I want my family to hear what I have been through and how it has affected how I relate to them?

- Do I want to think about ageing and death?

A combination of these and many more questions opens up avenues to explore, which may have eluded those who are despairing in the re-experiencing of trauma. Marsha chose to record her testimony rather than accept bereavement counselling. Irena focused on her relationship with her daughter as a present strategy, as against the confused, fragmented memories of her childhood grief. She reinforced this strategy through her enjoyment of travelling, to counterbalance her despair about her failed marriage. The process of choosing which way to proceed seems to release an energy that strengthens the fragile structure which binds survivors to this world. For Felix, these choices were less overt and obvious. Yet he chose to continue his encounters with me; he chose to keep living, despite the pain; he chose to accept practical help, such as the visits of the volunteer. We never lost sight of who he was and how he had coped before in his life.

The choices are not static, but change and evolve over the passage of time in the therapeutic encounter. These choices are multiplied many times when the range of services are broadened. We will look more fully at this when we turn our attention to the model of a therapy centre next door to a social centre later in this book.

The meaning of meaning

Fundamental to the subject of choice is the meaningfulness of the choices on offer to those who have undergone severe trauma. For example, to only offer counselling to someone who cannot verbalise the pain he/she is carrying is meaningless. To only offer talking as a therapy when there are pressing practical and social issues which are increasing the level of stress may also appear meaningless. Alternatively, to only offer practical help when there is a story which needs to be listened to would be meaningless. What is meaningful is individual to each survivor, and if we listen carefully, the survivor gives us clues as to what these may be.

The meaningfulness seems bound up with the question, 'What seems to help?' The following are a few of the remarks given as feedback from survivors I have encountered.

- It helps if there is a sense of being understood and believed.
- It helps if my behaviour is seen as a normal response to extreme trauma and not a mental illness.
- It helps if my coping strategies can be identified and worked with.
- It helps to be given choices, and not told what is best for me.
- It helps if I am consulted and listened to.
- It helps me to know more about the person who is helping me.
- It helps me if the person helping me is knowledgeable about the trauma.

Meaningfulness is being aware of the legacy of the trauma such as the Holocaust and how this is catered for in the therapeutic encounter. The choices which are explored in the therapeutic encounter must address the question of their significance to someone who has witnessed another world. To be significant, there must be links to that other world. Understanding and working with these links is at times intuitive, but when these risks are taken and they help, it is also liberating. Chava, for example, found great meaning in the ritual 'burial' of her mother and sister. Building on her own spirituality, and the meaningfulness of this in her current life, guided our work together towards this pathway. To only focus on the past, about which she could do nothing, would have reinforced her sense of hopelessness. To focus on something she could still do for her 'lost' family gave her strength and meaning in her life. Her writing then added to this sense of mastery and achievement, and she moved away from the sense of victim to one of survivor. Thus when further traumas are faced, such as her cancer and the deteriorating condition of her daughter's health, this mastery can be drawn upon again and harnessed as a strategy of coping. Such mastery is ultimately the survivor's victory over Hitler and the Nazis, which increases the sense of meaningfulness and purpose in the therapeutic encounter. 'Living well' is the best revenge on the perpetrator who is no longer present (Meichenbaum in Hoyt 2000, p.57).

At the entrance of the Tate Modern Art Gallery in London are three enormous works – named 'I do', 'I undo' and 'I redo'. They challenge us to deconstruct the familiar and to reform it in some other way. Allowing the vision of these structures to permeate my mind, I then viewed the art work within the museum with different eyes, and found meaning in works which I might earlier have dismissed. In the search for what is meaningful to someone who has witnessed horror, we are guided by these powerful edifices to think again, so that the stories may find different endings and different outcomes. It is the survivors' meaning, not our meaning, which must steer the therapeutic encounter.

Redefining the contract: restoring dignity and self-worth

A contract is an agreement drawn up to clarify the terms and conditions of a transaction. It is a word adopted in a therapy context to formulate the commitment to work together on defined goals. There are expectations concerning time for each session and frequency of sessions, and this may include discussion of fees in private practice. Brief or long-term contracts have become common language to describe the level of involvement in the professional encounter.

What meaning do such concepts have for someone who has been subject to totalitarian barbarism?

To address this question, let me tell you about Rachel, whom I have known informally over many years. I sat with her and other members in our centre as we commemorated Kristallnacht, 'the night of broken glass' (November 1938). There were readings and poems which captured that terrifying time, as well as prayers for the families who were destroyed in the Holocaust. As we had tea together, powerful emotions remained in the room. Rachel spoke to me about her distress at having lost touch with one of her grandsons, and her wish to see him again. She needed time to talk about it. Remembering the dead seemed to highlight a need for contact with the living. We arranged to meet. Rachel felt there were things she wanted to tell her grandson before she died, but earlier attempts to contact him had failed to bring a response. We sat together and compiled a letter to him. Instead of castigating him, she was able to convey her love for him, and the letter generated warmth and caring. Rachel felt satisfied that she had now left no stone unturned in her efforts to reach her grandson. She had told him what she wanted him to know. She was dealing with the last part of her life, and she did not want him to be left with bad feelings, even if she did not see him again. Is this a therapeutic encounter? I would say so, even though she may never come into my office again.

Often, fleeting moments such as these may constitute the beginning of a slow but cumulative series of 'testing the water'. These moments are not conditional upon further encounters, but must be accepted as gestures of a wish to trust, which takes a long time to rebuild.

The four illustrations of my therapeutic encounters (detailed in Chapter 6) did not have a prescribed duration. Massive loss is not subject to the finite nature of time. One day in Auschwitz would result in a lifelong memory. The passage of time does not relate to the depth of the trauma. With severe deprivation, as the three child survivors described, time must be found to nurture and address those missing years. Time was taken away from them, and time needs to be given back. Nine years and more will never heal the wounds, but we have seen how the commitment can make a difference. There is no pressure of time in the therapeutic encounter save the speed at which these traumatised people are reaching the end of their lives.

Together with the survivor, in our therapeutic alliance, we learn about the depth, breadth and shape which they wish the therapeutic encounter to take. Sometimes the dark shadow may be so engulfing that only short exposure to its spectre can be tolerated. Some survivors return many times to meet us, with passages of time separating clusters of two or three meetings.

Time is an essential luxury for these survivors, and they must regulate how much they want to take. The commitment to return again and again to meet with me was very high for the four people who speak in this book. In my view, this choice does not rest on the payment of fees. I believe that charging fees to someone who is suffering the effects of brutalisation would impose an additional injury. Their decision to attend the meetings is intrinsic and not dependent on external reasons. To be given time, and to be listened to, restores dignity and self-worth and gives back a sense of humanity to those who were dehumanised.

Towards a broader definition of therapy: rewriting the language of 'Wiedergutmachung' (to make good again)

I am often asked questions about the various claims which are currently being dealt with to compensate for suffering in the Holocaust. A language of compensation has emerged. Familiarity with that language, which includes words such as reparation, compensation and Wiedergutmachung, distorts the reality that, in fact, nothing can make good again the damage which was done. Yet somehow there is a sense that the slate can then be wiped clean, and those who give the money will be absolved of their guilt. Is this meant to produce a state of forgiveness? This is too difficult a subject for me to pursue as a non-survivor. Can the living survivors themselves forgive the perpetrators on behalf of those who were murdered? The answer cannot be simple. Nevertheless, survivors pursue their claims, even though their suffering cannot be measured in financial terms. It is perhaps a tangible way of addressing the unfinished business of the Holocaust.

The limitations of Wiedergutmachung guide us to rethink the language of therapy. Those who work with survivors are concerned to relieve pain and to repair the hurt and suffering. We can see, from the survivors who share their stories in this book, that we can go some way to alleviating the heavy burden which they carry with them. In our one-to-one encounters, we are limited in the extent to which we can facilitate healing. We have to look further, beyond the individual, to a wider context. We need to connect the individual to other healing sources which supplement what we can offer. Donald Meichenbaum (2000b), in his work with people who have undergone a wide range of traumatic experience, corroborates these observations made with Holocaust survivors. He sees the individual work undertaken as 'catalytic time' in which ideas and strategies can be formulated. However, he balances the one-to-one work with the 'homework' that needs to be done outside of the therapy room, in trying out new ways of dealing with people and life events (p.105).

As therapeutic facilitators, we cannot act alone. Our own work is strengthened through consideration of the concept of the family for survivors, and the concept of belonging to others who have undergone similar experiences of suffering.

Taking account of the family

For many survivors of the Holocaust, their entire families were annihilated. The creation of new families after the Holocaust became an overwhelming drive, to replace those who were murdered. The importance of these new families went some way to repair and compensate for the massive losses experienced. However, Wiedergutmachung often remained out of reach. Pressures on children to embody the dead could drive a wedge between the two generations. Living with the dead, as survivors do, separated them from their living children. Communication, which is often not clear in these families, gets transmitted into our therapeutic encounters.

The families speak in our encounters with survivors, whether they are present or not. Irena, for example, saw the dissolution of her current family as yet another form of suffering, having been wrenched from her parents who were then murdered. Her current family were ever evident in our individual meetings. Restoring a sense of harmony and communication among the members of her family became her wish in the last part of her life. To restore a sense of family would be her victory over the Holocaust. Thus, little by little, family members entered the space in which we met. I needed their help to assist Irena – talking about them was not enough. Each came in turn and Irena connected with them. As we worked with the living, so the dead could be buried.

For Chava, her daughter remained physically absent in our encounters, and yet ever present in the room. She could not help her daughter, but she became the catalyst for Chava to address the unmourned death of her sister, Sylvia. Chava saw these two people as closely connected. She saw her daughter's problems as a punishment for Chava's relief when Sylvia died. Her sister had carried the negative memories from their experiences in the Holocaust, which Chava wanted to forget. Seeing her daughter as a help rather than a hindrance enabled her to separate these two people, and allowed Chava to address Sylvia in the addendum of her book. In asking for her forgiveness, she let Sylvia rest. Her daughter remains a complex, unresolved problem, for which it is difficult to see an outcome. We focus on strategies that help Chava to cope with this wound that remains with her to the present day.

Taking account of the family also means seeing ourselves, the therapeutic facilitators, as part of the replacement extended family. Our significance goes beyond more direct ways of working with trauma. A survivor may be seen by more than one member of staff. He/she may be offered individual meetings and group meetings with other survivors. We work as a team, so that leave and sickness do not isolate the vulnerable survivor again to a sense of abandonment.

Taking account of a sense of belonging: making the outsiders insiders

The experience of severe suffering, as we have already seen, separated those who had gone through the unimaginable events from those who have not. That boundary largely remains in the therapeutic encounters with individual facilitators. To connect with others who have gone through similar experiences, to hear stories which echo one's own, reduces the sense of isolation and difference. Being with others who understand the world one has come from restores a sense of identity lost in the dehumanising world of the Holocaust.

This is evidenced in the group work which takes place in Shalvata, including the group for children hidden in the Holocaust, the group for those who came on the Kindertransport, the group for spouses of survivors, and the groups for children of survivors. As with the individual encounters described, the groups provide non-clinical opportunities for past and present experiences to be shared and understood. The content of these groups is not detailed in this book as access to the dynamics contained within is carried by those who facilitate the groups.

My task is to ensure that the groups form part of the whole therapeutic programme. I am constantly vigilant to patterns emerging which would benefit from being addressed in a group. As mentioned earlier, the Holocaust was a group phenomenon. Hence, bringing survivors together in groups, whether in Shalvata or the HSC, becomes an essential therapeutic prerequisite. For example, it allows people who were traumatised as children to have a peer group again and recapture some of that lost childhood. However, because of the setting in which the therapeutic work takes place, those who attend the group may also be meeting socially in the HSC. In this sense the groups, like the individual encounters, do not follow traditional boundaries and rules. They are not 'pure'. Nevertheless, in the positive outcomes which can be observed in the participants, it would seem that the content is meaningful and useful in their journey towards integrating the trauma into their lives.

However, the need to belong, and to be insiders rather than outsiders, needed a wider context than could be offered through a therapy centre, however creative and meaningful the approach.

Murder of close family, as we have seen, was a massive trauma for those who went through the Holocaust. Loss of entire communities meant that post-war recovery was impeded by an absence of structure, security and foundation on which to rebuild shattered lives. Bringing survivors together in small, informal, mutual support groups is one way of reducing the sense of being the outsider and increasing the sense of belonging. However, these disconnected oases, or pockets of hope, remained silent expressions of a wish to recapture something stronger and more lasting. Creating a new community in today's world became a driving force which would link the past to the present and the future; which would give a sense of home and identity to those who lived in a world in which they did not belong; and which would challenge the dark shadow which threatened to complete the work which began in the Holocaust. Bringing survivors together and helping them to build this new community threw a new light onto the therapeutic possibilities for severely traumatised people.

Building a new community with the survivors opened up avenues which could only be glimpsed in the small mutual support groups. Having reached out, having brought survivors together, having listened to how we can help them individually, in families and in groups, we now had a whole new world to explore. This would significantly augment and reshape the therapeutic possibilities. It was realised through the establishment of a social centre (the Holocaust Survivors' Centre) next door to our existing therapy centre (Shalvata).

Endnotes

1. *From the Kingdom of Memory*, by Elie Wiesel. Copyright © 1990 by Elirion Associates, Inc. Reprinted by permission of Georges Borchardt, Inc., for the author. Permission to reprint is also granted by Sheil Land Associates Ltd, London.

2. 'It Would Be Impossible to Keep Silent,' by Elie Wiesel, as published in *The Daily Telegraph*, July 31, 2000. Copyright © 2000 by Elie Wiesel. Reprinted by permission of Georges Borchardt, Inc., for the author. Permission to reprint is also granted by Sheil Land Associates Ltd, London and *The Daily Telegraph*.

Chapter 8

Building a Meaningful Therapeutic Service with those who have Undergone Severe Trauma

The Holocaust Survivors' Centre: the empty space

'I can take any empty space and call it a bare stage. A man walks across this empty space whilst someone else is watching him, and this is all that is needed for an act of theatre to be engaged' (Brook 1990, first published 1968, p.11).[1] In this new centre's raw, unstructured state, Peter Brook's concept of an empty space had resonance. To bring an empty space to life needs a creative leap. In this 'theatre' to be created in the Holocaust Survivors' Centre, many parts needed to be included – many voices needed to be heard. There were the silent voices of the murdered, the screams of those who suffered, and the muffled whispers of those hidden, whose lives depended on keeping quiet. Though the drama of theatre bears no comparison to the reality of severe suffering in the Holocaust, it nevertheless provides a window through which we begin to visualise a new scene. We will see how the space (HSC) allows a story to unfold that develops with the passage of time.

In 1989 I walked into an empty shell of a building – no ceiling, no inner walls, only greyness greeted me. There was no life, no shape, structure or form. It was a vast empty space waiting to be filled. Standing there alone, I thought of Marsha's words as she recounted to me her return to Auschwitz-Birkenau. 'The emptiness of the place struck me, and the absolute silence... only greyness could be seen – the greyness of ashes.' The vastness of

Auschwitz-Birkenau was an empty space waiting to be filled with death and misery. In the lingering void in which I was standing, the images of that past horror needed to be present. Those who had suffered had shared memories which were then scattered over the four corners of the world when the camp gates were opened. Now those same people were being brought together again in the HSC. The empty space embodied an almost fifty-year gap that separated the severe trauma in the war from the present – the two became linked in the unfinished business which had not been addressed.

That empty space in which I stood would be like an empty vessel into which the liquid memories of the Holocaust would be poured. These memories had found no resting place, except in the already tortured bodies of those who had witnessed the atrocity. I saw the HSC as a container into which the memories could be released and, by so doing, free the carriers from some of the heavy burden they had had to endure alone.

Thinking back to that time is like the blank white page now in front of me as I write. The page is waiting to have words put on to it, to fill the space and give meaning to the unfilled void. The words cannot be random but must have some order, plan and structure, which can be seen and understood. Words do not assemble themselves, but need a writer to translate them from head to paper. So it was as I embarked on this work in the Holocaust Survivors' Centre.

This centre needed to fulfil many functions for the diverse needs of those who had survived the Holocaust. The last time many of the survivors were together was in the camps. They may have been terrified, isolated children, experiencing atrocity no-one could imagine. The last time they were together may have been a time of chaos and confusion. Now, more than fifty years later, how would they begin again in this newly created space, coming together as though time had stood still?

Memories of starvation and fighting for one's life remain etched in the recesses of the mind from those darkest days. Never having enough to eat and suffering extreme cold and pain do not disappear when those tortures are removed.

Would this new centre be a place where the memory of death would be recreated, or one in which life and hope would triumph? In my heart, I wanted this newly created space to be a haven for survivors to escape to from the 'instruments of torture' which never ceased their vicious hold over those who had been at their mercy. I wanted this space to be a source of strength, to build a new foundation for shattered lives. I wanted this space to both memorialise the past and liberate towards a present and a future. I wanted this space to be a place to offer sustenance, humanity and hope. I wanted this space to symbolise a victory over Hitler's Final Solution.

While I am writing, the festival of Chanukah is being celebrated – a festival of light, miracle and hope. It brings to mind Rabbi Hugo Gryn's account of the festival of Chanukah at the Lieberose slave labour camp. He describes how his father

> produced a curious-shaped clay bowl, and began to light a wick immersed in his precious, but now melted, margarine ration. Before he could recite the blessing, I protested at this waste of food. He looked at me – then at the lamp – and finally said: 'You and I have seen it is possible to live up to three weeks without food. We once lived almost three days without water; but you cannot live properly for three minutes without hope!' (Gilbert, 2000, p.88)

Hope is at the core of survival. Hope needed to be central to this new centre. Hope reshapes and redefines the mirror which we spoke about earlier, and which brought the past into sharp relief against the present.

The dark shadow of the Holocaust, which the mirror reflected, helped to focus on the atrocity and to take account of it. The mirror needed to be wrapped up carefully in this new centre so that it should not be broken. A new and more multifaceted tool was needed to reflect the complexity of both darkness and light. A prism through which light is refracted would create new images for this multifunctional environment. The new centre would focus on 'play' as well as being a centre for remembrance. It would be a centre for creating new stories as well as bearing witness to the past. It would be a centre for joy as well as tears. Learning to live with life rather than with death, with enjoyment rather than despair, with sustenance rather than starvation, would provide a resting place, and a more peaceful interlude in the last part of these tortured lives. Deep within its remit, this new centre contained the concept of freedom – a freedom to create something new, which would move this arduous journey of survival along an, as yet, unexplored pathway. The concrete form of this new space converted the ephemeral into something which would last and remain for the future.

As I stood in that empty space, many years ago now, I felt it challenged every part of my being. It was both exciting and awesome. I remained steadfast even though I was fearful that I might fall short of my own expectations and those of the survivors. In the silence of that empty space, a turning point happened in my life – nothing has remained the same.

Endnote

1. *The Empty Space* ©1968 Peter Brook, is reproduced by kind permission of HarperCollins Publisher Ltd, London.

Chapter 9

Developing Services with Holocaust Survivors

Preparing the foundation

The beginning of another journey

In January 1993, about two hundred survivors and refugees from the Nazi Holocaust joined the newly established Holocaust Survivors' Centre. The SOS group and subsequent mutual support groups had grown in size and entered this new space, not yet knowing what shape it would take. Some survivors were ambivalent about the need for such a centre; some castigated it as an unnecessary expense; some were openly opposed to it, while many greeted it as the longed-for new home.

I believed that this centre would hold the key to converting a vision into a concrete reality. I knew we had reached the limit in the services we could offer survivors through our professional team in Shalvata and the mutual support groups. Survivors were growing older, and I hoped this centre would become a lifeline to them in the latter part of their lives.

In a time of economic recession, I had to make a very strong case to Jewish Care to invest in this scheme. I had written a two-and-a-half page document which was presented to Jewish Care's Executive Committee. I remember the day I presented the formula for this new centre with clarity – as though it had just happened. As I spoke, the words flowed out of my mouth with such ease and conviction that I scarcely recognised the speaker. I felt like a messenger for those fragmented parts which had been scattered, and now needed to be mended into a whole again. The urgency of their need inspired me, and the thrust of my delivery echoed the words, 'If not now, when?' In a few years' time it would be too late. The survivors had given the community a second opportunity to repair some of the untouched and unattended damage within their midst. The response from the Executive Committee of Jewish Care was unanimous – 'A centre for survivors must be established now.'

The empty space next door to the already established therapy centre, Shalvata, became the ideal location for this new centre. The recent departure of a tenant in that part of the building was fortuitous. It was a space waiting to be filled.

To translate the idea into something practical, a steering committee was formed. This consisted of survivors, the adult children of survivors, and professionals. They were drawn together in their quest to develop the new community. Initially the aim was to create a friendly environment in which survivors could drop in for a coffee and a chat. This modest blueprint was influenced by the SOS group as well as Café 84, a social project for survivors in Stockholm. Its founder, Hedi Fried (1997), stated that 'the concept behind Café 84 is to offer survivors a meeting place in a warm and accepting atmosphere, a forum that gives the possibility of opening up a dialogue. The survivors would be allowed to go at their own pace' (p.109).

The official opening of the centre by Jewish Care, and the naming of the centre by the survivors, gave the HSC an identity. The management committee then had to get involved with the running of the centre. They saw it as a centre 'for survivors, run by survivors'. Very soon the management committee meetings became dominated by a power struggle which emerged from a couple of the members, and this disrupted the urgent need to develop the day-to-day activities of the centre. The funding agencies (Jewish Care and World Jewish Relief) were seen by these two members as the 'enemy' and other members became caught up in this battle for control. Far from being a peaceful haven for survivors, anxiety and fear became commonplace emotions.

In my attempt not to appear to be the authority and 'Nazi' figure, I was not addressing the dynamic from the Holocaust past which had the power to destroy what was being created. Gradually members stopped coming to the centre for fear of being bullied into supporting those who wished to take over the running of the centre. The question may be asked, 'Why was the centre not given over to these survivors to run?' The answer lies in the issue addressed earlier in the book relating to the difference between mutual support and self-help (see Chapter 5). Owing to the hierarchy of suffering, owing to the competing needs of different groups within the centre, it was difficult for those who participated as members to balance the needs of all.

To overcome this intransigent and potentially destructive situation, Jewish Care decided to involve an outside ombudsman to assess the situation. His job was to listen to the survivors, to listen to the management committee members, and to listen to the staff. In his recommendation lay the key to our existence today. He suggested that an elected Advisory Committee be formed, comprising nine survivors from the different groups represented in the centre. Elections would be supervised externally for fairness, and would occur every year in order to maximise as wide a participation of members as possible. It was a consultative committee, but the managers of Jewish Care, it was stressed, must be allowed to make decisions. Those members of the former management committee who had instigated the turbulent fight to take control would have their membership withdrawn.

The members of the centre who had wanted a return to a peaceful life were relieved by the decisions taken. It was nevertheless traumatic for all those involved. There was, however, an important learning dimension to it. I had to accept that there was no easy way to relinquish my responsibility to steer the centre forward. For the centre to survive, I could consult, I could (and should) work in partnership with survivors, but I had to guide its development. Once this process was legitimised, and accepted by the members, it became possible to return to the task of making the centre come alive and to become the place the survivors wished it to be.

I have dwelt on this early difficulty at some length to illustrate the pitfalls that may be encountered and the lessons that can be learned from this experience. In a climate of 'user-led' services in a democratic society, it is politic to give power, authority and control over to the users. In the aftermath of totalitarianism, power and control were equated with bestiality and barbarism. In the recreation of a survivor community, there remain uncertainties about whose authority to accept and trust. Ambivalence by the designated authority (manager) of the centre opens up possibilities for power to be seized, thereby overthrowing the democratic possibilities. As manager of the centre, I became a guardian of that power. It helped power to be channelled back to the members as the community became established. The proportional representation of the membership on the Advisory Committee, the elections, and participation in the decision-making and strategic development of the centre enabled participants to identify with their centre. This still holds the centre together, but stormy seas are never far away.

My guardianship needs to protect the centre as a unique, separate and different facility within the larger organisation of Jewish Care. I also need to protect and ensure that the vision of the centre remains central to its internal development. The guardianship of the centre must ensure the survival of the centre, both now and for the future, through converting the vision into a reality.

The role of vision in the development of the services for survivors

Having survived the early turbulent days of setting up the Holocaust Survivors' Centre, I was entrusted to safeguard its progress and development, in partnership with the members.

My years of contact and listening to survivors could now bear fruit. Their vision of this centre could start to take shape. Before detailing the component parts of that vision, I would like to emphasise the essential nature of vision as an ingredient both in the foundation and progress of a specialised service such as the HSC.

If we look at a dictionary definition of vision as the power of seeing or, more figuratively, as an ability for imagination, foresight and wisdom in planning out a scheme, then this must be included in any discussion about setting up new and innovative services. It would be all too easy to replicate the warm, comfortable, caring environment which the parent organisation had established for the ageing population. These day centres for the elderly, which 'looked after' the increasingly frail members of the community, were the only models we had. Instinctively I knew that this could not be the model for those who had suffered severe trauma. A new format needed to be created which would directly or indirectly address the unfinished business of the Holocaust.

What have been some of the key components of that vision?

- The new centre would be a meeting place – a home-from-home for survivors as they grow older.
- The new centre would be a place where survivors would feel they belong; where they would not have to explain the trauma they

had been through; where they would have an identity; where they would feel understood.

- The new centre would provide a social programme through which they could enjoy moments of relief from the memories they carried with them from their past.

- The new centre would provide the social network they lacked as a result of family being murdered in the Holocaust.

- The new centre would provide practical support and advice.

- The new centre would help members to have a stronger voice in ensuring that their special needs are met, and that they are heard by the outside world.

- The new centre would provide a building in which the Holocaust could be memorialised.

- The new centre would help to strengthen the survivors through their active participation – where they would feel more like survivors than victims.

- The new centre would enable the establishment of a new community to replace those decimated during the Holocaust, and thereby give a sense of victory over Hitler's Final Solution.

In our day-to-day working life, different pressures sometimes distort and blur our vision so we no longer see our direction with clarity. An example of the precarious nature of vision was evidenced when I left my former post of team leader for a social work team in Jewish Care. As long as I was supervising the staff, as long as I was overseeing the intake of work, as long as I provided supportive groups in which staff could share the difficult nature of the work with survivors, the emphasis on survivors remained central, and grew in terms of the social workers' caseloads. There was interest and concern for this particular group, even though it was not the specialism it is today. However, very soon after I left the post, other pressing needs emerged in relation to the elderly and mentally ill. It appeared that there were very few survivors and refugees approaching the team, and soon its importance was submerged. Practical demands for care overshadowed the hidden emotional agendas of these traumatised survivors, and the commitment to this group was lost.

Vision depends not only on belief, but also the possibility to implement that belief. Vision does not last long without the means to particularise it in concrete terms. It needs a channel, a conduit into which its energy can be released. In practical terms it needs a dedicated person who becomes the ever-present reminder of its goals and mission. It needs a voice, or it will disappear into obscurity.

To be entrusted with the vision for this new centre required not only the survivors' authorisation, but also that of the parent organisation. To strengthen my position, my role changed from manager of the centres to Director of Services for Holocaust Survivors and Refugees for Jewish Care. As therapeutic facilitator alone, I would not have had the same vantage point to keep the vision on track. Demands by the parent organisation to provide written evidence to justify the centre's separateness and uniqueness were complied with. My managerial strategy will be looked at in more detail in the next section of the book. At present it is sufficient to note the steps which need to be taken to identify and appoint a person to a key post as the bridge between the vision and the realisation of it.

Building a bridge between a specialist service and the parent organisation

To translate vision into concrete reality necessitates money and support. However committed I was to the needs of these ageing survivors, I had to have the organisation's backing. The 'survival' of this new service depended on the relationship of this satellite specialist service to the funding parent organisation. The concept already mentioned in respect of insider/outsider dichotomy also revealed itself in the way the survivors' services were related to in the organisational matrix. The services for survivors were seen as the outsiders, while the parent organisation was seen in this context as the insider.

This dynamic was not evident immediately, but only as the service for survivors began to take shape. Initially, the creation of this innovative service produced a great deal of publicity and fanfare; Shalvata and the HSC were hailed as centres of excellence. This reflected very positively onto the parent organisation. The Jewish community seemed to recognise the important statement, even at this late hour, in terms of 'reparation' to survivors which had not been forthcoming earlier. This new development was perceived as a sign of life and vitality for the parent organisation which had recently completed an important merger.

I could not have set up this service alone. I could not have survived those early days of turbulence without the solid backing of Jewish Care. I owe a great debt to Jewish Care, the organisation which shaped me; gave me opportunities to grow and develop in my work; had faith in my ability, and invested in me and my commitment to work with Holocaust survivors and refugees. In turn, I worked to bring credit to the organisation by investing myself wholeheartedly in making this service unique and at the forefront in its field.

In setting up a service of this kind I would urge that time, care and attention are paid to the organisational context. A relationship of trust between the manager of the service and the organisation enabled inevitable differences to be addressed.

If I knew then what I know now, I would have perhaps been more alert to the tensions which ensued as the services became more established. Retrospect and hindsight are tools which are only available to me now, but they nevertheless allow me to share with you the complex dynamics which could have impeded the progress of this much-valued specialist service.

After the glorious setting-up phase, I was then left to steer these projects into permanent features. This became an all-consuming task. The centres grew; we began to reach more and more survivors. The year 1995 commemorated the fiftieth anniversary of the ending of World War II and the liberation of the camps. The centres received massive media coverage. Survivors were interviewed on TV, radio and by the press. As Director of these services, my profile was also augmented, and the work began to take on national as well as international importance.

As the services expanded, demand for greater resources increased, and the parent organisation had to feed this hungry mouth with more investment. The 'baby' (specialist service) was growing up into a child and reaching 'adolescence', with different needs and a louder voice, which was difficult to ignore. The service was developing its own identity. The difference between this service and the rest of the organisation seemed to become accentuated.

Instead of celebrating and acknowledging the difference, this new service became, for some, a focus of envy. The pleasant physical environment; the employment of high-calibre staff; the freedom to be innovative and to work creatively; the attention and recognition received by the 'outside world' contrasted particularly with the high caseloads of social workers in the parent organisation, plus the mountains of paperwork associated with a changing organisational culture. The new service's peripheral position *vis-à-vis* the parent organisation changed the meaning of autonomy to one of isolation and marginalisation – a major threat to its survival. The service, like the survivors, became an 'outsider' and similarly took on the label of 'disturber of the peace'. By degrees, the voice of the service, like that of the survivors, was not being heard and, consequently, was becoming increasingly disempowered.

The survival strategy was to make this satellite service both central and indispensable to the parent organisation. It was important for me to arrange meetings with social work teams to liaise over the work of the centres; to facilitate referrals from social workers to our specialist service; to offer support groups for social workers working with survivors in other settings; to offer written and verbal communication with managers in the organisation; to encourage visits to the centre by lay leaders and fund-raisers who were assisting the parent organisation; to produce an information pack about our work to distribute to the parent organisation; to increase transparency about the work undertaken in the specialist services; to increase the organisation's income through grants for this special work; to be seen on a regular face-to-face basis at head office. The success of this strategy rested heavily on its reinforcement through line management as well as lay leadership support. The strategy had to be legitimised in the parent organisation for it to succeed. It was essential for me to know the infrastructure of the organisation and how to harness the necessary power. My knowledge of the language and culture of the organisation helped me to access this support.

This complex organisational dynamic is certainly not unique to the service I was developing, but has much wider resonance. For example, the integration of psychotherapy in and with organisations is described by Hawkins and Miller (1994). They emphasise the importance of organisa-tional awareness by the psychotherapist in order to survive in different contexts. Psychotherapists in organisations have to be prepared to unlearn some of what they know, and to learn new things. They should avoid the 'dangerous temptations' (p.283) to pathologise individuals or systems, to look at process rather than talk, and to lose the focus of the organisation as a whole. The authors stress the importance of the psychotherapist's understanding of the nature of organisations and how they work.

Of particular relevance to the relationship between a parent organisation and its satellite project is the concept of the organisation as an open system. The analogy that Hawkins and Miller (1994, pp.267–85) make is to a biological organism. Organisations, they say, have tasks to perform in order to survive. To focus on a task, the organisation needs to maintain a sense of equilibrium. Anything that unbalances it threatens its system. This new service needed to be accommodated within the total system of the parent organisation if it was not to be a danger to it.

In addition to this internal linking, the survival strategy of the service was also enhanced through a national and international network with other survivor-related organisations. The respect and status accorded to Jewish Care's specialist service helped to affirm its position as a major contributor in the field of working with the effects of trauma. The development of training and consultation worldwide, the visits by those keen to learn about our way of working, plus the income from this work, reinforced the indispensability of the service. In a similar way to the survivors themselves, survival of the service was helped through a collective identity with other organisations involved with similar work. This crucial aspect will be looked at again later in the book, when we focus on current strategies which move us on into the future.

The schematic representation in Figure 9.1 – using a Star of David to reflect interrelationships between a specialist service for Holocaust survivors and Jewish Care, the parent organisation – reminds us of our common goals within the Jewish community. In partnership we work towards these goals, but the picture is multifaceted and complex. To complete the work of building the foundation for this service, much time and effort must be devoted to this task of making connections. In any organisation, to ignore this reality would be perilous.

Managing, supervising and directing a specialist service for Holocaust survivors
THE MANAGEMENT OF HOLOCAUST SERVICES

At the many international conferences I have attended over the years on the subject of working with Holocaust survivors and war trauma, no mention has ever been made about the managerial aspects of developing a specialist service of this kind. Establishing the service which we have today could not have been done on the basis of therapeutic skills alone. To make the therapeutic services effective, a particular style of management needed to evolve. This must be addressed at this point, as we continue our task of laying the foundation for working with traumatised survivors and refugees.

Managing such a service can be isolating and stressful. I would advise anyone wishing to embark on developing therapeutic services for severely

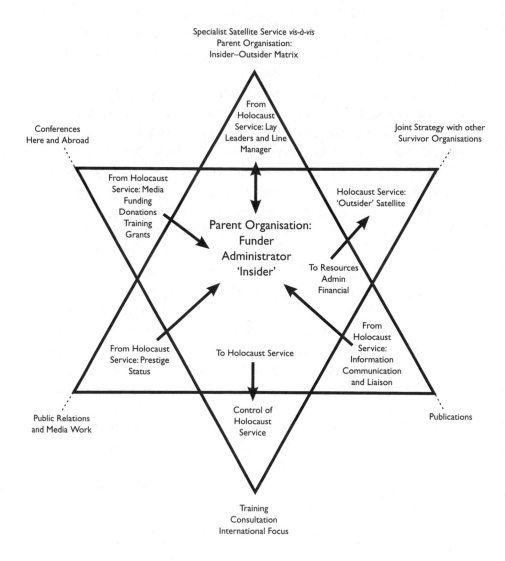

Figure 9.1 Survival strategy of a specialist service

traumatised people to ensure there is adequate personal support for them. We have already noted the complexities of the organisational dynamics. Couple this with the content of the subject matter of the trauma, and the manager of such a service would be in danger of burning out quite rapidly.

I would like to begin by focusing on the two consultants who work with me to strengthen me in my multifunctional role of Director, manager, supervisor and therapeutic facilitator. I want to give a voice to these silent contributors to the unfolding story of this service's success. I could not have achieved this on my own, and they must both find a place in my book.

Strengthening the manager: finding the source of strength

More years ago than I care to remember, I was introduced to Sonny Herman as someone who could help me in my work with survivors. After the death of Shamai Davidson, who was my inspiration, my teacher and my support, I felt bereft. My early meetings with Sonny mirrored this trauma and grief.

Sonny was, and still is, based in Holland working with Holocaust survivors on a daily basis. I needed his expertise and extensive experience to guide me in those difficult early days of not knowing or understanding the powerful and often chaotic world I was encountering. Alone, in that unknown world, I was in danger of being destroyed, and I was fortunate to be able to turn to Sonny. There was, in a sense, a survival instinct which was triggered, for I very much wanted to remain with the survivors, but knew I could not do this on my own.

Sonny questioned me, he challenged me but, fundamentally, he understood me and the heaviness I was carrying. We have been dealing with the raw, unadulterated horror which I share in my hours with him. Sonny has returned month after month to listen to me, to strengthen me and to guide me. His presence has enabled me to venture into that 'other world', to get closer to the suffering and the sufferers, but always to keep one foot in this world, the world of the living and life.

As I have grown stronger from the security and trust that has been developing through Sonny's input, I have begun to ask my own questions of him. We were, and still are, two very different people. Yet our mutual respect allowed a more equal relationship to develop, thereby mirroring once more the adaptation to those with whom we work.

There is a clear reflection between the nurturing, strengthening and empowering content of my meetings with Sonny, and the survivors with whom I journey. What I recognise in Sonny serves as a model for me, which I then form and reshape to myself. Sonny needed to be different; he needed an understanding of the 'outsider' quality of what we do, so let me tell you a little about him.

Sonny has worked for over thirty years with the filth and pain of suffering contained in the memories of those survivors who may be hanging on for another day. Sonny's work has revolved around helping the living to live, the living to die more peacefully, and those who see death as the only option to find some meaning in their lives again. Sonny was trained as a Jungian therapist, yet in his practice he redefines the parameters of the therapy. He returns year after year in the cold November days to visit the former death camps with survivors and their children. His whole being is invested in finding new and creative ways to help those who have suffered. As a Rabbi as well as a psychotherapist, he brings a spiritual dimension to his work, and can fuse that often important aspect into working with those who are nearing death.

Sonny is a powerful presence. When he enters Shalvata, it is a different day. Twice a month, on a Tuesday, Sonny undertakes the long and stressful journey from Holland. Though I am still left to deal with the day-to-day managerial and developmental aspects of my work, I feel a sense of relief that there is someone who communicates with me in the same language.

Sonny is a doer. If there is a group to run, he will run it. The group for children who were hidden in the Holocaust, as well as the group for the spouses of survivors, have moved forward significantly through his involvement. I observe the members of the group as they leave their encounters with him. He creates a space for the former hidden children to breathe, to find a voice and to belong. In the short time he has in London, he will go and visit one of the members who may be in hospital, or make a phone call to a member who may be temporarily unable to attend the group. By his actions he speaks loudly about his commitment and his care towards both the survivors and myself. In turn, I need to speak for Sonny for, though vocal on many subjects, he speaks little of himself. I write about him here because he does not write himself about the unique work he undertakes. Others should know what he has done, what he still does and who he is. Sonny shines through in the goals we have reached in Shalvata and the HSC. Without his presence, without his support and guidance, this story may have had a different ending. Sonny's non-conformist view of the world, his politics and his creative imagination were and still are liberating factors in developing my own thoughts. He gives me the courage to be different. He gives me the strength to speak up and have a voice in the organisation. He helps me find the

Jewish dimension in my work. He helps me to find the freedom to be who I am, and to use that to get closer to understanding and working with the severely traumatised survivors.

Balanced against Sonny's powerful presence is another source of strength: my former line manager and now consultant, John Bridgewater. Translating the language of suffering and that 'other world' into concrete form demands special commitment to make it work. It needs to have meaning for those who use the service, which can be understood by the organisation which funds it. Understanding that 'other world' is only part of the equation. In the vast arena of these two centres, chaos and memories of those other endless spaces – the death camps – threaten disorganisation and disintegration. To allow these centres to create something new, something different from that 'other world', they demand structure and form in the way they are managed.

As I got to know John, he listened closely to me. He asked me questions. He assumed nothing. In the details of staff appointments, staff supervision and budgetary discussions, he accepted the difference between this service for Holocaust survivors and other services in Jewish Care. In his powerful position in Jewish Care, he provided a non-authoritarian authority which helped to integrate the service into Jewish Care and ensure its survival. John has proved to be an excellent manager, helping to strengthen me at points of conflict and times of stress. He allows me the freedom to come to my own conclusions and to find my own answers.

As time went by, John's commitment to this service for survivors clarified itself. When he retired from Jewish Care, he agreed to continue meeting me as my consultant. Perhaps the most unique and profound dynamic is that John is not a Jew. He seems unburdened by the baggage of guilt and denial which affected some responses I had experienced from other colleagues. Through my voice John began to hear the voice of the survivors. It touched him, and his responses are compassionate and humane. In wishing to get closer to understanding and helping those who suffered, he attended meetings of the Advisory Committee. As a non-Jew working in a Jewish organisation, he knows the meaning of being an 'outsider', of being different, of coming from another background. As an 'outsider' he has developed a strategy which enabled him to become central to the organisation. This strategy has become a crucial model in ensuring that these services for survivors are not marginalised but looked upon as 'centres of excellence', as he calls them, which pay tribute to Jewish Care.

John's vast experience in managing therapeutic communities prior to Jewish Care gives a breadth of vision from which comparisons and differences can be formulated. He can identify with my multifunctional role, both as the manager as well as the developer of innovative therapeutic services. He perceives the isolation of being left alone to cope in a satellite service. He acknowledges the stresses relating to the content of working with severely traumatised people, as well as those relating to staff dealing with the same group of people. He protects me against burn-out – seeking out opportunities for me to grow and develop and find new meaning in what I do. He has encouraged me in my writing, always enquiring about its progress. He supports me in the options I choose to vary my work, whether this involves me in travelling abroad or attending conferences. He forms an important link between my current line manager and myself, digesting my words and making them intelligible to those who must support what I do. He acts as a catalyst in bringing me closer to those in the organisation I need to have on my side, whether they be professional or lay people.

Shamai Davidson's last efforts before his death to link me to those who could help me on my journey have not been in vain. Just as the survivors are strengthened by seeking out those who speak the same language of pain and suffering, so I too have worked hard to connect myself with those who are with me, for me, and fight for me to finish what I began. Sonny and John are with me most frequently, but others contribute to the total picture.

As John Donne ([1624] 1993) has written, 'No man is an island entire of it self.' The line managers who have supervised me, the teams I have worked with, the organisations I have co-operated with, the individuals both personal and professional who have helped me, have ensured my continuation. Opening myself up to receive help from those I trust is an essential ingredient in moving the service on from chaos to coherence.

Managing the manager

Sonny and John together symbolise the essential combination of tasks which need to be performed in developing a service for Holocaust survivors. To be a manager, removed from the day-to-day contact with the people for whom the service is intended, would have resulted in a different picture. As the manager of a social work team prior to my work at Shalvata, I continued to maintain my direct work with older people as well as people with mental health problems and later with refugees and survivors. I felt it was not possible to get a feel of the powerful dynamics the social workers were facing without being at the front line myself. My heart is still bound up in these personal encounters. Through Sonny, I remain close to the survivors. Through Sonny, I never become removed from the horror that they have encountered. Sonny keeps me on course. He understands how hard my task is, and helps me to return again and again to face the pain with them. Sonny's presence reminds me that this can never become like any other service for older people, but it must remain special and extraordinary.

John helps me to face my other role as the person who heads the service and takes it forward. At its root the concept of management has implicit within it both control and organisation. Also attributed to it are elements of authority and power – all difficult concepts when dealing with people who have been at the mercy of totalitarian regimes. The trust which has been built up over time, and the consultative process which has been developed between the survivors and myself, has led to an acceptance of my role as the Director of the services. As mentioned earlier, my role has evolved more as guardian of the power rather than as a threatening authority. Nevertheless, conflicts do still arise – for example, over funding issues between survivors and the parent organisation. On the whole, however, these conflicts are resolved through listening, through dialogue and through a sense that the concerns have been addressed and learned from.

Survivors who use the service do so because they feel it meets their needs and they feel comfortable in it. The philosophy which guides it must be given substance for it to work. Much of this substance is not overt, and the survivors themselves are unaware of the processes involved in creating the infrastructure which anchors the service.

Recruitment of staff, supervision of staff, budgetary issues, reports for various organisations, applications for grants, chairing of meetings, marketing the service, media and public relations work, consultation, strategies for future planning, networking with other organisations involved with refugees and survivors, and publications of the work are but a few of the complex and diverse tasks needed to be done.

I would like to look in a little more detail at some of these functions I undertake to illustrate the factors which need to be taken into account for the service to survive, and for the vision to remain central to its development. The appointment of staff has already been looked at earlier. However, what happens when these staff are in post?

SUPERVISION OF STAFF

The staff in Shalvata and the Holocaust Survivors' Centre form the backbone of the therapeutic service. Over the years, there have been team members who have brought in a vital energy in terms of their skills, strengths and exemplary commitment to working with the aftermath of atrocity. Some of these staff have made outstanding contributions to the development of this specialist therapeutic service for Holocaust survivors. The staff need to be nurtured in order to be sustained and to feel satisfied in their chosen work. The supervision can facilitate that process.

The range of skills and professional backgrounds in a team specialising in trauma work must be adaptable to the changing needs of the survivors. In Shalvata, these professional skills needed to include social work, psychology, family therapy, creative therapy, counselling and psychotherapy in order to address the trauma and its consequences. In the HSC, the range of skills includes administrative, culinary, organisational, reception and programme development in order to complement the work of Shalvata. My task has been to blend these diverse parts into one team.

As the work became more specialised and focused on war trauma, some staff found that the adaptations required were too difficult and went elsewhere. New staff were recruited using a new job description. The clinical component, which existed in Shalvata's early mental health work, gave way to more eclectic possibilities when Shalvata developed as a specialist service. The mental health work returned to Jewish Care. This separation was a crucial factor in evolving a different model in our therapeutic work.

The individual supervision needs to consolidate in practice the conceptual shift which this specialist service unceasingly demands. Having gone through these adaptations myself, I never underestimate or forget how difficult this may be. In the individual supervision sessions, in the detailed discussion of the work the staff were undertaking with refugees and survivors, we got to know each other better. Sometimes work would be closed prematurely, and I would question why. Was it too painful to listen to the trauma? Was it reminding the staff member of personal traumas or issues related to his/her own relationship to the Holocaust? We would also look at the content of the 'search among the ashes'. Was adequate time being devoted to practical issues for the ageing survivor? Was enough emphasis being put on the survivor's creative potential? Was there enough focus on ascertaining what the HSC could offer? In this two-way meeting, I was learning new things – for example, how images are used by the art therapist to express the content of the sessions. In the background, there was always the trauma and I needed to be clear as to how that affected the individual worker. When a member of staff is a child of survivors, I need to take account of the effect this may have. It has, at times, meant that the worker needed to be clearer about his/her personal issues before embarking on therapeutic work with people whose parents were Holocaust survivors. At other times, I have worked with staff who have used their personal experience of uprooting and dislocation as refugees themselves to facilitate their therapeutic responses. Instead of competing with the traumatised refugees and survivors, they used their sensitivity to find out more, to read as much as possible, to listen to these other stories of trauma, and then use supervision to test out and adapt their ideas and methods of working. These workers have tended to see these new approaches to trauma as liberating, while others reacted to them as a form of resistance against change. Each member of staff has his/her own reasons for working with survivors and each relates to the work differently. It is the task of supervision to enhance creative responses to the work, and to challenge the more resistant ones.

The mirror is there in the supervision, bringing the trauma into focus. The worker has to be prepared to look into the mirror and see himself/herself alongside the trauma. However, these supervision sessions are not meant as therapy. Decisions have to be taken as to whether the requirements of the work are compatible with the worker. The issue of boundaries is perhaps the most complex one to deal with. The rationalisation for maintaining more traditional therapeutic boundaries takes many forms. During my many years of supervising staff, I have seen how some have been fearful about the possibility of losing their professional identity through the less formal contact with survivors in the social centre (HSC). As a response, some have retreated into the comfort of their 'therapy' rooms in Shalvata. I have also observed, in their workloads, a tendency in some staff to develop a greater proportion of individual sessions devoted to children of survivors compared to the survivors themselves. I will now analyse the complexity of this process.

These adult children were approaching Shalvata for individual counselling or requests to participate in a therapeutic group. They therefore offered opportunities for the therapeutic staff to undertake work which was more familiar to their training and experience than the adaptations needed to work with survivors. In addressing this apparent professional preference, the argument was put forward by some staff that by helping the second generation, they were helping the survivors themselves. On one level that may be the case, but in so doing, little time and space was left in the workloads to outreach and work with those who had directly undergone the trauma. It is easy to get sidetracked from the vision of our commitment to the survivors themselves. The supervision allows the space to explore why traditional therapeutic responses may be adhered to as a reaction to the traumatic impact of working with ageing survivors approaching the end of their lives.

Understanding why staff may be reacting in a certain way is only part of the focus. Facilitating the shift to work in new ways is the challenge. Currently, with trust, new ideas have developed. A member of the Shalvata team goes on outings to the theatre with members of the HSC as a way of outreaching. She also facilitates the Solo group in the HSC for socially isolated members. The art therapist leaves his room in Shalvata to facilitate a singing group in the HSC as well as offering his skills as an art therapist to individual survivors. Another member of the team in Shalvata sees an individual Bosnian refugee to help her with her emotional issues. This same staff member facilitates an informal social lunch group for elderly Bosnian refugees who are also Holocaust survivors. A specialist worker from Shalvata accompanied a staff member from the HSC on a home visit when one of the members of the HSC was dying. All these changes are significant in the journeys that staff members are undertaking to make our service meaningful to those who use it.

My room also becomes the container of the fear, the powerlessness and the deskilling process which permeates our work. I pass on from my own practice the strategies which have proved useful. One such example, which I learned from my work with Chava, was the importance of ritual 'burial' for family murdered in the Holocaust. Some staff have used this idea in their work and experienced the positive effect this can have. Strengthening the worker against burn-out can also be done by adopting additional strategies. Staff appraisals, workload weightings, balancing direct and indirect work, informal meetings with staff and formal team meetings to share issues about our work, as well as individual and group supervision, may all help to contain the over-whelming feelings that arise in our encounters with survivors.

My combined tasks of supervision and management of staff are as complex as my dual role of being therapeutic facilitator with survivors as well as Director of the service. The issues of authority and leadership in my role as manager need to be delicately balanced with the professional development aspects of the supervisory task. Neither role can nor should be an end in itself. The supervision needs to facilitate the individual workers to develop their skills and interests in their work. However, these skills need to be managed so that the outcome enables the service to be enriched. In other settings these tasks may be separate and distinct. By combining them in this setting, it allows authority issues to be addressed in the supervisory relationship between supervisor and supervisee. How this is dealt with can then act as a guide to dealing with the issues of authority, power and control which are central to our work with former victims. It is important to understand these dynamics for anyone wishing to develop therapeutic staff working with those who have suffered atrocity.

My work spans both centres. My focus remains to bring them increasingly together as one unit. Just as the HSC provides a lighter, more informal setting for the survivors, so the supervision reflects its content. The emphasis is more practical; access to me is more flexible, and laughter is a more common theme. Yet there is structure; difficulties and conflicts are dealt with; staff issues are addressed and, in the process, the co-ordinator of the HSC learns about ways to work with trauma. There is a constant bombardment of the staff in the HSC, as is the case in many day-centre settings. In addition, like the staff in Shalvata, they hear indescribable stories of suffering. They are with these survivors as they grow older. They witness their illnesses and deaths on a regular basis. The staff in the HSC do not speak the language of therapy, and yet they understand what is needed to ease the survivors' pain.

Communication between these two sets of staff, in the two centres, offers opportunities for dialogue about different therapeutic approaches. The constituent parts of our therapeutic work meet face to face in our team meetings. The staff from Shalvata need to listen to issues that relate to the kitchen, the programme and the transport. The HSC staff get feedback about issues that may relate to a member who is seen in Shalvata and also belongs to the HSC. The freedom to cross these different boundaries opens up the work and protects against any preciousness in the therapeutic worker.

The working conditions, the pleasant environment, the variety of work and the opportunity to be innovative result in staff remaining for long periods in their jobs. The low turnover of staff and the low sickness record of workers give an indication that the needs of the staff are being catered for. However, it is not a cosy, cohesive situation. The hungry mouths of the survivors can leave a sense of emptiness in the pit of the stomach in the staff who work with them. There may be a competitiveness for 'food' and 'nourishment' resulting from the impact of starvation and its aftermath. This was illustrated in a staff meeting when we discussed the issue of some survivors expressing a view that staff should not use the café until the members had been served. Some staff members felt that as they were helping the survivors, they should not be restricted in this way. This issue is ongoing and the repetition of the discussion seems to illustrate how hard it is to digest. The supervision allows for such sensitive topics to be addressed individually.

The two centres are joined together through the administrative staff and the caretaker. They are instrumental in weaving the web which holds the two services together. The two administrators front the service. They are the first point of contact, especially in Shalvata, whether on the phone or for survivors who call in. The way they greet the survivors, the warmth they show in offering a hot drink and biscuits, their approachability as people – as the human face of the service – is fundamental to all that follows. Their efficiency in their administrative and secretarial functions reflects on the service as a whole. It is a difficult task to perform well and it has taken time to reach the pinnacle in the form of my current post-holders. It is a goal worth pursuing in creating an atmosphere and environment in which traumatised people can feel at ease. I have also come to realise how crucial these two people are in my work, in assisting me to do my job well. Supervision takes on a much more informal mantle, but the acknowledgement of their commitment and care gives them a special place in my book.

The caretaker is no ordinary caretaker. As a former refugee who is also a highly skilled professional, he has been forced to adapt to an unfamiliar situation, and to take on a more menial task. Despite the difficulty, he has endeared himself to the survivors and staff alike. I observe him helping survivors who are becoming frailer, with grace and sensitivity. He has made the job his own, and has combined it with personal attributes which find positive outlets in the way he applies them to his tasks.

The range of the supervision I undertake is broad and varied. I shift in and out, from looking at how the kitchen is run to the details of the social programme. I meet weekly with the Bosnian community worker, using my experience with the survivors to guide me into facilitating a meaningful service for the Bosnian refugees. I have in the process learned about the community in Sarajevo and why it needs to be preserved here. With the staff in Shalvata the dark shadow is faced, and we struggle to make our therapeutic responses meaningful. I am challenged and brought alive by new things I need to know, and creative ideas to try out.

I have always enjoyed supervising staff. I do not expect people to do what I myself would not be prepared to do. Before I end my work, I want more of my staff to observe what I do, to try out some of these ideas with me, and to keep them for the future. Nothing remains the same, but one has to know what was, in order to develop what could be.

FINANCIAL AND BUDGETARY ISSUES

There once was a time when I did not have to think about where the money would come from for my work. I had grown used to the habit of depending on the parent organisation to 'feed' the service it had set up. I was lulled into a state of complacency that this certainty, which had proved itself over time, would always exist. However, times of economic recession, and pressure and demands on limited resources, elicit different responses. Lack of input into the financial resources for the services affects the power balance. Total financial dependency produces a state of vulnerability. I had learned from the survivors that vulnerability could be a death knell, and this would also apply to the service.

It therefore became imperative that I searched for ways of identifying resources and ensuring an income for the service. The excellent relationship I had established with a sister organisation – World Jewish Relief – resulted in a regular, substantial contribution to the HSC.

I also began to submit claims on behalf of Jewish Care to the Claims Conference (Jewish Material Claims Against Germany) based in New York, USA – an organisation which distributes money to organisations offering services for survivors. This money has direct relevance for the services as it originates from Germany and is intended for former victims of Nazi persecution. Individual survivors can also apply.

The writing of this book has been greatly assisted through a fund made available by the Claims Conference. The applications which have been made successfully have included funding for the following projects: 1. the café project in the HSC; 2. renovations to Shalvata; 3. therapeutic work; 4. a social-work post; 5. an emergency fund; 6. outreach work; 7. a home-care service.

The offshoot of these applications has been threefold. First, we receive substantial amounts of money for our work from the Claims Conference. Second, it raises the status and profile of the therapeutic work undertaken with survivors and refugees in the UK. The members of the board from the Claims Conference were interested enough to visit our centres on a trip to London to see with their own eyes the services they are supporting. Some of the board members who are survivors themselves felt very positively about the work undertaken on behalf of their fellow survivors. Third, it has meant that we needed to join forces with other organisations in order to make the claims. The details of this development will be looked at in more detail in Part IV.

We also receive income from membership fees to the HSC, as well as generous donations by members. The members have raised money from bazaars which they organised annually. However, this has become increasingly irksome for them as they have grown older and frailer. Other members were involved in a fund-raising committee for the centres and organised events, such as the premiere of the film *Schindler's List*. It is important for members to feel that they are contributing in some way.

Another possible source of income emerged through the consultation and training services Shalvata offers to other organisations. I had to overcome my reluctance to discuss fees with other organisations wanting our expertise. It needed to be central to the negotiations. It became apparent that some organisations had considerable funds for training, and were generous in their offers. Others needed to understand why this service had to be funded, and was not free. Sometimes reluctance to pay gave way to acceptance in the wish to use our knowledge. The success of these consultancy services and the feedback we have received has affected the thinking about the role that consultancy and training should have in the future. In the struggle to survive with limited resources, necessity becomes the mother of invention. It has meant that this income could be used to maintain the policy of not charging fees for the survivors who come to Shalvata.

The income from all these sources together does not make a significant dent in the deficit which Jewish Care has to meet. Nevertheless, the contributions are a bargaining point when planning the budget for the following year. The success of our work increases the financial demands needed to cope with greater numbers and greater needs. I believe we have to tap into more and more alternative sources of money. This is a specialised task, and the future points to the creation of a post for this purpose. I am not an accountant, yet I diligently peruse my balance sheet, and I seek advice from my consultant as to how to ask the right questions to safeguard the service. John's advice to Jewish Care has always been 'never say no as a first response when you are dealing with someone who has known starvation'. It is a powerful and emotional statement which has produced a more open-minded response to our budgetary demands.

Those wishing to develop services of this kind for those who have suffered war trauma must ensure the service is fed through creative sources of funding. It is important to be active rather than passive in how this money is obtained.

REPORT WRITING

Writing for me is a way of clearing my head. It is a way of reflecting on events. It is an account of what goes on in our work, and the thinking behind it. Writing this book is a more detailed and more personal document, filled with anecdotes and treasured moments.

Busy managers and leaders of the organisation do not have time to read the detail of the journey of how we arrived at our destination. They want to see clearly where we are. They want their questions addressed, and they want to be able to draw conclusions. This demands a different skill. Précis exercises at school were challenging for me. They were always too long. I found it difficult to condense what needed to be said into a few words. At the time, I could not really see the point of the exercise but, today, I am glad that I had to persevere with that task – for, today, much rests on the succinctness of the many reports I have to write.

I often start with the end goal. This concerns what I want the report to achieve. I then work backwards, imagining what the reader may wish to know which will help them in understanding the content and, if necessary, to make a decision. This may include statistical information and budgetary matters. These reports are usually factual, but illustrated with enough human content to remind the reader who we are dealing with. For example, the reports for the Claims Conference will include examples of survivors who use our service and would benefit from the funding being applied for.

Reports are also a form of communication between the parent organisation and the satellite service. The Community Services Report I am asked to submit is included with other reports from Jewish Care's services within a single published document. These reports are a diary of events that opens up the service to the rest of the organisation and welcomes them in.

A well-written report gives status and dignity to the service. The written form is harder to ignore, and underlines the identity of this specialist service. It is important to do justice to what goes on in our centres and the contribution which we are making to the field of understanding trauma. With opportunities for face-to-face contact diminishing in this technological world, these reports are another survival strategy against the trend to dispense with difference.

Although report writing is often regarded as deadly and merely a chore to be done, I believe these reports are a life-force which gives a voice to the service. A collection of these reports over time becomes a testament as to how the service has evolved and developed. They need to be kept and looked back on. In the analysis we may feel more hopeful that progress has been made. They are documents for posterity. They bear witness to the struggle to survive and flourish as a service – a lesson gleaned from the survivors in their drive to record their testimonies.

In the future, different organisations working with war trauma can draw on these reports and learn from each other how their services have evolved – what is similar, and what is different, and why. They are tools of remembrance in a fast-changing world.

MARKETING AND PUBLIC RELATIONS

Many years ago now, I was sent by Jewish Care on a two-day media-training course. I attended with a select number of managers as it was recognised that my field of work had the potential for much media coverage. It was extremely daunting to see myself on television, being interviewed by one of the trainers. The sound of my voice, the grimaces and facial expressions, greeted me as though, for the first time, I had met myself head on. When I think back to what I learned, one very important aspect remains. I was told that when I am interviewed, I should have three points I wish to make. I should not be deterred or distracted from making these points, whatever the questions thrown at me. I should also make sure that I ask the interviewer what will be his/her first question.

I began to listen much more closely to the sound and tone of my voice. If you lack confidence, you can hear it. If you are arrogant, it echoes in your voice. If you are uncertain about your subject, it can be detected. The opportunity to test this out came in 1995 – the fiftieth anniversary of the ending of the war and the liberation of the camps. A whole day of BBC radio broadcasts threw me in at the deep end. This public exposure was stressful but necessary to put the services for survivors and refugees on the map. It was a way of reaching survivors who would not have known we existed. It was a chance to acknowledge Jewish Care's work in this field of trauma.

I never feel at ease with the media. A wrong word, an inaccurate statement, can threaten one's credibility. In the desire to make something newsworthy, images may be produced by the media which do not convey what is meant. Increasingly, the survivors began to speak for themselves. I became a conduit for them, linking them with the media. The power of what the survivors have to say is enhanced through the succinct, coherent interviews they give. Training which I received now needs to be offered to them, to maximise this potential. The survivors need to express the issues that concern them – combating revisionism; exposing the slowness of compensation for former slave labourers and other groups; clarifying the legacy they wish to leave for the future, to name but a few. Sometimes I join this platform with the survivors and we speak together on these subjects.

As Director of the service, I use Jewish Care's resources on marketing and public relations. I discuss the role we can play in enhancing Jewish Care's status as a lead organisation in the field of trauma services. I discuss the use of patrons who could be associated with our work without compromising those attached to Jewish Care as a whole. I discuss the role we could play in advancing the more academic field of trauma work through a series of lectures and public events. I inform the press officer at Jewish Care about current issues in the newspapers which we may need to comment on. I meet with a member of the marketing department to discuss ideas about how we can focus on our service. The potential for creative thinking is immense in this area. The current concerns about asylum seekers has a direct link with our work. We should not be shy about what we do, for we have learned a great deal from the survivors, and can now pass this on.

However, the marketing of the service nevertheless needs to take account of the sensitivity of the subject matter. For my part, the end must always justify the means. Press releases must never exploit the survivors for emotional gain. I now ensure that I see all press releases related to our service. Those who represent the organisations working with war trauma generally must heed the advice of the former victims in terms of the image they wish to project to the public. The repercussions of exploitation are massive.

Public relations includes our redesigned pamphlet. It includes the publication of articles, books and reports which throw a positive light on our service and enhance its image. The meetings attended by our staff, the assistance we can offer to other organisations and the respect we are accorded nationally and internationally reflect back and enhance what we do. How we look, how we dress, how our building is cared for are external pictures that show an image of how we regard others and how we want them to regard us. The survivors whom we have seen understand the importance of image in strengthening them. Those who work with them must do the same.

DIRECTING THE SERVICE

The managerial aspects of the service are perhaps the most overt and easy to perceive. However, the larger picture involves another dynamic in the translation of chaos to coherence. The overview of the service as a whole, the link between the service and the members, the interface between the service and the outside world, may be based more on intuitive and personalised features.

The directing of the service is more akin to the conductor of an orchestra, sometimes emphasising one aspect of the service over another. Directing is in a sense the freedom to develop the service in a unique way. Making it different, keeping it different and celebrating its differences are at the core of the director's function.

However, the charismatic nature of the director's role makes it difficult to institutionalise. Just as each performance of an orchestra is intricately linked to the conductor's mark on the music, so the director affects the orchestration of the service through the manner in which the sounds and voices of those contained in it are drawn upon. The director's role is in this sense ephemeral, and the future cannot take care of itself.

I have to think of that future. I have to plan what will happen when my involvement ceases and I also have to acknowledge that nothing will remain the same.

Developing the structure and infrastructure of the Holocaust Survivors' Centre

Having prepared the foundation on which to build this new community, the next stage was to give it form. I opened Part III with the voices of the survivors speaking to you, the readers. I believe that the life-force of our work resides with them. In the process of learning from them individually, we can also use this knowledge and that gained from the mutual support groups to inform us about how we adapt these concepts in a social setting like the Holocaust Survivors' Centre. The latter section of this part of the book pulls together all the concepts we have already looked at, and applies them to the development of this therapeutic model.

I think it is worth remembering some of those key concepts which have remained at the heart of the two centres, adjacent to each other. First we have to remember the critical components of the traumatisation. Then we will see how these factors are taken into account in the way these therapeutic services for Holocaust survivors are implemented.

Some key concepts in the traumatisation are:

- living with death
- witnessing murder
- vulnerability
- starvation
- lack of identity

- powerlessness
- dehumanisation
- lack of dignity
- victimisation
- degradation
- massive losses
- incarceration
- abandonment.

Naming the centre

No name, only a number, deprives a person of a basic human right – to have an identity. As faceless 'Untermenschen', many survivors lost their dignity and sense of self in the dehumanising environment of the camps. Once 'liberated', their identity as survivors did not facilitate a sense of belonging or status in the outside world. At times derogatory labels were attached to them, and so their identity as survivors of the Holocaust remained hidden. To be with other survivors was a reminder of the horror they had emerged from. To be with non-survivors reinforced a sense that they were 'outsiders' in a world that had not witnessed the atrocity. Identity was an elusive phenomenon. Changing one's name, covering up an Auschwitz tattoo, only masked the problem of identity.

Giving this new centre a name would in turn give survivors an identity. Much deliberation went into the naming of the centre. In the end, the most simple is often the best. Naming the centre after a person, giving it a Hebrew name to reflect its purpose, did not speak clearly of its meaning to the members. The Holocaust Survivors' Centre was a clear, unequivocal statement that this was a place specially designated for those who had survived the Holocaust. No elaboration was needed. Using its abbreviated form of HSC protected it for security reasons, and became like a password for those who belonged.

Membership of the HSC

Not everyone who went through the Nazi Holocaust could be catered for in this limited space in the HSC. A new country, a new language, multiplied manifold the sense of dislocation and alienation endured during the

Holocaust. Membership of the HSC was primarily for those who had been in Europe during the war. The excellent support of a self-help group for survivors, known as the 45 Aid Society, could not cater for the space which became increasingly necessary as the survivors grew older. The refugees who escaped only with their lives and no possessions (after November 1938) were also considered eligible for membership of this new centre. The current membership of the HSC numbers 750, of whom approximately 300 attend weekly.

Membership gives a sense of belonging. To be a member gives certain rights and privileges through the payment of a membership fee. However, survivors emphasised that the HSC is not a club. The centre is not a cheap option for a meal or playing bridge. To be a member involves not only benefiting from the resources available, but must also include active participation in the life of this new community. The privilege of membership requires involvement in the day-to-day affairs of the centre. Membership is not a passive state. Passivity is in the memory of the victim.

Being a member helps to overcome some of the stigma and vulnerability which is often associated with asking for help from a professional. We need to remember that exposure to persecution, torture and life-threatening situations left indelible marks on the victims which rendered them susceptible to the effects of future situations in which they again feel vulnerable. Consequently, the creation of a non-threatening social centre (HSC) for survivors allowed an entry point which avoided this sense of vulnerability. Becoming an 'insider', a member of the HSC, not only gave an identity, but strengthened the survivor through this sense of belonging.

The setting

The coldness, the vastness and the inhuman conditions of the camps tend to haunt survivors' lives when they enter institutional settings. For those who were hidden during World War II, the memories of cramped, airless dark pockets spring back into consciousness when reminders of those times are recreated in current claustrophobic settings. Many of these people today cannot travel by underground – they cannot be shut into a space without daylight or the means to escape. A sense of panic sets in and memories flood back to that 'other place'.

The setting of the HSC had to take account of those memories in order to create a non-institutionalised, non-clinical environment. The survivors needed to feel at home and at ease. Attention to detail such as the colour scheme, the small round tables, the paintings on the walls, the use of china crockery not plastic cups, the covers on the seats – all needed to be carefully planned.

Let me create a more detailed picture for you. Imagine a darkened room lit by candles. Clustered around small tables, people are listening to live jazz, the rhythm of the music propelling them into spontaneous dancing. The atmosphere is alive and vibrant. Who would imagine that this is a centre for Holocaust survivors? Who could imagine that those enjoying themselves had undergone severe deprivation and suffering as children in the Holocaust? Who would have imagined that this music, once banned under the Nazis, would be celebrated by those who had witnessed such atrocity? The meaning of the music speaks volumes for these child survivors who come together in this evolving community to which they belong. Younger in years than the older survivors, they can identify with the setting and allow it, even fleetingly, to reconnect them to their youth, which for many had been bypassed because of their suffering.

Anything that smacks of bureaucracy or institutionalisation is an anathema for survivors of the Nazi era. The inflexibility of the setting restricts the way in which services can be offered. I would like to illustrate this point by contrasting the setting of the HSC with a health service context. On the basis of a presentation I gave to an international conference on gerontology, about my work with ageing survivors of the Holocaust, I was invited to participate on an advisory panel concerning health needs of the elderly in the UK. As the only 'outsider' to this group of professional people, I could see how the organisation was influencing the way in which they were thinking. Their responses tended to take the form of reacting to the restrictions imposed on them by the bureaucracy. This led to fairly conservative ideas about change. My contribution was to suggest they could be thinking more about 'what could be' rather than 'what is'. Working in the voluntary sector rather than a statutory one, at that point, felt liberating for me. The voluntary sector I thought held great advantages in terms of innovation and the implementation of new ideas – the service for Holocaust survivors being a good example.

The setting of these meetings captured the shut-in feeling experienced by the participants. They were incarcerated themselves. I had to negotiate my way around a labyrinth of a building – drab, desolate and depressing. I was given a key (card) to open the many doors through which I needed to pass to reach the room in which the meeting would take place. Even though this was a temporary location, it seemed to underline the negative thoughts which were verbalised and, in addition, gave a sense of disconnection and isolation *vis-à-vis* the bureaucracy. Rules and regulations, structures and infrastructures separated the voices of those for whom the service was intended. This group I met with were the brokers, the messengers of the silenced elderly users. They needed to open doors, to free themselves from the suffocating space which this setting symbolised, and to challenge the bureaucracy which was inhibiting their freedom and creativity. My role was to help facilitate that process and to throw new light onto the concept of the victim.

For those who have been incarcerated, the setting must be liberating. Images of chairs positioned around the perimeter walls of a day centre for the elderly would be at odds with the needs of those who had been imprisoned and had lost their freedom. The setting must not be imposed, but evolve from its usefulness to those who participate. As the needs of survivors change as they grow older, the setting will have to accommodate this.

The café

At the heart of this centre for Holocaust survivors is the kitchen and café area. The centrality of food in a centre for people who have undergone starvation cannot be overstated. The galley-style kitchen is small, and becomes increasingly cramped as the numbers in the centre rise. The smallness in space, however, serves as a reminder that the production of food must be personalised and not mass-produced. It must be a reminder of the taste of home.

Thick, nourishing soup is a daily part of the menu – not the thin, watery imitation of 'soup' which constituted the camps' rations. Always making sure there is enough food for all allays fears of hunger and pain. A survivor reminded me that the two things he could not tolerate were being cold and hungry. Nomi, who manages the café, ensures that the daily menu is both imaginative and varied. Each survivor comes to the kitchen and is served individually. The food is matched by the warmth and caring which greets the survivors at the kitchen. Each one is known by name; each one has his/her own preferences for food, which are attended to. There is no waiting in line, no repetition of those endless queues waiting for nothing but a piece of bread.

What food can you serve in a centre for Holocaust survivors? Tuesdays have become a special day. A survivor and her husband are the catering team, working together to give a nourishing meal. Vegetable cholent has particular meaning for those from Eastern Europe. Stuffed cabbage and barley soup also echo the members' European origins. Nothing evokes memory like taste, and these wonderful dishes serve as reminders of good times.

At the Jewish festivals, food associated with those events connects the members to their Jewish backgrounds. Potato latkes and doughnuts at Chanukah and cheesecake at Shavuot offer the freedom to celebrate with tasty morsels.

The food alone would not be enough. The taste of the food is enhanced through the survivors socialising over their meal. To eat alone renders the same food uninteresting and characterless. To be together with enough food on their plate may soften the effect of those devastating memories. The importance of 'feeding' each other, and not only themselves, is generated through their social interaction. Some members only come to the centre to meet their friends and eat a meal with them.

The survivors also have the freedom to make themselves a cup of tea or coffee. There are always plenty of cakes and biscuits to be consumed during the day. They fiercely fight to defend their independence. Taking away their wish to use the kitchen as their own may threaten the therapeutic value of their sense of involvement.

The intimacy and warmth of a small kitchen and café has to be balanced against today's demands for health and safety. The non-clinical production of the food and the creative way that the food is made may challenge the strict demands of order and neatness. Hygiene levels have to be maintained to avoid any risk to health. At the same time, the individual character of this catering service has to be able to accommodate the sensitive needs of those who relate to food in a different way to you and me.

The café creates a space in which members and staff can informally meet together and can share moments which would be difficult to create in a more formal environment.

The consultative process: working in partnership with the members

If power has been taken away from you, if you have been ignored as though you did not exist, it becomes essential to counteract that experience through a process of consultation, empowerment and giving people a voice. Working in partnership with survivors has been noted as a vital interaction in ensuring their issues and needs are listened to and responded to. The concrete manifestation of this idea was the establishment of an Advisory Committee.

The Advisory Committee

The philosophy of the HSC rests on the principle of the active involvement of the members in how the service is offered. The elections to the Advisory Committee result from nominations and ballot along democratic lines, the three major groupings within the centre having a representative number of candidates. These groups were comprised of: 1. those who were in Europe during the war and were over sixteen years of age at the end of the war; 2. those who were in Europe during the war and were under sixteen years of age at the end of the war (the child survivors); and 3. those who came to the UK before the war as refugees after November 1938 (Kristallnacht) or as unaccompanied children (Kindertransport). To begin with, groups one, two and three had three representatives each, making a total of nine members as the Advisory Committee. With time, however, these numbers altered slightly. The HSC is the only centre in which survivors who were in Europe during the war have an identity and a voice. The camp survivors felt particularly strongly that they should have greater representation on the Advisory Committee. In consultation with the committee, it was agreed that group one should have four places, while child survivors (group two) should have two places as there were relatively fewer of them in the HSC. Group three would continue to have three representatives.

Bringing together these disparate experiences into one group did not happen smoothly. The camp survivors fought passionately for their voice to be heard, to have an identity, and to be given priority over other groups in the centre. Towards this end, they formed their own camp survivors committee, as well as maintaining a separate identity at their Sunday social events once a month. Having had their identity stripped away from them in the camps, this response was understandable. However, their exclusivity in their groups alienated them from others in the centre who wanted to participate in their social events.

The Advisory Committee became a forum to address these differences. The child survivors, like the camp survivors, had felt they could not share what they had been through with others who had not suffered in the same way. In the process of sitting together every two months, facilitated by a neutral chairperson, in dialogue with myself and the co-ordinator of the HSC, a common language had to be found. The agenda focused the members on the tasks. The side effect of this process has resulted in the committee members listening to each other and getting to know each other as individuals and people, not only as defined by their suffering. The elections of new members to the Advisory Committee brought other views into the discussion.

This is a far cry from the experiences of totalitarianism that many of the members had been subjected to. After several years of getting to know each other, we could focus on the work to be done. As an example, we began to talk about what it means for the survivors to grow older, and how they will accommodate members who become physically and mentally frailer. In a centre of this kind, this is not only a practical issue but an emotional one. Fears of vulnerability, dependency and frailty echo past memories of inhumanity and annihilation, for the frail were immediately exterminated by the Nazis.

The Advisory Committee is in a sense the think-tank for the centre. The Advisory Committee also act as messengers to and from the membership, encouraging them to think about what is important to them in terms of the services. To illustrate this point, a meeting was held in the centre, open to all members, to discuss its future plans. About forty members participated, sharing their ideas, speaking up and expressing views which reflected their thoughtfulness and identification with matters which related to them. They rejected the notion of a move to a new and larger centre, put forward by a few members, but focused more on the additional services which would be needed to complement the existing ones. They liked the 'intimacy' of the current centre, even though it was crowded at certain times. They identified the need for sheltered housing; home care; social work; volunteers, especially from the second generation; more money for transport to bring members in as often as needed; the support of specialist medical services; and fitness facilities to keep them as independent as long as possible. Their 'wish list' corresponded exactly with how I had identified areas for development related to the changing needs of the members.

This meeting was a unique and heartwarming example of a significant shift in the membership from an emphasis on 'surviving' for themselves to a concern for the group as a whole. They had come together and addressed the needs of all, in contrast to the hierarchy of suffering which existed in the different survivor groups. In my experience, people rise to the responsibility accorded to them.

Following this consultative process, a sub-committee from the Advisory Committee was formed and became the Strategic Planning Group. It drew some additional members, who were not on the Advisory Committee, into a dialogue with the managers of Jewish Care. I ensure that we meet regularly to identify the goals for the next five years, and we discuss the means to implement them. The harmony of purpose which emerges through these consultative processes become the key to unlock the door which opens to a future.

The Users and Volunteers Committee

Listening to survivors in the HSC, letting them guide us who work with them, is profoundly important as a meaningful therapeutic process. Not only is this so through the Advisory Committee, but also in the non-elected Users and Volunteers Committee. This group is open to *all* members. Much of their focus relates to the content of the programme in the HSC, and the internal day-to-day concerns that relate to the centre. They feel that they are in a sense the *heartbeat of the centre* – they are closely in touch with the members. The use of members as volunteers is a practical reflection of the involvement of the users – helping in the kitchen, making tea for the members and befriending members who cannot come to the centre are tasks which bind the members to the centre. The users and volunteers help to keep the centre alive. They make demands on the staff of the HSC. They express their views in this monthly forum about matters linked to the Advisory Committee, and present current issues which affect them as survivors.

I have dealt at length on the importance of this consultative process. It is a hard and demanding approach. It would be much quicker, very often, to make decisions about services without this more lengthy procedure. However, the advantages of following this route are manifold. It is not only political correctness which guides this democratic process. It is a two-way learning experience. Having recourse to a members group, for the managers of the service, allows delicate topics and discussion to be shared. The consultation is fundamental to challenging the stereotype of older people's acquiescence to others in the decision-making process. It is fundamental to giving former victims a voice, both in terms of the service itself and the link between the centre and the outside world. It is fundamental to the concept of the centrality of the survivor, and the strength of the survivor, in determining the future. It is fundamental to the concept of liberation, which is the root of the therapeutic process.

The programme

For many survivors, opportunities for education and recreation were stripped from them in the Holocaust. The reality of their harsh life left little or no room for fun and play, or for developing their untapped talents. Life was focused on surviving. After the war, a different struggle emerged. The need to adapt and to make a living took precedence, together with establishing new families to replace those who had been murdered. 'The need to recapture normalcy was paramount, as was the need to somehow erase the years of discontinuity' (Krell 1989, p.216). In this sense, the programme could become a survival strategy, aimed at catching up on those lost years in the trauma, and reconnecting survivors to those parts of themselves and their communities which they yearned to be in touch with again.

For many, retirement left a void which rapidly became filled with traumatic memories. The void created a challenge to find alternative ways of relating to the present. The traumatic memories needed channelling in particular ways, which would allow space and freedom to lift the survivors out of the nightmares which haunted them – even if this were only for a short while.

To fill the time only with activity and diversion would not have been enough. The programme had to have some meaning for those who had crossed to another world and whose eyes had witnessed unimaginable horror. We needed to deal simultaneously with the memory and remembrance of the horror through the testimony recording project and the education programme, as well as offering a social programme to lighten the darkness of their tragic past.

The testimony recording project

We have already noted the importance for survivors of bearing witness to ensure that all the suffering was not in vain, and those murdered will not be forgotten. A plethora of organisations became involved in recording testimony – the Shoah Foundation, the Imperial War Museum, the British Sound Archives, to name but a few. Why should the HSC also offer this facility?

Our project differed in several important ways. First, there was no pressure to complete the recording in a small number of sessions. Second, the testimony takers, who were mostly children of survivors, were offered regular training supervision and support in their work. Third, the survivors who became emotionally affected by giving their testimony could be supported by the HSC/Shalvata. They were not left to cope alone with the aftermath of reliving the traumatic memories.

The audio recordings were kept in the HSC. The survivors could also pass these on to any other organisation that stored these unique accounts of people's lives. The 'safe keeping' of the testimony gave some reassurance that the memories would not be lost once the survivor was no longer alive.

Some survivors recorded many times. The distribution of the testimonies to organisations outside the UK was like an insurance against loss in the future. The *raison d'être* of the survivors seemed very much bound up with the notion of their duty to the dead. Once released of that duty through the testimony recording, did they still feel they had a right to be alive? Did they have a right to enjoy themselves now that this task had been completed?

My discussions with survivors revealed that many did feel relief at having recorded their memories for posterity. However, the process of remembering was in itself traumatic. An interval of recovery time allowed a gradual reconnection to this world. Interestingly, as the testimony project is slowing down in terms of the numbers applying to record what happened to them, the uptake of the social programme in the HSC is expanding rapidly.

The collective memory which resides in the centres may be a liberating factor in freeing the survivors from carrying their memories on their own. The members, however, were clear that the HSC should not be an institutionalised setting for remembering the dead. Debates about having commemorative plaques in the centre for murdered families who had no graves met with negative responses. Instead, they preferred the idea of having plaques in cemeteries which they could visit, and negotiations were facilitated between the HSC and the United Synagogue for this to happen. In the HSC itself, a work of art was commissioned to serve as a memorial. The members chose an image which reflected their suffering, but also their hope. The reflection which shines through the coloured stained glass illuminates the boundary the survivors have created between the darkness and the light. The HSC creates an oasis in which to forget as well as to remember.

The education programme and public speaking

Many of those who have emerged from the darkest times have a commitment to ensuring that such horrific events should never happen again. Giving testimony tends to be a more solitary experience – the testimonies are often filed away after completion, and may never be looked at again except by researchers eager to find evidence to prove or disprove their theses.

It is, however, in the human encounter that the most healing potential may be found. Survivors who go into schools and speak to children about their experiences in the Holocaust are listened to, are asked questions, and often receive letters of gratitude and concern from those children.

The survivors who act as guides for those who visit the Imperial War Museum's permanent exhibition on the Holocaust help to individualise the experiences of extreme suffering and connect meaningless statistics into human reality.

Not every survivor wishes to participate in these educational programmes. However, for those who do, preparation may be needed to help the message to be conveyed in a way which is meaningful for both the speaker and the listener. Courses on public-speaking skills are part of the HSC's brief, as well as support for the speakers after their visits. Time and experience bring greater confidence, but stress often remains as a constant as the memories are relived again and again.

The HSC does not work alone on this project, but liaises closely with organisations involved in the educational aspects of the Holocaust – for example, the London Jewish Cultural Centre. In partnership with the survivors, we gauge with them how much exposure each survivor can deal with, when they need a break, and when they can resume their task again.

After years of the survivors' words falling on deaf ears, a new experience is created through their involvement in this educational programme. Speaking in schools, universities and museums is only part of the equation. Projecting the survivors' voice to the world at large, through media and publicity, has become a natural extension of this public-speaking programme. The year 1995 was the first occasion when survivors were invited to speak publicly, to be given a face and a voice and a sense of dignity. They marked this anniversary of the ending of the war and the liberation of the camps through images which spoke of their strength and coping – images of liberation which were in marked contrast to the emaciated victims pictured in the newsreel footage when they were liberated in 1945 from the death camps.

How the survivors come across in the media becomes a powerful tool in changing attitudes from the 'schadenfreude' response of pity to one of respect. Media training, being clear and succinct in getting the message across, is facilitated through the HSC. The significance of the image of survivors today, and the impact this has on how they are listened to and responded to, has a therapeutic effect on them.

Developing a group of spokespersons for the HSC ensures that survivors are not overlooked and their views are accurately represented. Britain has now established a Holocaust Memorial Day. Almost daily the media are in contact with me asking to speak to survivors. Many survivors now seize this opportunity to express their views. When I am asked directly to make a statement to the media, I always check with some survivors that my response is in keeping with the message they want to convey.

Survivors scour the press and are very alert to the world around them. Those who have gone through war and lived on a knife edge ensure each news bulletin is listened to. This is very much the case in Israel. Being alert is a pre-requisite to survival; complacency is potentially dangerous. The current affairs group which meets at the HSC and the Yiddish group bring issues that concern them and which need to be responded to. Unlike survivors in the USA and Israel, the survivors in the UK have tended not to form themselves into a lobby. Going public on so many subjects, rehearsing their skills in how to deliver their message, survivors have become more proactive in seeking out opportunities to air their views and influence public opinion. An example of this was seen in how they immediately responded with a letter of complaint concerning the fact that not enough members of the HSC were invited to the ceremony on the first Holocaust Memorial Day. The letter was written on HSC-headed paper, which they felt gave them their collective identity and status, but was signed by the membership who are empowered to express their views. The impact of this speaks for itself, and carries far greater weight than any manager speaking on their behalf.

How we develop this idea of a lobby of survivors will be looked at again later in the book. When former victims openly express themselves, when they are taken notice of, when they fight for what they believe is right for them, then they move a long way out of the dark shadow which has hidden them.

The newsletter and creative writing

THE NEWSLETTER

There is a bustle and frenzy as the committee of members who are responsible for the newsletter launch themselves into editing another edition of this eagerly awaited publication. Not everyone is able to speak publicly or be involved in the education programme in the HSC, but every member is able to make some contribution to the newsletter. Some write stories or poems; some share recipes; some review books; some write about events which have happened in the HSC, or outings for the centre they have participated in.

Is a newsletter merely *de rigueur* in a centre for Holocaust survivors? Is it only a voice for those who enjoy seeing their names in print? I think not. The HSC newsletter has become a forum for linking all members both in London and scattered around the UK. It is informative about issues that concern survivors, such as claims for compensation. It is a tool whereby those who cannot travel to the HSC nevertheless have a sense of belonging.

The newsletter is not only used to inform members, but holds up a mirror to the outside world about the events which take place in the HSC and the issues which concern survivors. The high standard maintained in its pages, and the sophistication of the presentation of the publication, led it to win an award in the Jewish community for the 'best newsletter'. The fact that this is no ordinary newsletter reflects the message that this is an unusual centre. It perhaps makes the 'outsider' curious; perhaps wanting to know more; perhaps wanting to visit to see what goes on inside. The newsletter is a stimulant for those who have kept themselves apart from survivors, fearing to be in contact with those who have suffered much. The newsletter opens a door between the 'insiders' (the survivors) and the outsiders (non-survivors). It is a non-threatening point of contact – a bridge – which allows those outside to peep in and to be touched by what they see. The newsletter tells the outside world that this community of survivors exists, who they are, and what they have achieved.

The power of the newsletter as a medium has been replicated in the Bosnian refugee community with whom we work. The creative imagination involved in its presentation and the quality of its contents defy the stereotype of the nameless refugee. These exiles are people who have been educated, who have careers and professions and have made major contributions to the communities they once lived in. Like the Holocaust survivors, they enrich our own community, if given a chance to do so. The innovative newsletters they produce speak loudly to the uninformed about what can be achieved.

CREATIVE WRITING

The ability to write, the skill of transferring thoughts to paper, does not come easily to everybody. As I sit here at the start of another day of writing, cups of tea fill the time of anticipation as I struggle with my thoughts. How much more difficult it must be for those who have experienced extreme trauma. Writing in a language that is not the mother tongue, describing events which defy description, would easily make this an impossible task. I sat with Chava in our sessions during the time she battled to write her book. The will to tell her story released a talent in her that had lain dormant. Jack, Anna and Chava have all used the medium of the written word to address the unfinished business of their trauma. The power of this creative approach gave each one of them a sense of mastery over what seemed chaotic and overwhelming thoughts and experiences.

Tapping into this often unknown and unrecognised ability in people who may have never had the opportunity to explore their talents became a core aspect of the HSC programme. The creative writing group facilitated by Jack was the catalyst which released an astonishing amount of hidden material. The critical analysis of the writing was not an easy path to follow. The frustration, the doubts, the fear of not succeeding became shared concerns in the group. They supported each other through the pain of both the memories and the telling of them. As the stories took shape and form, praise and encouragement saw them through to completion.

The catharsis which ensued from seeing an end product, namely a printed form which emerged from their 'hard labour', was not only personally satisfying, but helped to encapsulate the trauma in a concrete way. The covers of a book or the beginning and end of a short story or poem hold the contents within a structure. This was one way in which the powerlessness of the former victim could be channelled. The process of writing gave some sense of control back to the survivor as each one found their own individual way of telling their story. More and more survivors are now having books published based on their life experiences.

The group's collective publication of short stories called *Out of the Dark* (1996) was followed by another, named *Into the Light* (2000). The titles seemed to symbolise a sense of liberation which released the storytellers from having to remain locked in the darkness of the past trauma forever. This movement from darkness to light is, however, neither linear nor simple. The pendulum seems to swing forwards and backwards, the writing conveying pathos as well as humour. The endorsement of the members' contribution to these books came through the author Alan Sillitoe. He not only gave guidance in the publishing of the books, but wrote the foreword and attended the launch of the books. As a writer himself, and as an 'outsider' to the trauma, his validation of these works brought status to the event which broadened it beyond the confines of the HSC. A sense of dignity and respect was thereby accorded to the members of the creative-writing group. Not only were they recognised as survivors of extreme trauma, but were now being defined as writers who have the power to influence our understanding of trauma as well as enlightening us about the richness and variety of their lives.

The art class: an antidote to the void of despair in ageing survivors

Think back to the Appelplatz in the death camps – those vast open spaces where prisoners stood hour upon hour for their number to be called. Waiting…waiting, and for what? The futility and emptiness of it all. The pain of standing, sometimes propped up by fellow prisoners because weakness and exhaustion challenged the limits of the body's tolerance. Death was never far away, as day after day the relentless torture went on.

Keep that image in mind as age stealthily encroaches on the lives of survivors. As death approaches, memories of that vast nothingness come back again to haunt those who have remained alive. What is there to fill the wasteland between ceasing activity and death? No wonder survivors keep working as long as they can. Many have not had time to think about what will happen to them when work no longer serves as a distraction from the nightmare of their past.

Now, an unfamiliar reality of a slow and often almost imperceptible change is beginning to make its presence felt. Physiological and psychological adaptations to the passage of time are bringing death closer. This time, however, there is something different. Death would be a natural outcome of a natural process unlike the industrialised mass murder in the death camps. Between life and death there is a void to be filled, which would make that waiting time less hopeless and less despairing. The waiting time gives an opportunity to tap into new ways of relating to the world in the changing circumstances of ageing.

Unleashing creative energies helps to distract the mind from lodging in the hell of the Holocaust – not to forget, but to get some relief from the duty of remembering. The art class has become a medium for these positive thoughts to be set free. Through the skill and dedication of the art teacher, Barbara, an environment is created in which members feel encouraged to try out this new way of expressing themselves. Only one member of the group creates images of himself in Auschwitz. Initially this member sat alone at a separate table from the group, recreating memories on paper of the horror he and others in the group had experienced. This man, who is over ninety years old, travels for two hours every week to attend the group. He is someone who has dedicated his life to speaking in schools about his experiences during the Holocaust. He has also mounted an exhibition in memory of his wife and child who were murdered in the camp. As I observe him today, he has chosen to sit around the table with the other members of the group, still painting the same images, but somehow symbolically integrating himself as well as the past trauma into the present. His presence in the group reminds us that this is no ordinary art class.

In contrast, others in the group paint scenes from nature. Jewish themes, still life and their creative imaginations begin to adorn the walls of the HSC. Vivid colours and well-made frames set a standard of excellence in the work produced. Modest attempts soon take on greater confidence leading to proud public viewing of the paintings at exhibitions mounted through the HSC.

Fundamental to the process of painting is the sheer enjoyment and mastery which ensues from trying something new. I receive tokens from some members of the group – a card painted by one member, a framed picture to hang in my office by another. These serve as reminders for me that when we take account of the past, we do not have to repeat it. To fill the void with these pleasing images leaves a legacy of regeneration and not only of destruction, even at this late hour.

The bridge class

Focus on the word 'concentration', and then think about the different uses of the word. Sitting next to each other in the dictionary, concentration and concentration camp seem juxtaposed in the meaning they have attached to them. Concentration camp is a term used throughout this book. It conjures up images of inhuman conditions for the prisoner forced to remain there. Concentration, on the other hand, is an often elusive but much sought after quality that allows the mind to free itself in order to see clearly the matter in hand. The power of concentration is in this sense in sharp contrast to the powerlessness the victims felt in the concentration camps.

Talking to the survivors who play bridge in the HSC, they emphasise how the game helps them to focus all their attention on the cards. As they sit round the card tables, some sixty survivors are single-minded in their determination to play the game. They tell me how their ability to concentrate helps them to forget the memories of their traumatic past, at least as long as they remain involved in playing.

The excellent teacher Shirley, who circulates among the members, facilitates the skill in playing the game. The mind is wakened up from its slumbers in the challenge to succeed in becoming more competent. Differences and disagreements among members are suspended. A break for tea and cakes is the only acceptable interlude.

If an 'outsider' were to walk into the HSC on a Monday afternoon he/she may be fooled by what is seen. He/she may only see a group of elderly people playing cards – what, after all, is so special about that? Looking closer, bringing the scenes from the concentration camps back into focus, we can then see a scene in which there is a struggle going on to overcome the intrusion of traumatic memory. Keeping the mind active in this game prevents it from wandering uncontrollably to a different time and place. These short bursts of relief help time to pass and to reconnect the survivors with other positive experiences which may have existed in their lives before the Holocaust and afterwards. As I walk through the centre, as I often do, there is a shared realisation of the importance of this 'game'.

The Yiddish group: using a language of survival

Wednesday mornings are like a magnet, drawing me out of my room in Shalvata and towards the HSC. Soon after 9.30am, members slowly begin to arrive. They stop to chat to each other, helping themselves to a warm drink before the group starts. Some have a heaviness around them as memories linger from the night before or from the daytime reality that remains in their waking time. One such member is Jacob. He often acts as receptionist for his fellow members, greeting them as they come in. On one occasion, as I stood next to him, he recounted to me his inability to comprehend the mind of the Nazis. He contrasted two SS guards whom he encountered in the camp. One was vicious and sadistic and used every opportunity to beat the prisoners, including Jacob. The other also appeared brutal, always shouting at them and threatening to set his dogs on them, but never once did he carry out his threat. Jacob puzzled over why this should be. The paradoxical world he had witnessed made no sense to him, but he carried the remnants of it around inside him. Leaving these questions unanswered, Jacob joined the Yiddish group.

I have been privileged to attend the Yiddish group on many occasions. I would like to share what I experienced during one such event. I had done my homework in reflecting on and formulating ideas about why this group was so popular among survivors, and why the Yiddish language had special meaning for them. However, I needed to hear from the survivors themselves, and to learn from them directly about the centrality of Yiddish in their survival.

This one meeting taught me everything. I went prepared with a page of questions I wanted to ask them. As I left Shalvata and entered the HSC, I was greeted by a room overflowing with about fifty survivors, all waiting for me to join them. They had saved a seat for me around the huge table, and welcomed me into this special space. The warmth of their acceptance was voiced through Bettine, their much-loved, vivacious and very humorous facilitator. She explained to the members that I was writing a book, and I wanted their help in order to accurately represent the group.

I cannot speak Yiddish as neither my mother nor my father were familiar with it. My mother told me she only heard Yiddish after she had left Germany and came to England. It was generally not spoken by German Jewry. My father's Sephardic background (Jews from Spain and Portugal) meant that he spoke Ladino, but not Yiddish. Ladino is also a derivative language. My father recounted a story about a man who came to see him at the Sephardi synagogue where he worked. This man had a letter written in Yiddish. My father could read the letter as Yiddish is written with Hebrew characters, but could not understand what he was reading. The other man could understand what my father was reading but could not make sense of the Hebrew letters. Between them, the message of the letter could be understood.

My unfamiliarity with Yiddish could have made me feel like an outsider in the group. I need not have been concerned, as the members seemed to understand the importance of the task, and subsequently spoke in English or translated the Yiddish they used so that I could grasp what they were saying.

Instead of asking my questions, I listened to the members of the group. Each spoke in turn to tell me about their personal accounts of their relationship to this language. As they did so, they were noisy; they were funny; they were emotional; they were spontaneous. They spoke loudly and clearly using a microphone to draw attention to themselves. The atmosphere was contagious – there was a sense of enjoyment which seemed to feed the soul, both theirs and mine.

I would like to list some of these moving and powerful statements, and then reflect on them. First, comments on the Yiddish language:

'It makes my heart and mind feel better to speak in Yiddish.'

'Yiddish makes me think of my parents and grandparents, and happy memories of family life.'

'I came back to myself by listening to Yiddish.'

'In Yiddish I can express both sadness and humour.'

'Yiddish brings back memories of times past, of what I have missed, and what I miss now. It reminds me of the warmth of my family.'

'Yiddish is my mother tongue.'

'Through Yiddish we won't forget who we once were.'

'Yiddish binds us. I feel very near to someone if they speak Yiddish.'

'Certain emotions cannot be expressed in any other language but Yiddish. For example, "Sleep quickly, I need a cushion."'

'Yiddish is an international language.'

'You can curse in Yiddish. For example, "If you hang yourself on a sugary rope, you will have a sweet death."'

Next, comments by members about the Yiddish group:

'We are addicted to the Yiddish group.'

'We feel at home in this group. It feels like being with neighbours from home.'

'I lost my whole family in the camps. Coming to this group is like finding Paradise. Bettine is like our mother.'

'I came to the group because I had one hundred and fifty jokes to unload.'

'I feel the warmth of my family in this group.'

'This group is helping to keep Yiddish alive.'

They wanted to talk; they wanted to share with me and with each other what it was that bound them to the language and to the group. The process of the meeting was not a regimented, orderly one. As they thought of the curses or the emotions which could be expressed in Yiddish, each competed with the other in their remembrance of these treasured thoughts. Sad moments in the group were always balanced with laughter and jokes. One member began to cry when she told me that speaking Yiddish reminded her of her lost family. Another wept when Jacob sang a song for me, which he sang in Yiddish in the ghetto. All emotions were acceptable in this melting pot of tradition and memory. In an instant, a member would stand up and perform a song with gestures and movements to help convey the content of the story. Joke after joke began to pour out of their mouths, each one funnier than the last. Jacob, for example, who had been sad before the group began, was at the heart of this joke festival.

What would happen to the wealth of material enclosed in this group? Some spoke to their children in Yiddish with the hope that the language would not die. Most, however, found the next generation were not bound to it in the way that they were – it did not speak to them of their lost communities.

My own ear was beginning to become attuned to some of the sounds and meanings of the language. From my 'pigeon' German, I could surprisingly make out more words than I had imagined. However, when I commented that my German was not proficient, they were pleased. They wanted me to understand Yiddish. German for them was the language of the oppressor, and was therefore not an acceptable language of communication in the HSC. Yiddish as the 'mother's tongue' (*mama loschen*) binds the speakers of the language to those who were murdered. Through Yiddish, they bring their mothers to life. They connect with memories of childhood, from times long before the horror began. Elie Wiesel confirms this connectedness through Yiddish. He writes in his autobiography about his love of Yiddish: '…because it has been with me from the cradle. It was in Yiddish that I spoke my first words and expressed my first fears. It is a bridge to my childhood years… I need Yiddish to laugh and cry… Yiddish fills me with nostalgia' (Wiesel 1996, p.292).

For those who lost everything in the Holocaust, the Yiddish language was one thing that could not be stolen from the survivors. They celebrate this victory through their attendance in the Yiddish group. Yiddish binds the members together and gives them a sense of belonging and identity. There is a sense of not being alone. Being able to converse in one's mother tongue, in the language of home, is just as important for the Bosnian refugees we work with. Any displaced people feel comforted by their connectedness of language. The nuances of language bring much more than the language itself. Yiddish song, Yiddish theatre, Yiddish culture are the media through which the language can be expressed.

The sense of togetherness which the members feel in the Yiddish group was also evident in the death camps. Members of the group confirmed that Yiddish was indeed spoken in the camps. Jacob told me in the group that he was used for slave labour by the SS. For three months he was forced to build a road in sub-zero temperatures. It was so cold that the prisoners' hands stuck to the metal shovels. One SS guard occasionally left them for short periods. It was during these brief moments that they would stop working. As the guard approached once more, the prisoners would pass down the name they had given him in Yiddish from one to the other, and they would quietly resume work so as not to be beaten.

Yiddish and Hebrew, which were both used in the camps, were in a sense an act of resistance and defiance against the Nazi oppressors. Its symbolism was far more powerful than merely being a familiar sound against a background of violent, verbal, guttural abuse. In a covert way Yiddish protected the sacredness of the Jewish language, for its sound rested on Hebrew, which is considered a holy language. 'As they used to say, G-d writes in Hebrew and listens in Yiddish' (Wiesel 1996, p.292).

Yiddish, as we have heard from the group, has a special meaning for those who use it, whether it be in the telling of jokes, or in evoking the past with all its horror. The loss of the Yiddish language embodies the loss of an entire world from which the survivors were dislocated. Survivors have a special relationship to this language which gives them meaning and continuity. Recognising the importance of Yiddish in the lives of survivors may help to overcome their separation from the dead. Through being reunited with the Yiddish language, they rebuild the lost communities decimated in the Holocaust. By recreating these lost sources of strength and stability, they bring their former selves to life in this microcosm, which is the Yiddish group.

Working with Holocaust survivors, we have to understand how important it is therapeutically for Yiddish to remain alive. A group of this kind overcomes some of the limitations of a therapist who cannot communicate in this emotive tongue. The lost world is captured in Yiddish, it is made intelligible through Yiddish, and something is healed through Yiddish. 'The attempt to translate this world to the therapist may be experienced as hopeless, hence feelings of disruption and lack of continuity will pervade the survivor's sense of self in the present' (Hadda 1989, p.269). As the group drew to a close, I asked whether it would be more meaningful and helpful to them to recount their traumatic experiences in the Holocaust, or to record their testimony, using Yiddish instead of English. They did not answer the question as another joke took precedence for them. It nevertheless left me with questions about our work in Shalvata and whether survivors should be offered an option of speaking Yiddish there. It also left me wondering whether the link between the first and second generation could be made through the celebration of the Yiddish language and not only the legacy of horror and destruction. I also felt compelled to learn more Yiddish.

Some of the answers to the questions I posed myself were addressed after the group. Bettine and a few members decided that they would like to put on a Yiddish play. It would not only be for members but they would invite Jewish Care and other outside groups. Maybe our meeting together had served as a catalyst to go beyond the confines of this contained environment. When this group ceases, like the dead themselves, there may be no-one to remember what they carried. The sound of Yiddish needs to be heard and enjoyed by those who had never even thought about its significance.

As I returned to my room in Shalvata, I could still hear the laughter I had experienced that day, and many other days, as it penetrated through the walls of my room, demanding to be noticed. The experience of being with the Yiddish group and sharing with them helps me to rebalance the scales which tip backwards and forwards, trying to find an equilibrium in the aftermath of severe suffering. No wonder that, 'punkt', in the middle of the week, this most important group resides. It is a heartbeat, a life-force in this new community of survivors.

Parties and celebrations

The members of the HSC love parties and celebrations. The camp survivors have lunch together to commemorate liberation day. It is a joyous event with laughter and entertainment and full stomachs. The centre takes on a symbolic mantle in which it is safe and acceptable to celebrate in this way without the event being misunderstood. In these moments of enjoyment there is a sense of victory over the Nazis. There is also a sense of not being alone with the past. These celebrations are examples of living with life – they are life affirming and hopeful.

As I write, I have just returned from the launch of the creative writing group's book *Into the Light*. No event which can be celebrated goes unmarked. In the light-heartedness of the event, it is easy to miss the specialness of it.

Let us unwrap the mirror again and turn it onto the faces of these survivors who had come to celebrate their success. What do we see? Smiling, confident images which defy the trauma they carry inside themselves. As I looked around the room, I realised how many of these faces I had also seen in Shalvata carrying a more deathly hue, a more sickly pallor. The mirror now hides that image and releases the 'prisoners' to enjoy the evening's event. The invited guests could not see what lay behind the mirror's reflection. Captured on film by the press photographer's camera, these images of triumph would send powerful shock waves out to the community – no longer images of pathetic victims, but fighters against a 'war' which constantly threatens to engulf them.

For those who witnessed death on a daily basis, how juxtaposed are these images of sheer enjoyment. I thought once more of the powerful contrast to these positive reflections. I remembered the story of the survivor who encountered a different image while travelling on a train just after the war.

This woman, who had been released from a camp, wished to use the toilet on the train. As she opened the door, she realised that someone was inside and quickly closed the door again. A few minutes later she went back and opened the door again, only to find the same person inside. She repeated this several times until she realised that the person she was looking at was the mirror's image of herself. She had not recognised the emaciated woman with her shaven head. The image she carried was quite different. Even though she had seen others in the camp who resembled that image, she had no internal notion of herself looking the way she did.

Just as the mirror was cruel in the reality it threw back at her, so the mirror can be kind when it sees a smiling, well-nourished face peering into it. The celebrations and parties produce these pictures. When we cannot eradicate the reality contained in the aftermath of severe suffering, we can help to find temporary reprieve. Working from the 'inside' to the 'outside' with a person takes time, commitment and courage to confront the dark shadow. Working from the 'outside' to the 'inside' can also influence the way we feel, and how others respond to us. How we look, our facial expressions, how we dress can affect our mood. Working on the 'outside' can produce quicker results which, in turn, may impact on how we feel 'inside'.

The importance of self-image and external appearance to survivors has been referred to earlier in Part I when it was noted how prisoners struggled not to be seen as too pale as it could have been life-threatening. 'White hair, wrinkles, missing teeth, and so on, could be a death sentence' (Brainin and Teicher 1997, p.77). Taking a cold shower in the camp was a necessity in the struggle not to become a 'Musselman' (walking corpse) and so relinquish one's hold on life.

The survivors who come to the HSC do not dress like people who have given up. Their hair, their clothes, their make-up, their jewellery, their attention to detail in their appearance give a powerful message of defiance against the image of the emaciated, shaven spectres that haunt them from the past. The celebrations and parties give opportunities not only for enjoyment but serve as dress rehearsals for the roles they now increasingly play. When they give talks, when they appear on the media, their looks give them dignity, and they are listened to in a different way.

Encouraging these overt signs of being in control of oneself also features in other aspects of the programme. Beauty consultants and fashion designers focus on the external image. The importance of this in re-educating the public has implications beyond this group of survivors. For example, the labels and stereotypes attached to older people generally reflect a group of dowdy, unattractive end-of-liners. As I have talked to older people over my years of working, many have felt young inside but externally conformed to how an older person should look. In my work with them, I would challenge these stereotyped images and facilitate a process of self-expression.

I have to confess a personal passion for the importance of image in my life. Many of the survivors have no role model to help them develop their style and taste. I was fortunate to have developed this interest from an early age at home. I also feel that it binds me to my mother's three aunts, all of whom were dress designers in Mannheim. These three talented and beautiful women were deported and murdered in Auschwitz. Their positive legacy lives on in this connection I have to them.

How we look and how we feel about our appearance affect the way we celebrate events and enjoy ourselves. To see ourselves as younger versions of the older stereotyped model encourages us to be more active and alive. I attended last year's HSC celebration of Israel's Independence Day and a video was made as a keepsake for posterity. Spontaneous dancing and singing symbolised the importance of Israel in the lives of the survivors. Many feel that if Israel had existed earlier, they would have had a refuge from persecution in Europe, and the horrors of the Holocaust may never have happened. I shared a chair with Marsha as she joined in this joyous event. Out of breath from dancing, the survivors defied their age and health restrictions in this celebration of life.

As you throw your voice into the forest, the echo comes back. Similarly a smile may elicit a positive response in another person. Keep the image of the smile in your head, as Fergal Keane (2002) did when he revisited the widows from Rwanda's genocide. The smile may be a mask to cover over the memories of atrocity, but it is a way of coping against overwhelming odds.

Whenever we have an opportunity to capture the smiles that are evident in these parties and celebrations, the video camera is always ready. It witnesses what most would never believe possible out of the atrocity captured on earlier film footage as the camps were liberated.

The Sunday socials

Those of us who work, who are healthy and active, who have friends to meet, entertainment to pursue and money in our pockets, greet the weekend with open arms. A time for relaxation, a time to catch up, helps to rebalance the stresses of daily life. Those who cannot work due to ill health, those who cannot find work or those who have stopped working through retirement have to create their own structure to mark the passage of time. Without any form, days merge into weeks, and weeks into years – time is lost, never to be refound.

For many Holocaust survivors, leisure was a luxury. It was an unknown word in the vocabulary of survival in extremity. Hard work and keeping active became the antidotes to the haunting nightmares which had the power to overshadow the post-Holocaust lives of survivors. Now, time can weigh heavily for those who are together, as well as for those alone. Sundays and national holidays are often difficult hurdles to overcome rather than welcome breaks. This is true for many people with a surplus of time on their hands. For Holocaust survivors and those who have memories of extreme trauma, these days may reinforce their abandonment.

As a social centre for survivors, it therefore became essential to open its doors on these painfully long and threatening days. The Sunday groups contain the history of the development of the Holocaust Survivors' Centre, and embody in them a reflection of the Holocaust itself – for the original SOS group began on Sundays, as did subsequent social groups until the HSC began. The Sunday groups differ from weekly events in the HSC in the demarcation of identity related to the different experiences in the Holocaust. Only in the Sunday group did the camp survivors insist on meeting exclusively. Only in the Sunday group did the child survivors demand a space on their own. Other lonely survivors and refugees who did not fall into either of these two experiences could only attend the HSC twice a month on Sundays.

Fierce debate and confrontation surrounded the topic of the use of the HSC on Sundays. I recognised the need for both camp survivors and child survivors to have their identity reinforced through their insistence on exclusive events for their groups. At the same time, I was aware of the impact this had on those excluded. Even when only very few child survivors turned up for a Sunday event, and other survivors became angry, I had learned to wait, to be patient, and for time to change this intransigent pattern.

In contrast, during the week there was enough space, and enough food, for all. Repeated experiences of being cared for, of being able to trust more, of being valued and given dignity seemed to diminish some of the harshness. The programme during the week allows members to get to know each other personally, by name, through telling jokes, through giving lifts to each other, and by finding common ground through which to communicate. As a result, there developed a gradual softening of attitudes of one member to another. An abundance of warmth and comfort tends to reduce the fears and anxieties that earlier memories of hunger awakened. This centre is now another time and another place. In this climate, survival tactics used to deal with the past traumas gradually adapt to a less threatening environment. Learning to live with life rather than death, with enjoyment rather than cruelty, with hope rather than despair, with sustenance rather than starvation, gradually allows greater freedom for members to accommodate each other in this newly created space.

Though camp survivors continued to maintain that their suffering was incomparable to any other trauma, they began to acknowledge that others had also gone through very difficult times. The camp survivors' Sunday programme removed the words 'for camp survivors only'. They agreed not to turn members away, and have increasingly allowed non-camp survivors to participate – a major humanitarian step forward. Similarly, even the most vociferous of the child survivors have agreed to open some of their Sundays to other members. With no pressure on them to change, they are realising that soon they may not need a separate group on a Sunday. Many child survivors have participated in individual and group meetings in Shalvata which have addressed their particular issues of their lost childhood, and confirmed the fact that they have indeed suffered enormously. This recognition strengthens them against the older survivors' argument that they did not suffer because they were too young to remember.

The two remaining Sundays in the month have always been open to all the members. These afternoons of tea and entertainment can be both fractious and joyous events. The entertainers or speakers can stir up a variety of responses. A rota of staff from the HSC is on hand to facilitate these events. Perhaps the most important aspect to these Sunday socials is gleaned through a survivor's comments: 'On a Sunday, my children don't have to worry about me, and I don't have to feel dependent on them. I come to the centre and I feel at home. And then I can return to my other home, and I don't feel so alone.'

The power of the programme is the meaningfulness it has for the members. The Sunday socials are a statement of commitment by the staff in the centre to those who have suffered, putting their needs above the nine to five, Monday to Friday routine. The members' need to be together is paramount, and is met with flexibility by those working with them. We must remember always the pain of being alone, the torture of the memories of severe brutality and that 'What happened – really happened' (Carmi 1977).

The Solo group

As survivors grow older, their fears of what will happen to them, as death approaches, tend to increase. It could be argued that this would be true for any person growing older and left to cope alone. All too often, older people are prey to the vagaries of an ailing social and health system, and may be left susceptible to risk and danger.

For those who suffered during the Holocaust, a severe blow rained down on them through the destruction of their families and close friends. We have already heard from Irena and Chava about the emptiness and vulnerability that remained with them throughout their lives following the loss of their families. A more silent rupture occurred in the loss of their childhood friendships.

Memories of childhood friendships tend to stay with us. These early friendships tend to act as buffers which can protect us against a hostile world. In my own memory, I think back to my first day at primary school. Terrified and overwhelmed by this new world I had entered as a shy and timid little girl, I had the good fortune to be seated next to another terrified shy girl. Our fear bonded us, and we strengthened each other during that first day and for the next twelve years. Daily contact at school, in each other's homes or by phone sustained us. We worried about our homework, indeed we worried about just about everything, but we got through it together.

That friendship will live with me always. Only one other childhood friend has the power to cross continents and time to repeatedly reinforce and cement our bond. As an only child whose mother was forced to work, she spent more time in my home than her own. We giggled together, we talked together and we grew up together.

The special nature of these friendships cannot be repeated in later life. We are at a different stage in our lives. Though equally important, current friendships are not the same. I believe in friendship. I foster friendship, and I am nourished by friendship. Their numbers are few, but their impact is immense.

What would it have meant if these friendships had been threatened or destroyed? In Elie Wiesel's (1990a) book *From the Kingdom of Memory* he thinks back to his past and remembers his two close friends who were murdered in the Holocaust.

> Ever since, I have been looking for them. I have never stopped looking for them. Other friends have come to enrich my life, but not one has resembled either of them. When they left they took with them not only a conception of Messianic hope, but also the ideal of friendship. (pp.82–3)[1]

The value of friendship was a force for life even in the death camps. The relationship to other family members or other prisoners could be a crucial element in the struggle to stay alive. 'Even in the universe of ultimate horror, friendship was a haven' (Wiesel 1990a, p.83).[1] Like speaking Yiddish in the camps, friendship was also an act of defiance and resistance towards the Nazi oppressors.

After the war, some of the friendships forged in the camps remained. Groups of survivors in the UK met together, first in the Primrose Club and later through the 45 Aid Society (Gilbert 1996, pp.376–437).

Looking at these experiences of friendship, before, during and after the Holocaust, we see they are not the same. Friendship for its own sake has an intrinsic value. Against an outside enemy, in times of severe adversity, friendship can mean the difference between life and death. In the process of this severe suffering, being at the mercy of unimaginable horror affects how we perceive the world around us, and how that world perceives us. Nothing can remain the same after this catastrophe, not even friendship. When the fear of death is removed, relationships have to readjust to this absence of threat. What are these new friendships about? Who can you trust? Who can replace the void left by the annihilation of one's world and those closest to you? What are your expectations of friendship? Do you need friendship? Is the threat of loss too difficult to contemplate in the process of making new friendships?

These and many other questions remain as painful, unanswered reflections in the aftermath of the Holocaust – for, as Elie Wiesel (1990a) commented, '...the technicians of death tried to deprive us of it' (p.83).[1] Yet the antithesis of friendship could be seen as isolation and aloneness. How many times I have heard those two words spoken by survivors I have met. Those who were in hiding, those living in the forests, those who came as unaccompanied children on the Kindertransport, often describe a world created in a vacuum, an abyss, when they were separated and abandoned from family and friends. How do you get close again? How do you form a bond with another human being?

The fear of aloneness motivated many to look beyond themselves and forge some link with other human beings. However, social interaction did not necessarily reduce the inner feeling of being cut off and unreachable. For some survivors, these feelings return later in life when spouses die or when illness forces them to remain indoors. With no-one to care for them or care about them, they once more experience the sense of abandonment and, with it, both fear and depression.

In the HSC we have become increasingly aware how many members are struggling with life on their own. The responsibilities of day-to-day living take their toll. Days may go by when they receive no phone call – perhaps no-one would know if they died in the night. On the other side of the coin, how could they enjoy this time of their life more? Many have no-one to go on outings with or go on holiday with. We are a couple-orientated society, and people on their own are difficult to accommodate in a couple world. They feel like a fifth wheel with nowhere to belong.

With this in mind, the Solo group was set up. It is in a sense, as Elie Wiesel (1990a) put it, 'A Celebration of Friendship' (p.75).[1] It encourages friendships to form through practical as well as emotional attachments. Members may link up in pairs and phone each other daily to ensure all is well. They are encouraged to care for each other and to enjoy each other's company. It is based on Elie Wiesel's (1990a) wise comment, 'If you want to find the spark, you must look among the ashes' (p.85).[1] Caring for each other in this way brings people to life. They enjoy a meal together in the centres; they enjoy going on outings to museums and other places together; and they once more enjoy a sense of not being alone and anonymous.

The uptake for the group has been swift and enthusiastic. A member of the Shalvata team and a member of staff from the HSC facilitate the process of forming bonds and friendships through the programme and discussions.

Keeping fit in body and mind

Survivors do not like the words 'frail' or 'support'. In their memories, frailty meant extermination. They can see and feel the physical changes that go with ageing, but they try to postpone its impact. After the war, camp survivors such as Roman Halter and Ben Helfgott excelled in sports such as weightlifting – Ben went on to become weightlifting champion who represented Britain at the Commonwealth Games and Olympic Games (Gilbert 1996, p.382). The importance of physical prowess and strength reinforced the image of the survivor, in contrast to the emaciated, weak and frail victim.

In a snapshot of the HSC one day, I heard two survivors talking about their daily swimming; one, dressed in his tracksuit, had just come in from playing tennis, while a couple of others were sharing their common interest in ballroom dancing which they practise weekly. A young and enthusiastic keep-fit teacher entices more and more members into her weekly group, the modern music setting the rhythm of their movements.

In partnership with members of the centre, we discuss our future strategy. Keeping fit rates high on the list of priorities. Amenities outside of the HSC for swimming and other forms of exercise will be arranged for those who wish to participate. T'ai Chi, dancing and table tennis are on offer in the centre. Like most other aspects of the programme, the ideas emanate from the members themselves. It is not an imposed regime as part of a programme to keep older people fitter and in the community for longer. It is a central part of defying the perpetrators of a crime against humanity, which should have long ago resulted in the victim's premature death. In the survivors' physical strength, they challenge myths associated with them of 'lambs to the slaughter'. Never again will they be victims, at the mercy of such brutality. To be alive in one's seventies and eighties, able to walk around, able to think, would have been inconceivable and too miraculous to contemplate in the death factories in which many had been incarcerated.

Keeping the body active is only part of the equation. Keeping the mind alert can be helped through a range of activities. Playing chess or bridge; learning the lines of a play which the creative writing group present to the members; participating in the current-affairs discussions; speaking to schools and to the media; writing books and stories in the creative-writing group; learning a new skill fostered through lessons on how to use a computer and the internet – all defy the passivity associated with ageing.

Interestingly, in the years the survivors have been attending the centre there is little overt evidence of dementia. In their effort to ward off the horrific memories from the past, the mind of the survivor struggles to keep itself in the present. A wandering mind is potentially dangerous to the well-being of a survivor – for if one's mind lodges in the trauma of the past, it will once again be incarcerated, as mentioned earlier in reference to Elie Wiesel's (1992) novel *The Forgotten.*

Many day centres for the elderly adopt the fashion for 'reminiscence therapy' in an attempt to keep the mind active. The linguistic code of dementia makes communication difficult with those around you. In an attempt to make the unintelligible more understandable to others, focus is placed on reconnecting the mind to events earlier in life which still may be accessible to communication. I do not wish to enter into a critique of reminiscence therapy. Suffice to say that I have concerns about the issue of who feels good as a result of this enforced remembering – the older person or the helper? Is it perhaps a 'kindness' of the brain to assist the sufferer by becoming less aware of the dementing process? The problem remains of how to manage the dementia for those around him/her, but for the sufferer, it may be a welcome release from this creeping cruelty.

If we apply this to Holocaust survivors and those who have undergone severe trauma earlier in their lives, reminiscence as a group-activity programme would almost certainly bring back horrific memories. If the mind is lucky enough to reconnect to pre-Holocaust days there may be good memories to hold on to. The past is ever in the present for the survivors. As long as they can choose if, how and what they wish to remember, they must individually decide the form that takes. When they can no longer decide, when dementia takes hold of their minds, take good care of them, let them not feel forgotten, but do not force them back to a time which is not of their own choosing.

Feeding the soul: the Jewish dimension

The Final Solution of the Nazi era was meant to wipe every Jew off the face of the earth. The assimilation of many Jews in Germany and Austria did not save them from this brutal policy. Through the power of propaganda, Jews were perceived by the oppressor as hated, despised vermin. It became dangerous and life-threatening to be a Jew. The yellow star ensured that Jews could be easily identified and used as targets of violence and abuse.

Against unmitigating brutality during the Holocaust, some Jews lost their faith in G-d. On the other hand, some maintained signs of their adherence to their faith through some aspects of ritual, such as giving up their small ration of food on the fast day of Yom Kippur (Day of Atonement). Rabbi Hugo Gryn's father lighting the Chanukah candles in the camp was another specific example of the importance of maintaining ritual for some Jews, even if this meant putting themselves at risk. However, observance does not imply faith, and the question of where was G-d during the Holocaust remains unanswered.

I am not a theologian and do not wish to get embroiled in this complex debate about faith during and after the Holocaust. However, the question of Jewish identity remains a core issue for many survivors. 'Having suffered as Jews' during the Holocaust, 'they have already invested enormously in that identity. To walk away would imply that the investment had no meaning. To walk away would imply Hitler had won' (Haas 1996, p.158).

There were nevertheless some people who feared that an event like the Holocaust could happen again. Their response was sometimes to marry a non-Jew; to live deep in the countryside away from Jewish communities; or to deny their heritage in terms of their own children, bringing them up either in other religions or none at all. There was a fear that the ghettoisation of Jews was an inherently dangerous phenomenon. Keeping a low profile, merging with the background, assimilating into the general society, and being like everyone else, was a safer course of action. However, this theory, while understandable, is not borne out in reality, for in Germany, the hotbed of Nazism and the Final Solution, the Jews were very assimilated and many had lost touch with their Jewish identity. Many were Germans first and Jews second. The assimilation did not save Jews from being scapegoated as the enemy within, which needed to be eradicated.

Whatever decisions people made about their Jewishness before, during and after the Holocaust, these remaining years give an opportunity to address what was left as unfinished business, and to put one's house in order before death interrupts that process.

During my years of working with older people, I have observed their wish to return to their roots, to reconnect to their past and who they were. Those who left their Jewishness behind have returned to it as they grow older. Many wish to be buried as Jews. Is it fear, superstition or a genuine wish to be at peace with who they are that brings them to us – a centre for Jewish Holocaust survivors? As death draws closer, these issues take on greater significance. It is not a matter of orthodoxy, it is not a question of religious practice, but it concerns the centrality of Jewish identity in the heart and soul of these survivors.

I have had many long and moving dialogues with my colleague Sonny Herman on this oft-repeated theme of preparing for death. How do we help people who have witnessed death by murder and brutality to be able to face natural death with dignity and spiritual peace?

Some of the questions we are asked include:

- Who will arrange my burial?
- Will I be buried in a Jewish cemetery? (This refers particularly to those converted to other religions during the Holocaust to save their lives.)
- Who will say Kaddish (mourning prayers) for me when I am dead? (This particularly concerns survivors who have no close family.)
- Who will come to my funeral?
- How can I help my murdered family to be at peace?
- What will happen to me after I have died?

Sonny and I share a strong sense of the spirituality of our work. As a Rabbi, Sonny brings to me the possibility of exploring the relatedness of the therapeutic task to the care of the soul. However, there is a point beyond which I have neither the confidence nor the right to venture. An example of this was seen in the ritual 'burial' of Chava's murdered mother, and the importance of Sonny's part in it.

Nevertheless I believe in the centrality of the Jewish dimension as death approaches. I have never been afraid to be with people who are dying. My work has taken me into hospices, into hospitals and into people's homes. I remember a woman, not a survivor, whom I had been visiting in my early days as a social worker. She had developed a very disfiguring form of cancer in her face and was admitted to a hospice to die. I continued to visit her there. She had never been an observant Jew, but as death came nearer, she asked me if I would arrange for a Rabbi to come to see her. I had to force him out of his office to perform this pastoral deed. The woman died soon afterwards but I felt satisfied that she had died more peacefully. I wondered though what separated my world from that particular Rabbi in terms of the priority accorded to this spiritual comforting.

As Passover approaches once more in the writing of this book, Chava has told me that she will be making the Seder (the ritual ceremony to commemorate Passover) in her own home this year. It mattered to me that she was forging an ever-stronger link to her Jewish identity, and that her murdered family lived on in this way. It mattered to me that a member of the Shalvata team was pushing for a Seder to be held at the HSC. Against all the logistical problems, it became a reality. For those without families, this 'family'-focused event takes on particular significance. The HSC becomes their home, the participants become their family, and they become connected together through the tale of slavery and exile. What better place to tell this story of the expulsion of the Jews from Egypt than in the Holocaust Survivors' Centre?

Every opportunity to celebrate collectively the Jewish festivals is greeted enthusiastically. Rabbis visit the HSC to discuss the symbolism and significance of the Jewish holy days, but religion is never meant to overpower or drive away those who feel less committed.

Some survivors express their Jewishness through their devotion to the State of Israel. 'Am Yisroel Chai!' – the Jewish people live – is emblazoned on the stained-glass memorial window in the HSC. Survivors visit Israel frequently, even at times of political unrest. They support Israel in any way they can – they care deeply about the future of Israel. They welcome discussions in the HSC about any aspects concerning Israel.

People find their own level and own way of being Jewish. Their very attendance at a centre for Jewish Holocaust survivors allows a connection to be made with their Jewish identity, without having to connect to orthodoxy. By a process of observation or osmosis, something that may have become alien and unfamiliar may enter their lives again. Memories of their roots, who they were and what families they have come from may surface once more and can find expression in the multidimensional programme in the HSC. Finding out that which was lost, or rekindling that which is familiar, may warm the soul and feed it, ready for its last journey into as yet unknown territory.

To be able to leave, to be able to let go and die, there must be some sense that what happened will not be forgotten, and who they were will somehow live on after they are dead. The survivors' task was to remember those who were murdered, but how will the survivors themselves be remembered? Every year in the HSC, the survivors commemorate Yom HaShoah (Holocaust Memorial Day). Through prayers, ritual and lighting of candles, the murdered souls are remembered. After the ceremony, the survivors come back together to the HSC, have lunch and transit back to this world in which they now live. The survivors fight to keep these memories alive, they fight against forgetfulness and, through their remembrance, allow the dead to live on. Yet the second generation, the children of these survivors, were not prominent at the last Yom HaShoah ceremony I attended. Who will carry their candle? This will be addressed in Part IV when we look at the survivors' legacy.

The passage of time affects the power of memory. Something must remain in this world when the survivors are gone. As Elie Wiesel (1990e) wrote, 'Memory means to live in more than one world' (p.195).[1] The challenge for us, who will be left behind, is how to bridge the two worlds so that memory is not destroyed but acts as a link between the future and the past.

In concluding this detailed picture of the services which have evolved through working with Holocaust survivors and refugees, we still need to ask the following questions:

- Does the model make a difference in the lives of the survivors who use the centres?

- Are they able to live differently with their trauma?

- Does the service allow a different ending to the story which the traumatised person carries?

- Are the worlds of survivor and non-survivor, of insider and outsider, of life and death, any closer together?

These issues will become the focus of Part IV when we look at the different outcomes that we observe from the work my staff and I undertake with the survivors.

Endnote

1. *From the Kingdom of Memory*, by Elie Wiesel. Copyright © 1990 by Elirion Associates, Inc. Reprinted by permission of Georges Borchardt, Inc., for the author. Permission to reprint is also granted by Sheil Land Associates Ltd, London.

PART IV

Integrating Trauma

Introduction

The penultimate part of the book will begin by looking symbolically at how the two centres – Shalvata and the HSC – allow for survivors to live side by side with their trauma, finding a space for it to exist, but also offering a space to be free from its unrelenting hold. In the process of this journey, the centres have moved closer together, allowing the trauma to become more integrated into the lives of the survivors who use the service.

However, symbolic references or descriptive analyses of the services leave unanswered the question of their usefulness in the spectrum of working with the effects of severe trauma. We first need to look at the impact of the therapeutic services which we can observe in the lives of the survivors themselves. Second, and perhaps less obviously, we can also observe the impact on the people and the organisations working with the survivors which emerges from the lessons we learn from them.

This part of the book also represents the transition from the past and the present towards the future, opening up another door in the interface with the outside world.

Chapter 10

Connecting Two Worlds

One Monday afternoon, I found Rachel (a former survivor of the Warsaw Ghetto) in Shalvata, icing the chocolate cake she had made in the HSC kitchen the previous week. With meticulous care she inscribed the cake for a forthcoming birthday of one of the members in the Yiddish group. Dragan, our caretaker, was helping Rachel to store the cake carefully until it was needed. What did this small scene convey?

Rachel clearly felt comfortable about sitting in a space which she knew survivors came into to share their pain and suffering. She was proud of her handiwork, and I sat and watched her and talked to her as she completed her task. Rachel then returned to the HSC to continue her game of bridge. She invited the staff of Shalvata into the HSC where the cake was being cut, to make sure we all sampled this delicacy. After the Yiddish group, I met her again. She told me she was going to the cemetery that afternoon to visit her husband's grave, a task she always undertook before going away on holiday. She went there alone to confront her pain, but she balanced this with the love and generosity she was able to express through the cake she had made.

What was significant about this story? It perhaps encapsulates the ease with which survivors can enter Shalvata and to find their own reason for being there. Shalvata gave her a space to escape to in order to protect the 'secret' concerning the surprise celebration cake. The other 'secret' of the pain she carried inside her did not gain expression in Shalvata, but found an outlet for her in the more familiar surroundings of the HSC. Rachel is not someone who would seek out counselling or therapy in a traditional way. Her entering Shalvata, however, may symbolically enable her to make a connection to her suffering, and that is sufficient for her.

Though started as two separate centres with two separate entrances, Shalvata and the HSC challenge the boundaries that define where therapy takes place. Shalvata's life depends on being fed by the social centre next door. Referrals to Shalvata rest almost exclusively on the HSC being adjacent to it. Reaching out to survivors who may wish to use the services of Shalvata is greatly enhanced by its interconnectedness to the HSC.

The two centres together balance the opposing poles of darkness and light, despair and hope. If Shalvata had continued to exist alone without the HSC, purely as a counselling and therapy centre, I believe that by this time the staff would either have been out of work due to lack of referrals, or burnt out from the hopelessness and powerlessness associated with the dark shadow of the Holocaust trauma. If the HSC did not exist next door to Shalvata, the therapeutic choices on offer would have been much more limited. The sounds of music and laughter may not have reached our ears.

The two centres together can address the past, the present and the future. However, the model is not static, and both had to learn to live side by side and to find their respective meeting points. Though they continue to provide different resources, their proximity has the effect of being seen more as a part of a whole. The fragmented, dislocated lives of survivors of the Holocaust would not be enhanced through a disjointed, disconnected service. I have the daunting task of holding these two poles on one axis. Symbolically, these two parts (two centres) represent the mother and father missing in the lives of many traumatised survivors. Together they become the family. Together they represent the lost community. Together they make a home in which survivors can play and enjoy themselves, but also where they can turn to in order to discuss matters which need to be shared, which need to be understood and which need to be contained.

In the quiet space of Shalvata (Shalvata also meaning 'tranquillity' in Hebrew), in the smaller individual rooms which make up that part of the building, there is an intimacy created, which fosters the nurturing and feeding necessary to compensate for the years of starvation and deprivation. Compared to the chaos and turbulence of the Holocaust, Shalvata is also, paradoxically, more a reminder of a time when there was peace in their lives.

However, the HSC next door is a constant reminder to Shalvata not to become a sterile, clinical environment. The smell of cooking pervades both centres. The art work from the HSC has found its way into Shalvata, making a link between the two centres. The newly renovated Shalvata now shares the same carpet as the HSC, giving a visual sense of continuity between them. At large parties for the members, they have now asked to use Shalvata as an extension in which to sit and eat, thereby opening up the connecting door which formerly divided the two centres.

Both centres work together towards their common goals in the quest for survivors not to experience again the powerlessness of the victim. The two centres also empower each other, so that collectively the survivors' voices are louder and their identity clearer. The two centres can also support each other so that staff can borrow strength from each other. The co-ordinator of the centre often comments to me how difficult she would find it if she could not come in to see me in Shalvata and share her concerns. The knowledge of the other centre's existence, the crossover of staff from one centre to the other, opens up the creative potential for new interventions. Most recently, for example, the art therapist from Shalvata met with the members attending the Passover Seder,[1] to help them to learn some of the songs which are traditionally sung. In that way, they can feel more part of the service rather than 'outsiders'. That sense of belonging, community and link with their Jewishness could not be achieved through the work of Shalvata alone.

Together the two centres symbolise a memorial for the future when there are no longer any more survivors left to speak. Every day new stories emerge which both remind us of what was and also impel us to incorporate and remember them in our thinking and understanding about trauma and its aftermath. Throwaway remarks contain a wealth and richness of content which we cannot afford not to hear. Let me give you an example. I was standing in the HSC café waiting to choose what I was going to eat for my lunch. Two members were standing near to me dressed in their coats, waiting to go home after a morning in a discussion group. One of them told me that the subject of the Jewish ritual practice of washing bodies before burial had been raised. She said she did not like to think about such things. Our exchange sparked off a reaction in the other member, both of them having survived the death camps. She told me that the debate had reminded her of an incident in Maidenek camp when she was standing in the freezing cold. Next to her was a sick woman who was shaking with cold. 'I didn't know why I did it, but I knew I had to do something or she would die. I took off my knickers and gave them to her. She held them against her chest to try and keep warm.'

I asked her if this woman had survived. She told me that she had, but she had died recently. The talk of dead bodies and death took her back to that time. 'Now,' she said, 'I am ready to go home.'

The imagery of that horrific scene haunted me as I returned to Shalvata. She had given it to me for safe-keeping, and so it finds its way into these pages in the hope that you too will keep it for yourself and pass it on to others. It is this encounter and thousands of others I have heard over the years that have shaped the way the two centres have developed.

I began with a thought that perhaps I had to justify the model that has evolved in the hope that others may adopt it, and be motivated to adapt and develop it to their own circumstances. However, I soon realised that such an analysis would fly in the face of everything that had been said so far in this account of this long and arduous journey. The model is only good and workable if it is in tune with those who use it. Testaments to the model's usefulness include: the increasing use of the centres by more and more members; the feedback we receive directly from the members; the observations we make about the creative strategies survivors have adopted in the centres which help them to live differently with their trauma; their increasing involvement in how the centres develop their services; and their greater wish to have their voice heard, and to fight for what they believe is right – whether this be for compensation, for the truth about what they have witnessed, or for resources needed to help them as they grow older.

To return to the beginning of our journey, the model of these two centres rests on the fundamental principle of listening to survivors and learning from them about what seems to help them as they face their trauma again in the latter part of their lives. We need to be alert and accept when things do not work and then listen again, ask for their advice and keep asking questions. Those who work with survivors need constantly to be reminded about where the survivors have come from, what they have been through, and how they have coped in those interim years before they arrived at the centres.

As these pages move towards the final part of this unfolding testimony and I look back at what was and what is now, I see that these two centres have made a difference to many of the survivors' lives. Let me tell you about an event that I witnessed. I return again to two of the survivors who have guided our thinking. Between 2.30 and 5.15 one Monday afternoon, I met with Chava and then Irena in my room in Shalvata, one after the other. The morning had left me feeling as though I had been wading through treacle as I dealt with organisational and managerial issues that demand attention in my daily endeavours to steer the work on course. Some non-demanding administrative tasks, and the postponement of a half-day seminar later in the week, freed up my mind to enter into Chava's space when she came into my room. She soon began to tell me that she had felt overwhelmed at the weekend in relation to her daughter's illness and her inability to help her. Many tears were shed as she sat with me, and her despair was profound and worrying. We searched for the strength she had found, alone in her own home, which managed to bring her to me that day. She said that the spiritual dimension, which featured strongly in her life, helped her to focus on her love for her daughter. This seemed to help unblock the paralysis she had felt.

The purpose of recounting this event is not in the detail of what was discussed, but in the sequence which followed on that day and the next. Chava remained behind in Shalvata having coffee, talking to others she met in the centre, and also smoking a cigarette outside. Only when she was ready did she go home.

From the other direction to where Chava was later sitting, Irena approached my room, having spent the afternoon playing bridge in the HSC. The continuing wounds of her abandonment, her aloneness, her fears of ageing, filled the room which was already overflowing with pain and anguish. The tears which had been shed there over the years should by now have drowned me. That day, I felt them most acutely. They belonged there. They expressed the reality which these two women, and many others, carry with them daily. I felt relieved as the day came to a close. Emerging outside, the heavy rain seemed to compound the sadness that had hung around me during these encounters. To free myself from the weightiness that bore down on me, I went shopping for the ingredients which I would make into a cake later that evening. In anticipation of that sweet taste, I relaxed. Tomorrow would be another day.

The following day, I met Irena in Shalvata as she waited to have her hands manicured by her daughter who works as a volunteer manicurist in the centre. In the HSC, I met Chava who had an appointment to see Michael from our claims department to help her to put in an application for a fund which had become available. At lunchtime the three of us met in the HSC. We sat at a small round table with one of the other child survivors who had arrived to attend the Shalvata group for former Hidden Children. Irena and Chava were joking together. Chava suggested she should perhaps go to Israel with Irena during Passover. She also asked the other child survivor if she would teach her French as she had forgotten so much of her mother tongue. In the relaxed, informal environment of the HSC, more tears were shed, but this time they were tears of laughter, as joke after joke spilled out of Irena's mouth.

The contrast between the events of these two days, in these two settings, for these two people, speaks loudly and clearly about this model. Survivors would have their own different stories to tell about how they have used the centres to move on; how they may have been strengthened by being together in a community of survivors; and how they may see some glimmers of hope as they near the end of their lives.

Is the goal of 'liberating' these former prisoners from their victim past any closer to being realised? Do they feel their suffering has been better understood? Do they feel they have addressed some of the unfinished business transferred from their traumatic grief and loss in the Holocaust? Maybe these ideals cannot be verbalised or quantified in any systematic way because the dark shadow never really leaves them. However, it is possible to observe outcomes in how the survivors who attend the centres live their lives, how they relate to each other and how they connect with others and the outside world.

I would like to look at what evidence we see for this claim, and also to address this life-force which seems to emerge from the services which have been developed.

Endnote

1. Passover Seder – on the eve of Passover, Jewish families read in their homes about the exodus of the Jews from Egypt where they had been slaves to Pharaoh.

Chapter 11

Exploring the Usefulness
of the Therapeutic Services
in the Lives of Survivors

The outcomes for the survivors

Reconnecting to a life-force: redefining freedom

I have to think back to when my work began to remind myself how hard the struggle has been for survivors to hang on to life. The force at that time was the trauma itself pulling the survivors back to the horror of their past as it collided with their present lives. Now, many years later, the picture is not the same. The trauma remains ever present, but the balance has shifted. Living with the trauma is different to being overwhelmed by it. The thrust of our work in the two centres has been to use the therapeutic options to reconnect survivors to the world of living and life, to open a door which allows them to transit out of the world of death and destruction.

In diagrammatic form we can see that there is a continuum, a life-force which gathers strength as it revolves around the circle (see Figure 11.1). Some of that strength belongs to the individual, and some emerges from the strength that traumatised people give to each other. As the strength increases from these combined inputs, so the power released energises a process. This converts the negative effect of powerlessness and vulnerability in the victim into finding an identity and a voice. There is a sense of collective strengthening through being together which challenges the chaos, the darkness, and the hopelessness in the aftermath of trauma. The collective strengthening allows for a sense of belonging and meaningfulness – an 'insider' experience – but also allows the freedom to differentiate oneself as an individual. The impact of this strengthening is to hear the survivor's voice more forcibly. There has been a technological shift which has occurred as the centres have become more established. Now that this community of survivors exists, now that they are communicating more with each other in the centres, they are ready to identify themselves outside of the centres on a network. Not surprisingly, the interest by many survivors in learning to use computers and the internet seems to coincide with a drive to link with other survivors in the UK and worldwide. The momentum is gathering which allows survivors to address such important issues as their claims as former slave labourers, their rights to former Swiss bank accounts, insurance claims and reclaiming art treasures stolen from them by the Nazis. Survivors currently cannot be ignored, and this voice, this resistance which they are organising, feeds into the goal of liberation today.

I believe that central to this momentum for change are the survivors who participate in the centres. The centres facilitate the process through which the survivors redefine their freedom in today's world. In 1945, freedom meant the opening of the camp gates and the freedom from imprisonment. However,

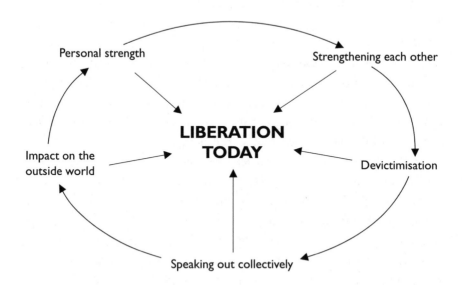

Figure 11.1 Diagrammatic representation of the life-force which contributes to 'liberation today'

that freedom, as we have noted, could be seen as a 'false' liberation. The trauma itself brought about an altered state in the aftermath of severe suffering, which again dislocated the sufferers who emerged from that 'other' world of pain and torture, and rendered them outsiders to the world of the living and life.

Symbolically, this community of survivors, established through the centre, became a conversion box to decode the language of the world of severe suffering. It meant we who work alongside them had to understand what had been taken away from these former prisoners which needed to be addressed in our services. We also needed to build on what had remained 'alive' in that world of death. Now, in this new millennium, a new language is being encoded as the 'outsiders', the survivors, have become 'insiders' in this new community. That new language embodies a redefinition of liberation today: a liberation which allows those who have suffered to live next to their trauma – never to forget, but also never to repeat it. The freedom to live differently with the trauma is encapsulated within the walls of the survivors' centres. In 1945, survivors had their freedom granted by their liberators. Today, survivors are liberating themselves.

> Your enjoyment in the centre, your involvement in the centre, offers a differ-ent experience to when you were all together so many years ago. Recon-necting with life is a second opportunity to celebrate 'liberation'. However, this time, now, today, freedom is not being granted by your liberators. When you begin to use this part of your life, these precious years that are left to you, to find some peace, to be kind to yourselves and to each other, then *you* are choosing freedom. And that is perhaps the greatest victory over Hitler and your oppressors. (Hassan 2001)

Choosing freedom connects survivors to this world. Freedom is not the chaotic aftermath of liberation in 1945. Freedom is the right to live one's own life, but at the same time means acknowledging the right to freedom of those around us. Freedom is not unconditional, but governed by the morality and code of ethics which define it. In that sense, the centres for survivors become much more than a haven for these tortured souls. They become much more than a respite from the pain and suffering. They become places of learning about regeneration out of destruction, about humanity in the aftermath of severe inhumanity, about how to live with life after atrocity. Those whom the Holocaust sought to silence forever are influencing the way we relate to their suffering. The survivors use us to test out new ways of being in this world. We are in this sense reaching a new stage, the beginning of another journey, which will continue long after the survivors reach the end of their lives.

When I look at the evidence of what is changing, when I see signs of new life and growth even at this late hour in the survivors' lives, it excites me and drives me to do more. As a sociology student in the 1960s, I was influenced by the powerful movements for revolution and social change which coincided with my learning. My politics became defined during that time, and impacted on how I viewed my role as a social worker years later. I had witnessed that society could change and hence the plight of the vulnerable should be challenged. I would fight for the rights of the elderly and mentally ill people with whom I was working. I would not accept the status quo. I believed change was possible and focused on the strategies to achieve this. I saw proof that the elderly and mentally ill people I worked with could change, could move on if they were motivated to do so. In the past and in the present situation, it is the challenge of what seems out of reach, of what seems hopeless and discarded by others, that gives meaning to my work. For example, after a recent meeting about developing a sheltered housing scheme for the survivors, some survivors as well as some staff commented that they feel it is a waste of time trying to get the funding for such a project. I said that we must keep trying. We must think of different ways of ensuring it happens, for what was clear was the high priority the members gave to such a resource. One staff member commented that I am always positive. It is essential to be so, in order to reach the goals. Positive thinking is as contagious as negative thinking. This element has also been a key feature in working towards the goal of a centre for the Bosnian refugees.

This positive attitude, however, must be fed, both from within and externally. Towards this end, I would now like to look more closely at these signs of life that emerge from the dark shadow of the survivors' traumatic past. I believe this part of the book, which focuses on the hopeful outcomes from our services, may be a motivating force for those who struggle with the despair of atrocity when working with survivors from other genocides and war trauma.

Fighting for justice: the outcome of empowerment

In the lives of victims, keeping a low profile, keeping silent, was a way of surviving. Through the emphasis on empowerment, through the involvement of the survivors on every level of the HSC's functioning, they have found a voice.

This voice, which was strengthened through the HSC, resulted in a group developing to fight for the claims of former slave labourers.[1] When the originators of this small group came to see me together with Jewish Care's Executive Director, they wanted this large organisation to take up their cause. Instead, another strategy was adopted. The aim was to encourage the survivors to expose the German companies that had become rich through exploiting slave labourers whom they intended to work to death. The HSC gave the administrative backing to their fight for justice, but the survivors remained at the forefront in this arduous task.

The commitment, the fortitude, the determination of these survivors to achieve this compensation grew, despite the obstacles put in their way. More and more forms were completed at the HSC. These survivors took the initiative. They contacted lawyers; they attended meetings in Germany, in the USA and wherever their voices needed to be heard. One of the survivors was featured in a documentary film shown on Channel 4. They spoke to the media on behalf of all those who had suffered a similar fate at the hands of the Nazis. Information was disseminated through the HSC and support was offered to strengthen them in their fight.

These survivors went as far as they could in drawing attention to the gross inhumanity meted out to the former slave labourers. Their fight here was echoed in other countries around the world, and survivors collectively demanded to be noticed. Their goal has still not been fully realised, but the process speaks volumes about empowerment and the will to fight back against the injustices which were done to them.

These survivors act as an example to others who have suffered without receiving compensation. The Bosnian refugees we work with are now wanting to return to Bosnia to claim back property which belonged to them. The survivors change the face of the victim. They are not prepared to just accept the compensation that is handed out to them. They shame those authorities that delay the payments for compensation. They challenge those who again wish to silence them, claiming that their demands for this money produces an anti-Semitic backlash. These are not individuals fighting for themselves, but a group who speak collectively and more powerfully.

As I write, an announcement has been made by Germany to release the money to former slave labourers. It is too little money, and has come very late in the lives of the survivors and their suffering, yet it reflects how these survivors have moved on in their journey. It is at a cost, for those who have dedicated themselves to this task have been under great strain – yet the benefit is far greater than the money itself. It is far greater than the recognition of their suffering. It turns the tide in the role that the survivors play in their lives today and how they impact on the world around them.

The experience of this group of survivors involved in the claims has had repercussions in other situations in which their collective voice needed to be heard. They respond rapidly to issues related to Nazi war criminals, and to revisionists who deny the Holocaust. The survivors want representation and a platform to express themselves on subjects that concern them. An opportunity arose when the President of the Jewish Board of Deputies was invited to the HSC to give a talk about her work. This major organisation has delegates from all the communal bodies which comprise the Jewish community. It is a powerful voice representing the community as a whole. The members have often expressed the view that they wished to be part of that forum to express the issues that concern Holocaust survivors. Having felt like 'outsiders' in the Jewish community, the time had come for them to have their voice heard. The centre had given them an 'identity', and they wanted that identity to be recognised. The question was put to the President concerning the possibility of a delegate from the HSC. The response was positive.

The task is not an easy one, but is essential in the integration of survivors into the world which has not witnessed atrocity in the way that they have. I will ensure that the necessary public-speaking training and support are provided to contribute to the impact of the survivors' voice.

Choosing life and facing natural death: the outcome of mourning and memorialisation

During the years of the Holocaust, only the Nazis decided who would live and who would die. We have seen during the course of this book how certain actions by the survivors themselves could assist in passing another minute in the hell of that other world, but ultimately they were not in control of events over life and death.

In 1945, revenge on the Nazi perpetrators was an option open to those who had suffered. Most chose not to take that option, arguing that such revenge could have reduced them to a level of behaviour from which they were trying to escape. Today there are arguments put forward that retribution and revenge destabilise society in the aftermath of trauma, and may lead to further bloodshed. Truth and reconciliation in South Africa, for example, have been offered as an alternative response to atrocity. I do not know what those who have suffered severely at the hands of their oppressors feel about these criminals who committed crimes against humanity being free to get on with their lives again. Does it bring the two worlds of the oppressor and the oppressed closer together? Does it heal the rupture in humanity that allowed these crimes to take place? Will it prevent further atrocity from taking place? These remain unanswered questions which we must contemplate in the light of what we observe.

The Holocaust survivors teach us that there may be another way. If we take the dictionary definition of revenge to be the 'deliberate punishment or injury inflicted in return for what has been suffered', then fifty years and more after the event, revenge by the survivors has taken on a different mantle. The rage associated with revenge has become encased within the walls which surround the centres for survivors. Channelling the rage through the therapeutic options opens up new ways of learning about how to deal with revenge. There may be positive and not only negative, destructive aspects to it. If survivors had responded in a way that belonged to that other world of inhumanity and bestiality, they would tend to fit the dictionary definition of the term. However, the centres' acting as interpreters of the language that bridges the two worlds produces responses that may have different manifestations. Revenge could be seen as choosing life, about living well, and about holding on to humanity – for that is what the totalitarian regime tried to wipe out.

Let me illustrate what I mean. When I visited Ruth in hospital, she had undergone a triple heart bypass some six months earlier. Her life had been suspended during that time as she hung between life and death. Unable to move, unable to talk, her only visitors were her devoted husband and daughter. From the HSC, we had kept a close eye on the reports about her, but no-one was allowed to see her.

I had got to know Ruth informally over many years. She was an important member of the Yiddish group. She contributed to the centre through volunteering in the kitchen. She regularly went to Israel to visit her family, and she would chat with me about this and on many other areas of her life which she enjoyed. Ruth, who had survived Auschwitz, is one of the few survivors from Salonika. As time went by, she found it harder to deal with the memories of her suffering and the massive losses she had experienced. She asked me to introduce her to a member of the Shalvata team, whom she saw for some time. I never lost contact with Ruth, and when she became ill, I was aware of her absence in the centre. Her fellow members who cared for her in the HSC were also greatly affected by her severe health problems. During six months of barely being conscious, she touched death once more as she had done many years earlier in Auschwitz. Once she had regained consciousness, I asked Ruth's husband if she would like me to visit her. She readily agreed.

As I walked into the hospital room, Ruth lay in bed and still found it difficult to talk due to the tubes in her throat. Her smile though, and her bright eyes, contrasted with the Auschwitz number visible on her arm. I sensed the fight she had been through, I sensed the trauma of her current dependency and vulnerability but, at the same time, I sensed her determination and defiance in returning to life. The few words she spoke were contained in the short sentence, 'I don't have to tell you, you know.' In that sentence, the two worlds were bridged. I took my cue from her in encouraging her to return to the centre rather than detailing her illness.

The following week Ruth moved to a rehabilitation unit. She became depressed as she struggled to be independent again. She asked me to arrange for a member of the Shalvata team to come and see her. A few weeks later, she was ready to return home, walking again without assistance. Ruth rejoined the Yiddish group which she missed so much during her illness.

Ruth had not been ready to give up her life. Her connection to her family and to her friends and 'family' in the HSC joined her to the positive things in her life. Of course, the medical care Ruth received played a great part in her survival. Nevertheless, Ruth's own determination, not only to survive, but to live her life again, and to die when she herself is ready to let go, also speaks to other survivors about illness and recovery, in contrast to the memories of unnatural death through murder. Ruth was not meant to survive Auschwitz, but she did. She may not have survived this severe illness, but she did. She talks to us about her connection to this world which she has rejoined. By doing so, she puts her past trauma in its place, as part of her life rather than part of her death. As an outcome she changes the patterns of the past repeating itself in the present. It is as though Ruth herself represents the door which opens between the two worlds.

Ruth's story inspires us to think positively about the last part of people's lives. We have seen how our therapeutic work has offered opportunities for survivors to mourn for those who were murdered, to help survivors ritualise the 'burial' of those killed, and to memorialise them through their testimonies, education programmes and museums. Addressing the deaths of those murdered leaves space for survivors to prepare for their own end. Facing natural death, spiritually, emotionally and practically, is the outcome of what Ruth teaches us. We are now planning a group devoted to that task. The dignity and sense of peace which more survivors feel as death approaches confirms the differences between the past trauma and their lives today.

Cohesiveness out of chaos: the outcome of 'feeding', dignity and building trust

It is difficult to describe the raw, unadulterated chaos which featured so often in the early days of the HSC. In my professional life, I had never encountered the dynamics which surfaced so forcibly as these survivors came together. It was my initiation into a world of destructiveness which my sheltered existence tried in vain to comprehend. It was made clear that in terms of the death camp experience, I was on the other side of the barbed wire. I needed to be kept at a distance, viewed suspiciously, despite my attempts to assist in the process of bringing this community together. It did hurt, it did pain me; this paradoxical confusion of my threatening helpfulness came close to concluding this chapter of my work.

I contrast that time to the world I observe today in the HSC – a world in which compassion and humanity have a place. That is not to say that tensions do not exist, but the way in which those stress points are dealt with is different.

I would first like to look at a couple of examples which reflect the shift towards a more cohesive response, which seemed out of reach even a few years ago.

A senior American official from the former Clinton government was visiting London for a meeting to discuss the subject of compensation to former slave labourers and forced labourers. Some members of the HSC involved in dealing with the claims felt it was important for him to come to the HSC to address the members. This suggestion came very late in the day, and there were concerns that only a handful of members would attend. The official agreed to meet with the members, which was an important acknowledgement of their collective identity as a group of survivors. The centre was their official voice. I was asked by the survivors to chair the event, and the meeting was due to take place on a Sunday at 2pm. I arrived well in time and found a room already overflowing with members – one hundred and twenty survivors had thought it important enough to participate. One hour had been allocated for the event. The official gave an opening address and members were then invited to ask questions. The emotive content of the subject for the survivors, plus the sheer volume of their numbers, was a potentially overpowering dynamic. However, this was a very different experience to those earlier chaotic meetings I have referred to.

The members of the centre raised their concerns about the delays in payments being made, that time was running out for them, as well as more specific issues relating to payments for former child survivors. Apart from these important issues which needed to be aired, it was the way the meeting was conducted which spoke so eloquently about how the survivors had moved on. They allowed me to chair the meeting; they waited patiently until each member had raised a question and the official had responded to it.

Halfway through the meeting, a member of the centre asked to speak. Unlike some of the more vocal and coherent members, this survivor spoke with a strong accent and struggled to express herself in this language which is not her mother tongue. As she took the platform, she shook physically as she talked briefly about her time in Mauthausen and the death-provoking hard labour of carrying heavy boulders up steep slopes in the quarry. She carried the emotions for the whole group. In the present day, she struggles to have enough money to live on and emphasised her need to receive this compensation in order to make her life a little easier. It meant so much to her that her voice was heard, and she found me after the meeting, and at the 'liberation' lunch, to tell me so. Giving space to these more silent voices acts as a balance to those who speak more loudly. It moves us towards a greater acceptance of difference in a community who have competed in terms of their suffering.

Even though members were angered at the slowness and inadequacy of how their claims were being handled, they nevertheless treated the US official with respect and restraint. The dignified way this meeting was conducted was a moving and powerful example of the survivors' capacity to lift themselves above their trauma and to focus on the task in hand. The mirror image was not a return to the death camps, even though the subject matter related to that experience. It was not mirroring the bestiality and extreme inhumanity of the death camp world, but gave a hopeful pointer to man's capacity to adapt again from the world of death to that of life.

This move along the continuum from chaos to cohesiveness, which this meeting exemplified, did not happen overnight. As we have noted, plenty of food, warmth and space create a very different environment from that experienced in the trauma. In addition, a major contributing factor to the cohesiveness is the basic everyday happening of survivors living side by side in this community. The vociferousness and exclusivity of camp survivors and child survivors has lessened as their respective identities have been confirmed.

Sitting on a coach on one of the many social outings from the HSC, members chat to each other and get to know each other in these relaxed and enjoyable events. They identify themselves less by their survivor category, and more by their names and who they are. Sitting over lunch in the HSC on a daily basis, the members eat meals together – refugee and camp survivor, partisan and ghetto survivor. In the writing group, the plight of the Kindertransport is expressed and acknowledged by others who write about surviving the camps. In the singing group, they join together with one sound and reproduce the songs which unite them, or learn songs which may be less familiar to one group and more familiar to another.

In this home which they help to create, they are neighbours. You do not have to like all your neighbours, but life is better for all concerned if you can accommodate each other in some way. The term 'neighbour' may in itself have negative as well as positive connotations for some survivors. Neighbours could have been enemies, informers and brutal persecutors, collaborators, and even murderers. Indeed, *Neighbours*, Jan Gross's book (2001), horrifically describes how half the Polish town of Jedwabne murdered the other half, namely the Jews, in 1941. Therefore, in this community of survivors, the word 'neighbours' needs to be redefined in the light of repeated evidence of trust and concern for each other.

Let me give a few examples. At the luncheon to commemorate the liberation of the prisoners' incarceration in camps, ghettos, from hiding or any other oppressive experiences, I had assumed that only those who had actually gone through these traumas would be invited to attend. That would be one occasion in which it would seem appropriate not to open the event to all members. However, with the passage of time, friendships have formed with other members in the centre who may have a refugee background. Thus exceptions were made, and some refugees mingled with those who had been liberated from Europe at the end of World War II.

By the same token, only those who participated in the liberation in 1945, either as fellow prisoners or as liberators, have been invited as guest speakers at the lunch event. In the year 2001, however, I was invited as guest speaker. I was not even a refugee, and did not directly experience the atrocity of the Holocaust. I thought long and hard about whether I should accept, owing to my non-survivor status. My decision to accept the invitation rested on the symbolic recognition of this closer connection between the two worlds. I believed the survivors were making a statement to me about the shift in the relationship between the insider and the outsider. I believe that the invitation was the culmination of the observations the survivors have made about me. As one survivor put it at a public meeting which I had been asked to address, 'Just as Judith observes us, the Holocaust survivors observe her. They see she is with us, for us, and when it comes to pressing our case, she does it ferociously.' I believe I was invited to this liberation event not merely because I have facilitated the services which the survivors engage in but, more particularly, because I provide evidence of having opened myself up to be touched by who they are, what they have been through, and how they would like to be remembered in the future. I am on their side fighting with them for justice and liberation today.

If there is one memory which will remain etched in my mind for all time, it is the response of the survivors to my presence with them that day. In a sense it embodies the joint efforts of both the survivors and myself to live side by side and to be touched by each other's worlds. Allowing them to give me food, to make sure I enjoyed the event, to listen attentively to me when I addressed them and to ask for personal copies of my talk made this event different to any other I had experienced.

How the survivors relate today to myself and to each other is in evidence in many different ways. We have seen how they were initially unable to tolerate the frailer members of the community, and advocated alternative resources for them. Today, they believe our resources need to be adapted to accommodate them. While they continue to have difficulty in sharing their centre with the Bosnian refugees, they nevertheless regard our Bosnian caretaker as their good neighbour. They see him helping them, treating them with respect and caring for them despite his own trauma from the war he experienced. They know him personally as a kind human being, not a refugee who competes with their suffering. When Ruth was in hospital, both he and my Bosnian community worker volunteered to visit her. When she returned to the centre, she specifically asked them to join her to celebrate her return. At one time, some of the camp survivors' group felt their committee should be run in a different way. Today there is more acceptance that different approaches can co-exist.

Eradicating conflict is not the aim of the centre. Total harmony would not allow survivors the opportunity to express themselves in ways they may need to. Learning new ways of living with each other contributes to the cohesiveness we have witnessed as the centres have developed. A final example of the survivors' adaptation can be seen in the participation of six survivors in a training event for professional staff. Twelve delegates from Paris asked to visit Shalvata and the HSC to hear and observe the way we work with survivors. As many of these delegates could not speak English, we asked those French-speaking survivors to join us over lunch. In their eagerness to meet with the delegates, the survivors arrived very early. They began speaking informally to the delegates prior to the formal start of our meeting. I needed to make a decision as to whether to ask them to return later, or whether they should remain to participate in the event. I chose the latter course of action as it sat most comfortably with me and my experience of learning from the survivors.

I gave an introduction about how the centres had developed, and how they had evolved from listening to the survivors about what had helped them. Members of the Shalvata team gave short presentations about different aspects of our work. Throughout this time, survivors commented on the value the service had for them. They established a dialogue between the delegates and ourselves. They became the link through translating the language of our therapeutic work into a language (French) which all the delegates could understand. One of the survivors present had been the scribe for the book which the art therapist helped to illustrate for one of the members. In this meeting, her handling of this delicate situation was extremely professional. Personal issues were restrained and she focused on translating the art therapist's words.

This event demonstrated vividly the interconnectedness between the two centres, the two worlds, as well as the partnership between the staff and the survivors. The fluidity of these movements inspired the French delegates to rethink what they called their more compartmentalised view of their work. The survivors gave very positive feedback about their experiences that day. They felt they came together with the staff, and did not feel stigmatised by the subjects discussed. They felt they were contributors to this important event, and had been given a role to play in this educational process.

When dignity is restored, when humanity is in evidence, then it is possible to live differently with trauma. The cohesiveness and neighbourliness are overt manifestations which can be witnessed both internally in the centre and in the interface with the outside world. The cohesiveness frees the survivors to get on with enjoying the time they have left to them instead of struggling with each other to 'survive'.

The neighbourliness, the greater acceptance of who these very different people are in this home they have created, began to feel more like the place I had known as a child – the home in which all nationalities met together and which had shaped my world.

Redefining the legacy: regeneration out of destruction

It is not pleasant to die Lord if nothing is left in life
And in death nothing is possible except on the basis of what is left in
life
It is not pleasant to die Lord if nothing is left in life
And in death nothing is possible except on the basis of what one
could have left in life.

(Cesar Vallejo's poem 'The Windows Shuddered'[2])

These words by the Peruvian poet Cesar Vallejo (1978) teach us about the importance of planning for when we are no longer alive. It is a theme echoed many times over by writers, philosophers and others concerned with the transitory nature of existence. Perhaps one of the most beautiful books given to me is a collection of Shakespeare's sonnets (1988). Sonnet No. 3 speaks directly about remembering and remembrance which we must address while we still have time:

> Look in thy glass, and tell the face thou viewest
> Now is the time that face should form another,
> Whose fresh repair if now thou not renewest
> Thou dost beguile the world, unbless some mother.
> For where is she so fair whose unear'd womb
> Disdains the tillage of thy husbandry?
> Or who is he so fond will be the tomb
> Of his self love to stop posterity?
> Thou art thy mother's glass, and she in thee
> Calls back the lovely April of her prime;
> So thou through windows of thy age shall see,
> Despite of wrinkles, this thy golden time.
> But if thou live remembered not to be,
> Die single, and thine image dies with thee.

As I was sitting with Branko, the Bosnian community worker, he was describing the sadness and nostalgia that the elderly refugees felt when they saw a documentary film of life today in Sarajevo. It was less to do with the destruction of the war which affected them, and more to do with the images which reminded them of the good times when they were there. Their sense of loss was focused on their disconnection from their home and community. It was as though they had never existed. There was nothing to mark their former presence in that place and, with time, no-one will remember them. They also have less time to put down roots in this country, as their age robs them of the luxury of starting anew. These already traumatised Holocaust survivors touched me, and I felt impelled to make some response. A fitting sculpture or some other concrete reminder of their lives as part of Sarajevo might ease some of that pain. I encouraged a discussion on this theme between Branko and the group, and busied myself with ensuring the logistics for such an event to happen.

People often ask me what will happen to the centres when there are no longer any survivors alive. Thinking of the future, in this penultimate part of the book, guides me towards thinking about the legacy of the survivors which will continue long after their death. As long as the survivors are alive, they have pledged to remember those who were murdered in the Holocaust. In the work we have undertaken, we have listened to the survivors and have assisted them in recording their memories for posterity. The documentation of these recordings has helped to give some of the survivors peace of mind in the latter part of their lives. They continue to write their books, which continue to be published. More and more of them are speaking to the media and ensuring their truth is told. More and more are going to schools and speaking publicly to ensure that what happened in the Holocaust will become known to as wide a range of people as possible.

We have also seen an increase in the numbers of survivors who return to the camps and their places of birth. They relive the memories of where they have come from and what they have been through. Some find this helpful, while some do not. Some have their worst memories confirmed, while others are shocked by the commercialisation of places of horror, such as Auschwitz.

However diligent the survivors have been and however supportive and facilitating our services, there is a fragility and vulnerability about how the memory will be preserved. Books were burned by the Nazis during the Holocaust. Elie Wiesel (1990d) writes vociferously about trivialising the memory of the Holocaust (p.171). With time, the reality of what happened becomes distorted and then forgotten. For example, while the subject of the Holocaust is now part of the national curriculum in schools in the UK, the number of hours devoted to it is very small. While National Holocaust Memorial Day has become a public recognition of the horrors of the Nazi Holocaust, the survivors fear its uniqueness will be lost. While education through schools, museums and memorials has helped enormously in assisting survivors to leave a legacy of their past, a large part of that success is due to the participation of the survivors themselves.

The question therefore remains about the power of this legacy once the survivors are no longer alive. The survivors today are the living legacy for those who were murdered – but what of themselves? Who will remember them in fifty years' time? Who will feel committed, as they have done, to fight for that remembrance? Those who have never seen war see the world differently. There is a tendency to become more complacent. There is a fear of being reminded of what has been sacrificed for peace. In this sense, monuments and museums will become the conscience of society in relation to that legacy, but how will the feelings associated with the suffering be preserved? Does a list of names of those who perished in the Holocaust have the same impact on us compared to a sculpture of a single jacket with a yellow star on it, draped over a bridge to commemorate the deportation of Jews from Germany? What makes the latter different from other memorials is its simplicity as well as its evocativeness. We can identify with this garment as though it belonged to someone we knew. The power of this type of legacy is that it touches us personally, and therein lies the key to its future security.

I remember some years ago meeting with a group of eminent historians specialising in the Holocaust, as well as with those responsible for Holocaust education. The meeting took place in the HSC to discuss the subject of the legacy of the Holocaust for future generations. There was much self-congratulatory talk about what was being done to remember the Holocaust. I felt the discussion was very academic and it did not reassure me regarding my concerns about the future, and how memory fades and how memorials can crumble. I tried to express the view that 'when the Holocaust is part of each one of us, then the goal of the survivor will have been reached'. We needed to be part of the legacy and not just observers and recorders of what happened. The change had to be experienced rather than described. I found it hard to form the words to convey this urgent task, and I was met with blank faces. Not surprisingly, further meetings did not materialise, and I realised I needed to think more carefully about the different ways that the legacy could be preserved for posterity.

The legacy of Holocaust survivors has until now rested primarily on remembering the dead, the horror and the pain. To counteract Holocaust deniers, that remembrance is of paramount importance. The survivors feel that the duty to remember must be passed on to their children, and this is where we encounter a divergence between the two worlds. We have already noted how the children of survivors have often felt reluctant to carry the legacy of their parents' and grandparents' suffering. It is often too heavy a burden for the child of a survivor to be given the name of a murdered member of his/her family. It is sometimes too difficult a duty to be the 'memorial candle' for the parent's pain. As a child of survivors commented, 'I want to separate myself from these dead people, who have always stuck to me, inside my soul. I want to see them and talk to them and even begin to love them, but I don't want to be buried with them any more!' (Wardi 1992, p.213).

The two generations seemed to reach an impasse. Before the centres for survivors began, those who witnessed atrocity felt isolated in their task of remembering. In their desperation for the memory to be preserved, they turned to their children as the vessels into which they poured these memories. These adult children, in danger of being drowned in the blood of the victims, would have readily abdicated their role in the legacy for the future. These adult children of survivors often receive the negative impact of the legacy from the Holocaust, as it struggles to find meaning in their lives today. Their parents came from the world of death and they carried these spectres into their present life. For the two worlds to meet, for the survivors and their children to begin to communicate in the same language, they need to redefine the legacy in a form with which their children can identify.

A major thrust of our therapeutic work with the survivors is in addressing the life-forces which allow the survivors to have an identity which is not only defined by their suffering. The survivors who are alive today are distinguished from those who were murdered in the Holocaust in that they have a post-Holocaust experience. Talking to one of the members of the HSC who had come to see me about making a donation to the centre, I asked him in the course of our conversation what work he had done after the war. He told me he became a fashion designer and had travelled the world in his chosen profession. Again, asking certain questions elicits a richness of responses. Chava worked in marketing; Irena was a primary school teacher. Lawyers, architects, librarians, writers, academic professors, engineers and musicians were but a few of the life-enhancing contributions which emerged from the ashes of the Holocaust.

Against all odds, and without the help of families, there emerged a will to succeed. Many survivors excelled themselves in their fields of work. Recognition is given to the contributions and achievements made by refugees who came here before the war, but I feel not enough focus is put on those who came after 1945, having survived such extreme atrocity. The energy needed to succeed in this occupational diversity left little strength and time to mourn for all that was lost. Celebrating success may have seemed incongruous against the overwhelming memories of the trauma. In a similar way, the acts of humanity in the death camps had paled into insignificance against the horror. Unless we focus on those years of *regeneration out of the destruction*, we could easily miss a most important contribution to the redefining of the legacy. Why did certain survivors get involved in certain careers and occupations? Was it important for the fashion designer, for example, to create possibilities of external attractiveness to mask the memories of dehumanised skeletons? What did the architect see in his designs of buildings which perhaps allowed him to rework his memories of the structure of the death camps? Was it liberating for him to move into an open space and create something new and innovative?

In redefining the legacy, we may be able to open up new ways of channelling the negative experience of the traumas to release a life-force which can be carried and understood by future generations. How this manifests itself can be seen by returning once more to one of the survivors you have come to know – Chava.

Chava told me that she had been asked by a friend of hers if she would make a dress for her daughter. This seventeen-year-old girl had been invited to a party and wanted a sophisticated design to make her feel special, confident and grown up. The mother and daughter chose the material and the pattern and took it to Chava. The black silk material and halter-neck design inspired Chava and she agreed to take on this daunting task.

During our meetings Chava spoke to me in some detail about the skill involved in bringing this dress to life. The dark, sensuous material challenged Chava as she painstakingly laid out the pattern and cut the shape. In the process of creating the garment, memories of her father came back into her mind. Chava only mentioned this in passing, but I brought this connection back and made it more central to the story she was telling. She remembered watching her father, who was an experienced designer of women's fashions, using his skill to create beautiful designs for his customers. She thought of the patterns he had made hanging from the walls of the room ready to be transformed. Those memories inspired her, and guided her hands as she cut into the material. No mention of her father's abuse of her this time. No mention of her running away from the trauma she experienced when she was a similar age to the girl whose dress she was creating.

Chava had never had any formal lessons in dressmaking. Each handmade stitch was a triumph. Unpicking and reworking the material to achieve the best fit for the young woman gave Chava a sense of mastery in this creative field which linked her to her father.

The final fitting session arrived. Chava felt ill with anxiety. What if the dress did not fit? What if this young woman was not satisfied with it? Would she have failed? Would her father's view that she would never succeed in her life be confirmed? Her doubts, her uncertainties, her fears seemed to reside in the blackness of the material. Without form, the darkness of the material seemed at that moment to have the potential of overwhelming her. What happened next transformed that darkness as the young woman tried on the dress. The material shimmered as the light caught the fabric. The fit was perfect and the young woman was overjoyed with the result.

Chava had overcome many obstacles in the journey of making this dress. She felt the dress had helped her to get closer to her father than she had ever been. She realised that her father lived on in her through this talent. She had inherited something positive from him, and that seemed to help her to let go of some of the anger and resentment which left her father 'unburied' for her. Remembering her father as a creative and talented person was the legacy she could live with. His cruelty and abuse disconnected her from him and made it difficult for her to accommodate him in her life. This living memorial to her father has inspired Chava to pursue these talents by enrolling in dressmaking classes. The final touch for the dress was symbolised through an embroidered label, bearing an abbreviated version of her father's surname. Chava felt this would be her designer label in the future.

The story of the black dress becomes a metaphor for describing the mechanism I had failed to make explicit at the meeting of the historians I mentioned a little earlier. It is a mechanism which may speak more directly to the grandchildren and subsequent generations of those who survived the Holocaust.

Having seen how a survivor can redefine the legacy for herself, I would also like to return to Irena with an example of how she assisted her children to engage in the process of forming a link between the past and the future. Irena had only one photograph of her father, which her uncle in Sweden had given to her as a remembrance. She said she could not bear to look at it because it reminded her of all she had lost. Thinking about the legacy, as I have done during the process of my writing, I asked her if she had ever thought of giving a copy of the photograph to her daughter and son. Her daughter had remonstrated about the absence of grandparents in her life. This photograph of Irena's father, smartly dressed, with an air of prosperity and calm, could provide her daughter and son with a positive image for the future, in contrast to her own memory of the atrocity. This photograph contained the essence of this double legacy – the remembrance of the death by murder of Irena's father, and the memory of the life of a man who was her children's grandfather. What a treasure for her children to keep and pass on to their own children.

These illustrations raise the issue of the connectedness in survivors' lives. The decisions they take and the work they choose link their pre-Holocaust lives, their Holocaust experiences and what happened to them subsequently. It is this connectedness which the adult children of survivors are also seeking, and it enables them to get closer to their families in order to find some meaning in the legacy for themselves.

> When the mists of death disperse...a clean and sharp family picture is revealed: great cities teeming with life and towns in the heart of pre-war Europe; extended families gathering together on happy occasions or at times of sadness and death; and babies, children and young people who are none other than their parents before they were enveloped by the smoke of the crematoria. Then the 'memorial candles' find their place in the chain of the generations and, as links in this chain, their task in transmitting the family heritage to the coming generation. (Wardi 1992, p.258)

These 'memorial candles' become more like living memorials, like trees reconnected to their roots. The roots feed them, and they are nourished and grow strong. In today's world, genealogy has become a fashionable area of study. There is a thirst to know who our ancestors were, our family trees. When we look closely, we can see patterns emerging through generations of talent, whether they be musical, artistic, theatrical, or perhaps trades and professions, which span across many generations. In continuing the links between the contribution of these ancestors to the choice of work and self-expression of the second generation, the latter may be preserving the memory of those who are no longer alive. Many of these adult children work in the fields of film, media, journalism and the helping professions. As living memorials, they are perhaps giving expression to a vanished world, and channel these inherited characteristics in positive and overt ways.

In general terms, the therapeutic work with the adult children of survivors usually offers opportunities for them to express the pain of their burden of remembering the dead and their wish to reject this unwanted legacy. In our work with both generations, we need to facilitate the opportunities for each of them to reconnect to life, and to communicate that wish to each other.

I have already noted how my own family, and others connected to me, live on in both the work that I undertake and the interests I pursue. Shamai Davidson guides my thinking and comes to life in the interpretation and application of what he has taught me. The home my mother created, to feed and nourish the displaced and isolated, lives on in the model which has emerged in the centres. My father's spirituality, tolerance and care for those who have suffered finds an outlet at the interface with the survivors. Nothing gets lost if these positive connections are maintained. My sister, Ann-Marie, carries in her name the link to both our grandmothers. When my niece describes making a recipe she received from her maternal grandmother, the legacy lives on. When my nephew returned to the birthplace of his maternal grandmother in Germany, he acknowledged a connection. On a daily basis we carry these positive transmissions if only we can see them in the struggles which make up our everyday existence.

Addressing the survivors as we do in our centres, we share the legacy with their children. If living with the dead was the survivors' only memory, I believe many of them would themselves not be alive today. Through their participation in the HSC and Shalvata, these terrible memories have found many outlets, and in the process have begun to be mourned. Through being listened to, through being believed, the survivors shared their pain. We who work with them carry them on a raft through troubled waters, helping them in their mission never to forget. We hold up the raft they are travelling in, so that they should not drown with the weightiness of the load that they carry. In the process, other currents have passed beneath the raft and taken them in other directions, as we have witnessed in the therapeutic content of the work. Those of us who work with them are often affected by the dead they carry. However, unlike some of the survivor families, this newly created 'family' of professional workers tries not to compete in terms of their suffering and breathing space. Out of the deadness, we have to find a new way of learning from their responses to atrocity that will remain long after the survivors have all died. We help them to package the legacy differently. They rehearse with us how to pass their legacy on to their children, and we can prepare the adult children to receive it.

The centre has become a powerful medium through which the legacy can be redefined. However, preparing the legacy is only part of the equation. To bring it to life, it needs to have some practical applications and an interface with the outside world. The next section will focus on how we move from the inside to the outside, and how we create possibilities for the legacy to find an outlet.

The impact on the people and organisations working with survivors: the application of the lessons learned from survivors

A great deal of emphasis has been put on the work we have undertaken to give the survivor a voice, to have an identity and not repeat the experience of the victim. The concepts of 'liberation' and empowerment have been translated through the centres for survivors to help them live differently with their trauma in the latter part of their lives.

I have already described some of the observable outcomes that have emerged for the survivors from their participation in the centres. Their reconnection to a life-force which allows them to bridge the world of the dead with the world of the living has had an impact on the outcome of their story.

Today, as I write my own story of that long journey I have been on with the survivors, I see a reflection of a similar process which has changed the way I see myself and my relationship to my work. As I tell this story to you, the readers, I realise that I have also become a participant in it. I have tried over these pages to give an account of how to undertake this work with those severely traumatised; to give pointers covering the changes which need to happen personally and professionally to make this work meaningful; and to encourage some creative process to be triggered whereby new and innovative ideas can be released. In my determination to develop these services for survivors, and in my efforts to pass on to you what I have learned from the survivors, I have been drawn towards a mirror image of how these processes have impacted on me.

My critics may argue that I have become so over-identified with my task that I cannot differentiate myself from the survivors – yet I do not see myself as a survivor. I can go home at the end of the day and pursue a life that is separate from my work. Night is not a torment of nightmares for me, as it has been for some of the survivors I have seen.

I enter in on every level of the survivors' lives. I will share certain events with them. In the Advisory Committee and Strategic Planning Group, we work together for the centre. They will approach me whether it is for writing a letter, asking advice about a claim, making a complaint about someone or something in the centres, or to resolve a dispute between members. Being with the survivors on a daily basis over such a long period of time has proved invaluable. There were so many ways of making mistakes, so many ways of getting it wrong, so many ways of losing the trust. An inappropriate word, an unhelpful gesture, could daily have overthrown the equilibrium in my relationship to the survivors. Without trust, without mutual respect, we could not have reached the situation today.

Let me describe an event from some years ago now, which may serve to illustrate how easy it is to get it wrong. Dealing as I do with the survivors of the Nazi Holocaust as well as the more recent refugees from Bosnia, there seemed to be a possibility of linking these two groups who experienced war trauma. There was a suggestion that the Bosnian group could use the HSC in the evening once a week for their social activities. As a community centre, this would have been a usual practice and would be more cost-effective than hiring a separate facility for the Bosnian group. The survivors who are older do not like to go out in the evening, preferring to come to the centre during the day. Logistically, therefore, it would have made sense for it to be used in this way. After all, the Bosnians had also suffered uprooting and dislocation, and hence there was some connection as compared to some other Jewish group.

As with all sensitive discussions connected with the centre, I was not prepared to act as a manager without consulting the Advisory Committee of the HSC. Consequently, the matter was raised at a meeting and was proposed as a short-term suggestion until the Bosnians could be found a centre of their own. The response by the majority of the committee members was to reject the proposal on the grounds that this was their home, and they did not want it used by anyone else when they were not there. They argued that this was the only home the survivors had and why should they have to share it. Some recalled memories of how their homes were taken over and strangers came to live with them. They crowded them to suffocation, in what had formerly been their haven. Others argued from a different perspective, saying that if the Bosnians were able to use the HSC, Jewish Care would never agree to move them on. Whatever the argument, the vociferousness of their objection both touched and troubled me.

A long discussion with my consultant and advisor, John Bridgewater, helped me to see more clearly for myself the divergence of the two worlds. In my world, I had come from a land of plenty, a land of security, love and warmth. The sharing of my own home with strangers was not always easy, but it emanated first from the compassion my parents felt towards these displaced people and, later, it provided the economic means for my mother to be at home for my sister and myself in our formative years. Those who had gone through the Holocaust not only lost their home but their identity and their dignity. Sharing their home, therefore, meant something very different. The fear which sharing seemed to provoke in the current situation needed to be understood in the light of that reality.

The initial pain I felt at their responses to the Bosnians therefore moved towards a different conclusion. To ask the survivors to adopt my own view at that moment in time would have alienated me from them. It was in a sense my problem, not their problem. I had to resolve this conflict within myself in which my own sense of morality, based on my own life's experiences, did not coincide with a world in which morality had been seriously undermined.

The interpretation of the survivors' language of atrocity, the acceptance of the reality of their suffering, drew me ever closer to their trust. The decision to concede to their wishes was endorsed by John. He understood perfectly that the upset which would be caused by overriding their arguments may endanger the centre as a whole – a centre in which they come to find some peace of mind. These decisions, and many more, can be seen as markers along the road to moving the centres on.

Acceptance of the survivors' world does not mean I think in the same way. For example, I continue to fight for the rights of the Bosnian refugees. I enhance the possibilities for caring within the centres of one survivor towards another. However, what this example demonstrates is how I have learned to hold back; never imposing my own view; respecting the impact of the survivors' suffering while, at the same time, maintaining my sense of self and who I am. This has become the essence of trust, with the result that I, in turn, have been accepted by the survivors. This stage of the journey has only culminated recently. It was made explicit and verbal following my participation in the liberation commemoration. One survivor commented, 'You have come closer to us than any other person who has not gone through our experiences.'

The Camp Survivors Committee has invited me to sit with them during their meeting instead of remaining in my room in Shalvata. This could not have happened even a year ago. However, I do not rest with any sense of complacency. On the contrary, I feel we need to go beyond mingling our tears with theirs (Wiesel 1990d, p.172)[3] and use the empowerment that comes from their trust to act as a springboard for action in how we further strengthen the services now and for the future.

The empowerment of organisations

Time is of the essence as the survivors grow older. We have no time to waste through duplicating services with other organisations, or competing with them for precious funds. We have seen how the individual was threatened through his/her isolation in the death camps. The formation of groups was a survival strategy during the Holocaust, which became translated through the Holocaust centres into a collective identity.

In contrast, the history of the services for refugees and survivors has been parochial by nature. To maintain power and identity, the organisations working with survivors and refugees developed separately, and there was little communication among them about the needs of the communities they were serving.

Envy and rivalry are dangerous concepts in the strengthening of services for the survivors. Some years ago, I formulated a report which I submitted to Jewish Care recommending a shift towards joint projects with other organisations. I knew from my own experience about the positive effect of linking into a network outside of the parent organisation. I had strengthened my own position through worldwide connections which opened up the horizons of my work. However, trust needed to be built up for the organisations to move on.

The impetus for change was enhanced through external pressures which supported my earlier recommendation. The need to administer a Swiss humanitarian fund for Holocaust survivors brought many of the formerly separate organisations together around one table. The meetings were convened through the Board of Deputies, and the representatives faced each other in their common venture.

Some of those meetings were fraught but, as we met face to face, we began a dialogue which paved the way to new ways of working. On each occasion, I was accompanied by one of the survivor members of the Advisory Committee. In keeping with the commitment to a partnership approach with the survivors, I needed their voice to be present in the room. This survivor and I talked before the meeting and reflected afterwards on what had transpired. The dynamic of his presence, the content of his contributions, gave the meetings a reality.

The second impetus for development thrust itself upon the separate organisations that were independently making claims for funds to support their services. The claims were submitted to an organisation called the Claims Conference for Jewish Material Claims Against Germany, which distributes funds worldwide to assist programmes for services supporting ageing Holocaust survivors. It was revealed that Jewish Care (HSC) and the Association of Jewish Refugees (AJR) had submitted similar projects for consideration – namely their outreach work. The applications, we were told, would only be considered if they were joined together.

As a consequence, I began to meet with the Director of AJR and, ultimately, the application was successful. As a result, it allowed me to support AJR as the key organisation in outreach work. It thereby released funds which had previously been budgeted to pay for our own community outreach worker. The details of the scheme were fine-tuned through the representative from the Claims Conference. He insisted on my continued involvement regarding the needs of survivors, as AJR predominantly cared for refugees who came to England prior to the Holocaust. Shalvata would offer training and consultation for the outreach workers and thereby dovetail the respective expertise of the two organisations.

On a grass-roots level, AJR and the Jewish Refugee Committee (JRC, World Jewish Relief) became our partners, and more and more opportunities to share our work developed. The JRC have been important partners in the HSC, as well as in our work with the Bosnian refugees, which I would now like to detail.

The stress of working with severely traumatised people takes its toll. There are also the pressures of managing the services, the staff and the constant pressure of making decisions. When I begin to analyse the issues I deal with on a daily basis, I realise the weightiness that hangs upon my shoulders. A stream of sleepness nights could have been the outcome of meeting the high expectations I have of the service and myself. To support the load, I welcome opportunities to share with colleagues, and I would like to give an example of how that helps both those who work with trauma and those who have suffered the trauma.

My colleague from the JRC had been invited to the Bosnian Club to speak to the refugees about her recent official visit to Bosnia. I had also been asked to attend. I welcomed this opportunity to meet the group of refugees again in their setting, as well as hear about the current situation in Bosnia. My colleague had suggested we meet for a meal prior to our visit to the club, and I took the opportunity to talk to her in an informal environment. Over our meal, we discussed many issues related to our common work in helping these more recent refugees as well as the Holocaust survivors. We shared our concerns about finding a centre for the Bosnian refugees, about funding, about their citizenship issues, about our good feelings related to the successes within that community. Interspersed with these work-focused discussions were more personal issues that bind us as people, and make the task we have undertaken easier to carry.

We moved on to the meeting at the club. My colleague showed photographs she had taken in Sarajevo, and spoke about the places she had visited in the former Yugoslavia. I sat silently as she spoke. I looked at the photographs, and I looked at the sad expression on the faces of the people gathered in the room. My colleague finished her presentation by telling the group about the work of the JRC and invited me to talk about the work Jewish Care has undertaken with the Bosnian refugees. Like blotting paper, I was mopping up the unshed tears which abounded in the room. I felt nothing could express better how our two organisations dovetailed than through my question to this audience about what it meant to them to look at these photographs and to hear about the home they had left behind. The sadness, the loss, the longing expressed itself readily. They had made their life in the UK, but they would not forget where they had come from. This opened up the opportunity to talk about the idea of a 'home' for them, a centre where they would feel they belong, and where they could recreate something new after all they had lost.

My colleague was able to suggest practical ways of continuing to assist the refugees – for example, by hiring a lawyer to deal with their pension issues from Bosnia. Together our two organisations, which we represented, carried the responsibility of ensuring the needs of this group were addressed. Symbolically, a photograph taken of my colleague and myself with the group in the club captured the essence of our joint venture.

The key to this enhanced functioning of the organisations rests largely on regular dialogue and bonds which have been built up with colleagues. Sharing, working together and putting the services before ourselves have changed the pattern of the way we work. The trust and respect which have emerged then reflect back into our individual organisations.

Once this groundwork had been done, the next stage was to have one umbrella organisation in which we could look at how to make more public these informal grass-roots interconnections. A common brochure detailing the work of all the organisations involved with refugees and survivors was seen as a first step. *Into the Light* – the survivors' book which emerged after *Out of the Dark* – would also have been a fitting description for this new brochure. It seemed like a way forward from the more ad hoc arrangements which had disempowered the services as well as the survivors themselves. Further joint applications were submitted – for example, an emergency fund which would allow the different organisations to make payments directly to survivors in need.

Within this Umbrella Group, the managers of the organisations, as well as the directors and lay leaders, all meet together. The survivor who had accompanied me to the earlier meetings continues to perform this task. The next phase will be to develop strategies together. We pool our skills and expertise, assisting each other to move forward.

An outcome of this process brought me into an ultra-orthodox organisation which deals predominantly with Holocaust survivors. This organisation, which is part of the Umbrella Group, wanted to develop some therapeutic services for its survivors. I was asked by the Chairman of the Umbrella Group to ascertain the requirements for this work in the residential and sheltered housing projects that were being run by them. Though I was experienced in our own therapeutic services, the setting and the level of orthodoxy of this group differed to the work with which I am familiar. Despite this fact, a meeting with some of the survivors there revealed similarities in terms of their needs. A reworking of their submitted plan opened up therapeutic options to help these frailer survivors. In terms of the level of orthodoxy, I would appear to be secular in my outlook. Nevertheless, I was welcomed into this survivor group and was moved by their openness to accept me in my capacity as Director of Jewish Care's Holocaust services. Crossing into unfamiliar worlds, we realise that the differences which separate us are not as great as originally thought.

In the Umbrella Group, we talk together, we share refreshments together, we meet in each other's 'homes' (places of work), and we begin to come closer to a common language. I have noticed over time the greater tolerance when I speak, or when others express themselves. We have the potential to strengthen each other and to have a more powerful collective voice. The survival of our services I believe rests on this important cohesive dynamic. As a consequence of our dialogues, I invited a member from AJR and Otto Schiff Housing Association (OSHA) to attend discussions about the strategic planning of our services at the HSC. On a daily basis, we all touch the needs of those who have suffered during the Holocaust. Together we fight more effectively for the services to meet those needs. The parallels with the groups for survivors already referred to are clearly reflected.

The sharing and strengthening of the organisations described here could be applied much more widely in bringing to the forefront the issues of displaced and traumatised refugees and survivors. The benefits, in terms of accessing resources, of pooling expertise, of developing creative ideas, increase substantially when these frontiers are crossed. At a time when refugees and asylum seekers are receiving such bad press, we have an opportunity to speak up for their rights more powerfully. This can be done much more effectively when organisations concerned with these issues find ways of speaking together and working more closely together. The organisations for Holocaust survivors and refugees provide a hopeful message for the development of trauma services more generally.

Getting to know our 'neighbours' who also work with war trauma may begin to influence those for whom war trauma is an empty concept. Part V will develop this theme.

Fighting for justice: dealing with the claims

The organisations in the Umbrella Group all felt inadequate in dealing with the huge number of applications for compensation currently being processed. The former slave labourers had done the groundwork for their claims for compensation, but the administrative and organisational ramifications needed to be developed. Constant updating on information about the different claims needed centralising and co-ordinating. Survivors needed support and assistance with the arduous and sometimes harrowing task of processing their claims.

A central office for claims was funded by the Umbrella Group. The creation of this new post opened the floodgates for those who had been waiting for such help to be offered. In the world of trauma, therapeutic services cannot stand alone. The Umbrella Group brought together a cross-section of professional people who pooled their expertise. As we began looking for the right person to deal with claims for survivors, this raised different expectations among the professionals. The fact-finding orientation of the accountant may have chosen a particular type of applicant who would focus on the financial aspects of the claims. The lawyer may have wanted to focus more on advocacy. The therapeutic staff may have emphasised the emotional repercussions of making a claim.

In the event, the task of finding a suitable applicant was delegated to my colleague in the Association of Jewish Refugees and myself. Out of this melting pot of ideas, a person emerged to take on this daunting responsibility. Michael, who was appointed, learned about the specialised nature of his task. He gathered information and has become aware of action that needs to be taken on behalf of some of the claimants. The appointment of a lawyer as an assistant to Michael underscored the advocacy aspect of the job. The 'political' background of one of the workers, and the legal prosecution background of the other, combined to become a dynamic force for the survivors' sense of injustice to be heard.

The original notion of this claims work merely being an adjunct to the current services on offer to survivors began to take on a new momentum. Some of the members of the HSC who were former slave labourers were being drawn towards joining with a foundation in the USA to give strength to the issues that concerned them. Survivors were expressing the need to have a pressure group or lobby. These survivors wanted representation and the power to influence decisions about themselves. They were beginning to define themselves politically.

Frank, an Auschwitz survivor, sat on one chair in my room expressing these views. On the other chair sat Michael, who had become the counterpoint to Frank's arguments. Dealing with the claims highlighted a general need to become more active, more vocal and more 'political'. The survivors had the freedom to be political. However, I was under no illusion that the role I played in assisting the survivors needed careful thought. I had always been told that as a charity we could not be seen to be acting politically. However, I have come to believe that the politics of justice veers towards ethics and morality. Therefore politics defined in this way must be associated with the specialised work relating to the aftermath of atrocity. Our services have assisted in giving the survivors a collective identity and a voice. The survivors now seem ready to use it, as they have begun linking their issues of justice with the subject of the claims.

In turn, those associated with the injustices of the tortured, the humiliated, the victimised, in whatever setting and circumstance, must not ignore the political nature of their work. Special training, or specialised staff who are able to carry these issues and know how to respond, is an essential ingredient in the progress of the work. It helps us to make the shift from the bystander referred to earlier in the book to being an active participant in alerting others to the dangers of inactivity. It is a response that speaks directly to the world which has not touched trauma, and which imagines trauma will never affect it. Learning from the survivors of the Holocaust about how to respond to atrocity, we must heed them when they warn us about the consequences of not getting involved. This theme will be developed in Part V.

Life and death issues of the organisations

The organisations are moving with the survivors towards the interface with the outside world. As we prepare for this new challenge, we have to look at the dynamics of the infrastructure which will support this movement. Moving from the inside towards the outside is symbolised through the Umbrella Group. Moving from the darkness towards daylight, the umbrella shades us from the brightness of the light. We have been in transition from the world of death to the world of life as described throughout the book. In this process, some aspects of the organisation's functioning change. Do the tools we have used to develop our work continue to have the same usefulness a decade or more on? The survivors are ten years older. Their needs have changed. Many have talked and talked about their trauma. Many have recorded their testimonies and gone to schools to share their experiences. What remains is the time left to them: a time in which to maximise the positive life-giving experiences as long as they can, but also a time in which to adapt to their ageing bodies. So much was left unfinished for those who perished in the Holocaust. Those alive today have a chance to deal with the end of their lives differently.

As the reality of that end draws closer, those who work with these ageing survivors have to take an honest look at whether we maintain the status quo in relation to the services we have developed, or whether we rebalance the component parts to reflect the changes that are happening.

Let me look at this issue by focusing on the Shalvata/HSC model. Having developed Shalvata from its inception, having acknowledged the positive aspects of the range of therapeutic approaches in it, having fought for its continuation when it came under threat during the course of its life, I have clearly invested a great deal in its continuing existence. I have seen survivors start to 'live' again from the care and skill they have received from the highly trained and committed staff with whom I work. What is becoming clearer, however, is that fewer survivors are referring themselves to Shalvata. Does that mean that our work in Shalvata is coming to an end as we have known it in the past? Does it mean that the HSC is providing increasingly for survivors' needs and hence they do not need this additional service?

In analysing these questions through my regular contact with the survivors, it would seem that the most pressing needs relate to practical issues that are needed to help the members cope with ageing. More home visits are required. More assistance with home care, medical problems, financial and housing needs take precedence in their lives.

To meet these changing needs, the most recent appointment to the team has been a community-orientated social worker. The focus of this post will be to concentrate on the day-to-day difficulties that are compounded by the lack of personal support many of these traumatised people experience.

I have already mentioned how the staff in Shalvata have begun to interact increasingly with the survivors through the groups which take place in the HSC. As the survivors grow frailer, I believe that the staff in Shalvata will need to focus their work increasingly in the HSC. So much is revealed when I sit in the HSC. I see Susan, one of the members, having great difficulty with walking due to the severe pain in her knees. She talks to me of that physical pain, but also expresses her fears about the increasing limitation on her life imposed by her driving licence being taken from her. She would not come into Shalvata to shed the tears which her dependency triggers in her.

I do not believe in change for change's sake, but if Shalvata is not being used sufficiently, and if the strain on the HSC staff increases due to the needs of the members, then we have to think creatively about how to accommodate this factor. Our budget dictates the limits of intransigence. The space in Shalvata for the dark shadow to be expressed must continue to be an option, but the amount of space may need to be adjusted. To include wheelchairs in the HSC may necessitate knocking down another wall which interfaces with Shalvata. The need to take time out to discuss these pressing matters with the staff has been increasing. The model must always remain flexible and adaptable to facilitate its survival. Its *raison d'être* is to meet the needs of those who use it. Any therapeutic model which does not keep this concept as a primary focus will die from its lack of use to the people it is intended to serve.

However, death ultimately cannot be averted. There will be an end to the work as we know it now, even though it may take some twenty more years. The last stage of my working life is present in my mind as I reach the closing part of this book. There is still one more aspect of the work I need to undertake which will continue after all the survivors have died, and my own contribution has ceased. It stems from the survivors' concerns about the legacy for the future, and my own concern that all they have taught me will not be lost.

Preparing a legacy: a place of learning about the Shoah

So much has been learned from the survivors: so much to pass on, so much to reflect upon. To keep that solely to myself would not do justice to the depth of my learning, or the generosity of spirit which the survivors have shown me as we came to know each other better. I have witnessed the suffering of these severely traumatised people as they grow older. I have been privileged to develop with them meaningful ways of living differently with their trauma. I have been fortunate to have found the capacity within myself to record what has transpired in my work with the survivors, which in turn shapes the way I respond to the trauma of others who suffer.

Before moving on to the final part of the book and the application of what has been learned to other experiences, I would like to look at the ways of documenting the uniqueness of what the survivors teach us. For the learning to remain as a legacy for the future, it needs its own place, it needs its own home and its own identity. I believe the word Shoah must exist in its description, for that word exemplifies what was particular about the Jewish experience of the Nazi Holocaust.

I have tried over the years to combine the practical aspect of the work with teaching, consultation and publicising this specialised subject through papers and contributions to various bodies. People have visited our centres and learned about how we work. At international conferences I have been invited to have a platform to share the particularness of the response to the trauma of Shoah survivors. These ad hoc arrangements were excellent preparation for me to conceptualise the thinking about the work, but these opportunities had to be fitted into the overall responsibilities which my job has entailed.

I believe the time has come to focus more directly on this aspect of my task. A separate part of the organisation devoted to sharing what has been learned would help to consolidate our position in the field of war trauma. As a working title, I will call it the Shoah Institute, though I have concerns that the institute should not become institutionalised. It would be a place of learning, but not an academic environment. It would not only be a place for imparting knowledge but also of receiving and developing new ideas about dealing with war trauma.

The publication of this book will, I hope, serve as an introduction to this new development. It could not have been written in the particular way it has evolved without my being in daily contact with the survivors. The life-force which has fed the contents of the book described herein would be the blueprint for the style and content of the Shoah Institute. Let me now analyse some of the possible component parts of the proposed Shoah Institute in order to indicate what it may contain.

RESEARCH

Almost every day I am contacted by students researching the subject of the Holocaust, or media researchers looking for a programme to develop. I vet the bona fide status of the researchers and also the content of their proposed research. Exploitation of the survivors' experiences has to be carefully guarded against. There are some survivors who wish to share their experiences, and we have assisted in this process.

However, research has not been a feature in our work at the centres for survivors. External research is a matter of choice for the survivors, but research with people who come to the centres for a different purpose could be confusing. When asked if I had undertaken research for my book, my answer has been that twenty-five years of listening to survivors and working with them has provided the necessary background information. This is different to systematic research. I have always been at pains to create an environment in which the survivors would feel relaxed and at home. To become academic researchers in this environment may have threatened the trust which needed to be developed.

Nevertheless, the Shoah Institute may provide a way of looking at patterns and details which may enhance our understanding of severe trauma and how people cope with it. As a separate entity, the Shoah Institute may convey a sense that survivors are not being compromised if they choose to participate in helping us to learn lessons for the future. I believe that research as an end in itself would not fit the aims of the Shoah Institute. However, research as a living testimony of the trauma may assist both the survivors and ourselves in terms of a legacy for the future.

PUBLICATIONS

At training sessions and at conferences, people often ask me for written papers which will help them to think about the work they are doing. Jewish Care's Executive Director many years ago encouraged me to present an article for *Community Care* about my work with Holocaust survivors, and I thank him for his belief in me. That first published paper laid the foundation for a lifetime's devotion to the written word. It has helped me enormously to think. If I did not write, then all that I have learned, all that I have witnessed, would not be recorded, and would be lost with the passage of time.

When Elie Wiesel (1990f) asks the question 'Why do I write?' he replies, 'To wrest those victims from oblivion. To help the dead vanquish death'[3] (p.21). The gift he has – to express the inexpressible – is perhaps only within a survivor's remit. My task is different and less noble, but nevertheless important in passing on to others what I have learned. My publications contain hope. They are a record of the progression from naivety to a greater openness to develop new and creative responses in how we work with trauma.

Many academics regard publications as an essential part of one's professional status. I find no relevance for myself in such statements. If the writing of a paper encourages us to read, focuses our thoughts, helps us communicate in language which can be understood rather than hidden in jargon, then the exercise will prove to be worthwhile.

I believe the Shoah Institute should collect together papers which have emerged from our particular work. I believe we should organise seminars and conferences to bring the outside world into our remit. I believe we should join together with others struggling to make the work with trauma intelligible. Publications bring honour to those who have helped us understand a little better the meaning of their severe suffering and how we may be able to help. These publications will also be the memorials for the future about how two worlds have drawn closer together.

TRAINING AND CONSULTATION

Preparing for a training session takes time, imagination and effort to master the technology that has overtaken the presentation. Training in another country demands the additional dimension of interpreters, or attempts to speak in another tongue with which I may be only vaguely familiar. My work has taken me to Israel, Sweden, Holland, Germany, France, Hungary and Slovakia, to name but a few countries.

On the many occasions both here and abroad when I have undertaken this task, I have felt an immense sense of satisfaction at passing the message on about how to work with survivors. I get a feeling which perhaps reflects the survivors' description about the times they speak to groups of children or adults. That moment in which the 'language' one is speaking is understood and taken in by the listeners is unique. When the groups I have spoken to tell me that they can identify and use the ideas and practical manifestations in their work, it inspires me to continue to make these journeys.

I would like to detail one particular training/consultation session which I was asked to undertake in a mental health residential unit within the private sector in London. This was not a Jewish setting, but the person they wished to discuss was a Holocaust refugee. There were about twelve participants who came together with their manager to share their concerns about this man. I gave an introductory talk, which laid the foundation for its application to working with this person. The group focused on the behavioural problems they experienced with him, and wanted to understand how this might link to his Holocaust background.

The refugee they described had been a teenage boy in Austria, forced to leave on the Kindertransport after the Nazi annexation of Austria (the Anschluss in 1938). All his family, apart from his sister, was murdered by the Nazis. He came to the UK but remained isolated and depressed, unable to deal with his past or his present. He had now reached the age of seventy-eight years, having been institutionalised in mental health units for most of his life. He had been locked into this trauma which had never been addressed.

The staff recounted the numerous times he had categorically refused to help them and the residents to clean the unit. As they spoke about their frustration, images of Austrian Jews forced to scrub the streets in Vienna as a means of humiliation by the Nazis came clearly to my mind. Sharing this background and perspective opened up the issue of the intransigence of his resistance, as well as the staff's frustration with him. Even though the manager of the unit required the man's co-operation, I believed that greater sensitivity to the reality of the refugee's persecution could open a door which may help this resident to feel that someone had heard his cry. The staff's attention was drawn to the particularity of the trauma for this man. At the beginning of the meeting, they had felt that he was similar to many of the other residents in terms of his behaviour. It is true that many who found their way into this mental health arena had gone through traumas of their own. Coincidentally, or perhaps not, my meeting that day fell on Yom HaShoah (the Jewish Holocaust Memorial Day). It seemed appropriate for this refugee's voice to be heard, both for himself, and for his murdered family who could not speak. My presence there that day allowed that event to happen.

I helped the staff to convert their sense of helplessness in relation to this person into concrete action, and encouraged them to listen to him and to learn from him. That action included opening the door to hear about his experience, and asking questions which would help them to understand him better. I also believed they could help him to prepare for the last part of his life and his death. Helping him to record his testimony, linking him in to our centres, finding out about his creative abilities, addressing the ritual related to his family's 'burial' and focusing on his identity as a Jew were but a few of the possibilities with which they could work.

A bridge was also being built between the staff and myself. In the short time we had together, they wanted answers, and they wanted solutions for their frustrations with this man. By the end of the meeting, they realised they were still at the beginning. They asked for more sessions to test out and develop the thoughts which were germinating.

As we work against time to reach out to survivors before they die, these front-line workers, who care enough to come together to focus on this one person, give us hope. In opening themselves up to the suffering, they are touched by events with which they have no personal connection. It is a very different experience to visiting a museum or reading a book about the horrors of what happened. In personalising it to one man's experience of trauma, they begin to address issues in themselves. They could so easily have labelled this man as 'hard to reach' or 'mentally ill'. Instead, they put themselves in the house next door to trauma. They are affected by him and, as a result, they respond differently. They are no longer bystanders.

Though my focus had been to impart to these workers how to respond to this person's suffering, they were also teaching me about the importance of using the particular to understand other worlds – the space which is inhabited by our neighbours who may also be suffering.

While the uniqueness of the Shoah is contained within the walls of the HSC and Shalvata, the Shoah Institute has the potential to bridge two more worlds at its interface with others who have experienced extreme trauma. This training/consultation session exemplified the possibility of maintaining the unique nature of the suffering of the Shoah in helping others to understand its lessons. Nothing would detract me from my primary responsibility towards the survivors of the Shoah. However, the fear that the uniqueness of that experience would be lost if other genocides are addressed needs to be examined rather than discarded. The Shoah Institute could pave the way towards thinking further about how we ensure that the legacy left by the survivors of the Nazi Holocaust remains current and alive when they have ceased to exist.

Endnotes

1. Jewish slave labourers were among those forced to make munitions and other goods including German army uniforms. Many were treated as though they were totally expendable – their lives were unimportant. They were beaten and subjected to starvation rations and extremely severe working conditions. Survival rates were low; once dead they were replaced by new prisoners. The largest slave labour group was around Auschwitz. The Jews not selected for the gas chambers were sent to arms factories, coal mines and the synthetic rubber and oil production plant such as the one at Buna.

2. 'The Windows Shuddered' (1978) by Cesar Vallejo is reprinted by kind permission of University of California Press.

3. *From the Kingdom of Memory*, by Elie Wiesel. Copyright © 1990 by Elirion Associates, Inc. Reprinted by permission of Georges Borchardt, Inc., for the author. Permission to reprint is also granted by Sheil Land Associates Ltd, London.

PART V

A House Next Door to Trauma

Particular and Universal Dimensions

Introduction

Addressing the particular and the universal in relation to trauma

In November 1987, Elie Wiesel addressed the German Reichstag as follows:

> Thus, in remembering them [those murdered in the Shoah], we remember today's victims too. We remember our hunger so as to eliminate starvation. We remember our anguish so as to proclaim the right of men and women everywhere to live without fear. We remember our death, so as to denounce the insanity of violence and the absurdity, the ugliness, the shame of war. (1990e, p.200)[1]

The identification with other people's suffering is sometimes confused with the comparison of suffering, and universal statements about the similarities of genocide. For those who have been subjected to extreme and prolonged suffering, it is sometimes difficult for them to go beyond the boundaries of their specific experience and embrace others whose human rights are being violated. As we have already seen, it is perhaps the primary duty of the witnesses of atrocity to ensure that the particularness of that experience is preserved for posterity.

Elie Wiesel never forgets the uniqueness of the Nazi horror but, at the same time, guides our thinking towards a world in which suffering goes on next to us. He writes about his participation in the march for the survival of Cambodia and the dilemma he faced when he realised the event coincided with the anniversary of his father's death in the Holocaust. 'As a Jew I felt the need to tell these despairing men and women that we understood them; that we shared their pain; that we understood their distress because we remembered a time when we as Jews confronted total indifference.' However, in memory of his father and others murdered in the Holocaust, he is careful to add that, 'of course there is no comparison. The event which left its mark on my generation defies analogy' (1990b, pp.132–133).[1]

The fear of being misunderstood by those who suffered systematic murder and annihilation under the Nazi regime inhibits our responses to other traumas. For those of us who work with these survivors on a daily basis, who unlike Elie Wiesel are not survivors ourselves, we walk an even finer line between the particular and the universal aspects of suffering.

In the process of confronting this closing chapter of the book, I reread Terence Des Pres's book *The Survivor – An Anatomy of Life in the Death Camps* (1976), as well as a small book *Rescue in Albania* (Samer 1997), which focuses on the Jews in Albania during the Holocaust. Des Pres's book is a constant and necessary reminder of the horror of day-to-day life in the death camps. He includes the appalling witness account in Neumark concentration camp for women in the winter of 1944.

> It was hard to believe the women on the ground were still human beings. Their rigid bodies were skeletons, their eyes were glazed from long starva-tion… The meagre bundles of straw on which they lay were putrid from their urine and excreta. Their frozen limbs were fetid and covered with wounds and bites to the point of bleeding, and countless lice rested in the pus. Their hair was very short indeed, but the armies of lice found a home in it. No stretch of the imagination, no power of the written word, can convey the horror of that tent. (Des Pres 1976, p.45)

That was life in extremity. A life abandoned by the outside world. A world which remained silent, even though more and more evidence reveals there was knowledge of the fate of the sufferers. Indifference, inactivity, standing by and doing nothing endorse the oppressors' philosophy.

In contrast was the experience of Jews in Albania (Samer 1997), one hundred per cent of whom survived the German occupation. Indeed, there were more Jews in Albania after the war than before. Jews who escaped from Greece and other countries were protected in the same way as the indigenous Jews. They were welcomed into this predominantly Moslem country as 'guests', with whom they shared their bread and their homes. The moral code of the Albanians positively guided their responses and thereby vastly affected the lives of those in danger of deportation and death.

What lessons do we learn from these two contrasting situations? The population in Albania and other countries such as Bulgaria, Finland and Denmark give us hope against the inevitability of man's destructiveness and violence. Speaking up, speaking out, being active belong to the realm of the living. 'Silence constitutes the realm of the dead' (Des Pres 1976, p.36).

The combined effect of reading these two very different accounts of life under totalitarianism invites us not to ignore the suffering of those around us. In the war in Kosovo, the Kosovan Albanians were themselves on the receiving end of violence and war trauma. A child survivor of the Holocaust who became a democratic congressman in the USA spoke at the hearing of the House Committee on International Relations in March 1998: 'We have a moral obligation to identify with the people of Kosova. They have been persecuted, discriminated against and killed by a police state. Kosovar Albanians have suffered enough' (Cloyes 1998). Staying on the edge, not getting involved, 'Presiding over Genocide' (1998), as Shirley Cloyes called it (Balkans affairs adviser to the Albanian American Civic League), does not protect those who are at the mercy of others' cruelty. It is not 'their' trauma; it is our trauma. Even though these different wars may not be close to home, in today's world, everything is close by; everything has the potential to touch us.

Trauma knows no boundaries

If Auschwitz had been in Hampshire
There would have been Englishmen to guard it
To administer records
Marshall transports
Work the gas ovens
And keep silent
The smoke would have drifted over these green hills.

...And the smoke will drift over these green hills
Our culture makes us barbarians
It does not allow us to live humanely
We must create a new culture
Or cease to be human.

(Edward Bond's poem 'If' [2]*)*

Bond's poem poses the right question when he asks us to consider the possibility of a death camp on our doorstep. He cautions us not to be complacent, and to guard against the notion that such extreme bestiality has no part in our civilised, cultured society. How would we have behaved; how would we have responded if the Germans had invaded the UK? Watching the TV reports on the desecration of cemeteries, listening to the venomous outpourings against the Asian community in England's northern towns, in today's world, reminds me that very little space separates us from earlier times.

Moving from the particular to the universal necessitates broadening our thinking about our proximity to other suffering. Trauma exists around us all the time. To be touched by it, we have to open ourselves up to its presence. In our therapeutic settings we need to allow the impact of the world around us to penetrate the walls that protect us. Our therapeutic work can become a microcosm for change. In this sense, the therapeutic task may be more than helping the oppressed live with the injustices they suffer or have suffered. It may also be involved in confronting injustice more directly.

The concluding sentence in *Rethinking the Trauma of War* emphasises this point. 'This is a plea not for therapy, but for justice. It is a plea which the international community, UN agencies and non-governmental organisations may well ignore, but at an enormous cost' (Bracken and Petty 1998, p.192). I believe the therapeutic task may encompass both listening and responding, supporting and empowering, as well as helping the traumatised fight for justice.

Living side by side with the survivors of extreme atrocity is like living in a house next door to their trauma. The walls are too thin not to hear the echoes of that other world, and some of us are compelled to respond to what we hear. Those who do so cannot close their ears to that suffering, and when the door to their world is opened, it changes us.

The aftermath of working with survivors of the Holocaust has alerted me to others who suffer. War trauma knows no boundaries; we cross frontiers, we cross continents, and the chaos and devastation in the wake of extreme violence becomes a universal phenomenon.

The lessons learned from Holocaust survivors about how to respond to atrocity have taken me on another journey which had not been envisaged when my original journey began. It has drawn me towards other experiences of war trauma. The work with Bosnian refugees has been like a testing ground for the usefulness of the therapeutic responses gleaned from the Holocaust survivors. It has given me the courage to begin to explore the aftermath of other war trauma as related to Rwandan refugees. The following illustrations of my involvement with these two examples will emphasise how the difference between the respective experiences of war trauma are taken into account while, at the same time, incorporating the essence of the teaching taken from Holocaust survivors. The adaptation of one to the other widens the scope of our understanding about war trauma and how we can respond to its aftermath.

Endnotes

1. *From the Kingdom of Memory,* by Elie Wiesel. Copyright © 1990 by Elirion Associates, Inc. Reprinted by permission of Georges Borchardt, Inc., for the author. Permission to reprint is also granted by Sheil Land Associates Ltd, London.

2. 'If', *Plays 4,* (1995) by Edward Bond is reprinted by kind permission of Methuen Publishing Limited.

Chapter 12

Like a Mother with her Second Child

Work with Recent Refugees from War Trauma

Working with a group of Bosnian refugees

In 1992, as the bombs were falling on Sarajevo, the Holocaust Survivor Centre opened its doors to welcome in the survivors and refugees from a war that ended almost half a century earlier. What I learned from the severely traumatised survivors from the Holocaust would guide me into making responses to a group of Bosnian refugees who fled from their homeland to save their lives.

Throughout this book, I have interwoven illustrations of the parallel thinking in terms of the therapeutic responses which emerged between these two very different experiences of war trauma. I would now like to look in more detail at the development of the work with these Bosnian refugees, linking it to the lessons learned from working with Holocaust survivors. I will focus on how the model has been adapted to their particular needs, and how we may begin to influence policy decisions on the issues that relate to asylum seekers and refugees more generally who come to the UK. The naivety which abounded in my early work with the survivors and refugees from the Nazi Holocaust has, over the past twenty-five years, given way to more informed understanding of severe trauma and how to make our therapeutic responses more meaningful. Like a mother with her second child, there is more confidence, based on experience gained over the years of trial and error, and the observations of how the services have thrived. Yet each child is different and individual, and so to some extent I needed to return to the beginning, and get to know these newly arrived refugees.

I was not involved in the early stages of the Bosnian refugees' reception into the UK. This group, numbering about one hundred and twenty refugees, was assisted in practical ways by the Jewish Refugee Committee (JRC). They were initially housed in north-west London in the 'Jews' Temporary Shelter' until council accommodation could be found. The JRC was active in negotiating help with benefits, general financial issues, housing and obtaining English lessons. Their commitment to help was exemplary. Negotiations with the Home Office over asylum issues and the appointment of an immigration lawyer experienced in these issues to speak on the refugees' behalf were major contributory factors in giving the refugees a sense that they were cared about. They were shielded from some of the difficulties relating to the entry of refugees into a new environment. The appointment of Branko, a refugee from the former Yugoslavia, as the community worker assisted in overcoming some of the language and communication problems. The staff at the JRC got to know the individual families, and helped to reunite members of these families who may have been left behind in Bosnia. The refugees received an empathetic and sensitive response to their displacement and trauma. The reception of the refugees played a very important part in all the subsequent work which followed. Accounts of how other refugees are received, the racism they encounter and the bureaucracy that they have to face tell a different story, which I believe profoundly affects their integration. However, even the JRC could not provide for all the needs of the Bosnian refugees, which continued into the next phase of their integration.

My partnership with the JRC and their generous support for the work in the HSC made it natural for them to use my experience in the continuing work with the Bosnian group. Branko began to have meetings with myself and my line manager at Jewish Care to familiarise us with the issues these refugees were facing. My own immediate response was to encourage Branko to transfer from the JRC to Shalvata. Shalvata symbolically represented a 'home' in which the ongoing effects of war trauma could be addressed and responded to.

I had lived so long next door to the trauma of the Holocaust survivors that I was highly tuned to respond actively to the sounds of these more recently traumatised refugees. Just as my own home had been a sanctuary for refugees in the memories of my childhood, so I felt Shalvata should open its doors to welcome in the Bosnian refugees.

I saw this new development as an opportunity rather than a burden. It seemed right that my years of struggling with the Holocaust survivors to find ways of living with their trauma could now be of use to help these uprooted refugees. There was so much to offer, so much richness and depth which could be drawn upon in reaching out to this new group. However, Branko's transfer would involve Jewish Care in the payment of his salary. The JRC would continue to pay all other costs related to the refugees, and that seemed a reasonable combination. Despite the urgency, despite the validity, questions were still being asked about whether Shalvata should get involved. I argued that when bombs are falling, they do not discriminate between Jew and Moslem – death is a danger to all. A humane response resulted, and I thought of those whose lives had not been saved prior to World War II, and who could perhaps have been, if Shalvata had existed then.

Branko was given an office space amid the multidisciplinary therapeutic team. Branko, an architect by profession, was learning how to help members of his community to adapt to their new life. I met with him regularly and I remember having pen and paper in hand as he began to teach me about this group of people with whom I was not familiar. I knew nothing about the world they had come from. Even their names were difficult to grasp. Branko clarified for me the fact that these refugees had not been persecuted as Jews in this war, that they were largely inter-married with Moslems; that many had lived under a Communist regime; and some of the elderly had been victims of the Nazi era. The complex politics of the war needed to be understood, as did how Serbs and Croats could be accommodated to live side by side in this new community. I had to be aware of Branko's own background, as this could influence his inaccessibility to certain members of the group.

I learned about life in Sarajevo, and the Judaeo-Spanish (Sephardi) tradition of the Jewish community. I learned about the range of professional skills in their community, as well as the cultural heritage the refugees brought with them. I needed to understand the context from which they had emerged and the particularness of their traumatic experience. I knew from my work with the Holocaust survivors that I could make no assumptions about their experiences, but needed to listen very carefully to what may help them.

Placing Branko in Shalvata was strategically important. I needed to get closer to others from the group to begin to reach out to them more directly, and not only through Branko. Members of the community would come to see Branko for a variety of reasons. Sometimes they came to participate in the committees which were set up to develop the club or their newsletter, *Salon*. I also began to be invited to some of the events at the club, and informally made contact with many more. My experience with the SOS group, in laying the foundation for the therapeutic work to begin, had direct relevance in this situation as well.

The majority of the refugees were not coming to Shalvata for therapy or to talk about their traumatic experiences. Shalvata became a safe and familiar place to meet. Making a cup of tea in the reception area allowed a few words to be exchanged, and a smile and a handshake to make a connection. The non-clinical setting of Shalvata allowed it to have a different purpose for these refugees. A very small number did ask to see a member of the therapeutic team in Shalvata to help them with their emotional problems, but mostly they were concerned with finding work, retraining in their professions, ensuring their children's education, and other practical problems that related to the continuing adaptation to their new homeland.

Shalvata was therefore adapted to the needs of these refugees. From being a therapy centre it became an informal meeting place and information centre. In the world of war trauma these different approaches can co-exist. The beauty of Shalvata is in its flexibility to adapt to the needs of each group. I learned from the Holocaust survivors to focus on the strengths which the refugees brought into their new community, and it was from that premise that I started to build.

Branko reminded me of the primary importance of employment as a therapeutic response to trauma. A programme was started involving refugees as volunteers in Jewish Care in a variety of departments from training to accountancy. They shadowed employees, and some were later offered jobs as a result of this programme. An outcome of this programme also meant that the refugees became known to Jewish Care as capable employees, and this resulted in a slight shift in attitude towards these outsiders.

Their refugee status, which gave them exceptional leave to remain, meant that they could work, and they needed it to give form to their lives. The structure of time at work gave a sense of 'normality' once more. Some needed more help with preparing CVs due to language problems. Jewish Care's Employment Resource Centre began to run groups specially to help the refugees. Doctors, architects and other professionals needed to retrain in order to get work. Some, already in middle age, lacked the motivation to do so, and some took on menial work to earn an income. Some were left with a great deal of time on their hands compared to life before the war. Tensions at home and low morale, due to a drop in status and income, were danger signals in terms of their emotional adaptation. This needed to be taken into account in our responses.

Attempts to connect families to those from the host community proved difficult. The elderly were particularly vulnerable to isolation following their dislocation. Remembering Jean Amery's (1999) words mentioned earlier in this book about the problems of ageing in exile, we gathered the elderly members together into a group which began meeting at Shalvata. They can speak together in their mother tongue, they eat lunch together prepared in the HSC café and they enjoy painting classes with the art therapist from Shalvata, or listening to speakers, for example, on issues that relate to their health. In addition, Branko and one of the therapeutic staff in Shalvata take the group to museums and other places of interest and help them negotiate their way around this large city of London. They enjoy being together and have continued to attend the group regularly. Giving these elderly refugees their own place in Shalvata speaks clearly to them that they have not been forgotten. Conveying this in a language which they understand gives them a sense that their trauma is being recognised.

Branko became more and more the advocate for the members of the group, accompanying them on visits to hospitals, housing departments, the Home Office, the Department of Social Security (DSS) and other institutional bodies. He could act as their interpreter, as well as being a support to them. We would discuss the details of these interventions, and I could help him to develop a strategy which would reach the intended result. I have heard Branko challenging hospital authorities over treatment plans for some of the refugees. Turning to someone who may not understand their English would have increased the sense of vulnerability and powerlessness of the refugees. The importance of a designated person to liaise directly with the members of the community cannot be overstated. None of my therapeutic staff in Shalvata could have provided that essential ingredient needed to develop this service for the Bosnian refugees.

One of the most powerful messages that we hear from the Holocaust survivors, which has resonated throughout this book, is how their traumatic experience rendered them 'outsiders' to the community at large. The world of war trauma impacts on those who experience it and separates them from those who have been unaffected. How to make outsiders feel like insiders, how to create possibilities for these refugees to feel they belong, needed therapeutic responses which would address these vital issues.

If I were to summarise the underlying process in helping traumatised refugees adapt to their new environment, I would say that it has more to do with integration than assimilation. Assimilation would render the refugees indistinguishable from the rest of society. It would annihilate the difference in culture which has given them their identity. Enforced assimilation, the dispersal of refugees all over the country, ignores the healing effect which emanates from the slow and gradual shift between the world they have come from and the unfamiliar world they now find themselves in. These refugees are not here by choice. They are here because their lives were endangered by the war. If there had been no war, they would have continued to remain in their homeland. This group of Bosnian refugees has been housed in relatively close proximity, which gave us the opportunity to establish the club, The Friends of 'La Benevolencija', which has already been referred to. The once-a-week club was a beginning which allowed us to lay the foundation for a centre, in a similar way to the development of the HSC from the SOS group.

I had listened to the Holocaust survivors' wish to be with others who had suffered, where they would be accepted and not have to talk about their suffering. They had recreated a community which had been lost in the Holocaust and this new 'home' gave them an identity and a voice. The Bosnian club had served a similar purpose. In that oasis on a Wednesday evening, they could speak in their mother tongue, and eat food which was familiar to them. In that space, they could share information about issues that affected them, support each other and feel some sense of continuity between their former lives and their current ones.

The realisation that they had very little to return to when the war ended highlighted the fact that the difficulties they experienced would continue to be part of their lives. The losses they had faced in their uprooting needed to be catered for in a more permanent centre than the club. They had nowhere concrete to put down roots, as the club was used by other groups. They had nowhere to hang the art work which emanated from the artists among the refugees. There was nowhere to store food and belongings which would be safe from other users of the club premises. In the club they continued to feel like refugees.

Together with Branko, I consulted with the group about their wish to move to a more permanent centre which they could use on a daily basis. The therapeutic idea behind it would be the involvement of the members' skills in converting an 'empty space' into a 'home'. Throughout the following description relating to the centre for these Bosnian refugees, the vocabulary used will echo the language and ideas we have associated with our therapeutic work with Holocaust survivors. In designing this new centre, there are architects who can help with design and layout; there are engineers and electricians who can help to renovate it; there are artists who can paint the walls and design the décor. This idea met with great enthusiasm, and a committee was appointed to steer it forward. Once more, my colleague from the JRC joined me to give voice to this new concept in order to release funds from Jewish Care as well as from her organisation. The new venture was seen as a partnership between the refugees and the funding bodies.

It would have been very easy merely to maintain the club with a view to phasing it out once the refugees had been settled. There were few overt signs of emotional problems among the refugees and most of the practical issues had been attended to. However, I had learned that the suffering that accompanies adjustment after war trauma and displacement can be easily overlooked. Branko, within the structure of Shalvata's framework, helps to ensure there is no complacency about the 'success' of the refugees' adaptation. We know from the Holocaust survivors that their apparent adaptation to life after the Holocaust merely masked the trauma they continued to carry, which then resurfaced in later life. By remembering the long-term effects of trauma, we became more vigilant in responding more immediately to the sometimes hidden voices of the refugees.

If the trauma cannot be dealt with directly through talking about it, then we needed to offer different choices which would speak more meaningfully to the refugees. The new community centre for the Bosnian refugees would be a place in which the participants could gain strength from each other without having to ask for help from a professional. It would offer a link between the past and the present. Memories can find a resting place in a centre. Without a centre, those displaced by war may cling together for fear of being lost through dispersal. A centre is a safety feature in an unsafe and alien world. Knowing it is there gives a sense of confidence that it can be returned to. There is less fear of being victimised again.

Without a centre, the isolation among refugees makes dissemination of information or practical help that may be available much more difficult. Without this means of containing anxieties about benefits, asylum issues, about family left behind in the war, problems are more likely to erupt and overwhelm both the refugees themselves and those trying to help them. In contrast, self-advocacy can emerge from the combined knowledge contained among the members.

It is intended that the recreational content of the programme will foster creative outlets for talents already present, as well as encouraging new ones to develop. Like the club, the centre will have a kitchen in which the established cookery competitions already in operation in the club can be developed. There are writers, artists, actors and other talented members who can help others in the group develop their own abilities. Recognising these 'artists in exile' gives status to the group and links them to other refugees. The programme, like that in the HSC, will offer respite from the trauma they face in their everyday lives. The centre emerges from consulting with the members as to what is meaningful for them in adapting to their new situation. A centre will allow them to play host to non-refugee guests, and begin to form a bridge with the outside world.

Having a building, as we have seen in the HSC, makes it easier to attract media attention and sources of funding. The Bosnian group have already organised concerts and art exhibitions to raise funds for their community. A building gives status and dignity to the people who use it. To have a building and resources gives a sense that you are worth something, and you are worth investing in. It restores self-respect to those who have undergone drastic changes in their circumstances.

The aim is for the centre to foster independence rather than dependence. The strengthening which emerges from the refugees being together will, it is hoped, empower them and give them a stronger voice to express their needs.

It may be possible that through having their identity confirmed, the refugee label will gradually be left behind.

Clearly the investment needed in such a project is a major consideration, but the pay-off in terms of preventing the long-term impact of the trauma as the refugees grow older would argue in its favour. Thinking about a project of this kind changes the therapeutic language in how we respond to atrocity. With a keepsake from their old life, a new life can be regenerated.

I would like to include here some statistical information which reflects interesting developments in the process of integrating the refugees (see Table 12.1). Such information has been useful as evidence in making the case for investment. It translates the therapeutic outcomes of the work into a language which organisations can understand – namely, facts and figures. In advocating the services for refugees, we have to be able to transmit the message in this format to non-therapeutic staff. Once established, this centre for Bosnian refugees may become a flagship for other refugees and asylum seekers whose war trauma is compounded by insensitive responses to the trauma they have suffered. This new centre is needed now, but it may not be needed in ten years' time. We must be guided by the participants into their own future.

It is important to note that the therapeutic model for the Bosnian refugees has not evolved in exactly the same way as the Shalvata/HSC model for the Holocaust survivors. While the physical layout of the model is not the same for the two experiences of war trauma, the philosophy and conceptual thinking behind the services are similar. The model must always remain flexible and adaptable as we have already noted in Part IV. Not forcing an identical model onto these more recent Bosnian refugees has allowed more appropriate responses to their needs.

In analysing this, we see that both models emerged from mutual support groups. However, the newly arrived Bosnian refugees tended to focus on their practical issues rather than the emotional repercussions of their trauma. In the initial stages of our work, the role of Branko as advocate and community worker in helping with the pressing needs of interpretation superseded any wish to talk about their trauma. Shalvata's specialist team therefore did not need to be housed next to the club. In contrast, the Holocaust survivors, who were already established here for many years, needed to have an opportunity to address the unfinished emotional repercussions of their trauma. Hence

Shalvata's proximity was crucial to the therapeutic options which needed to be offered.

Table 12.1 Statistics on the Bosnian refugees at Shalvata, 2002			
Total number now in the community		109	100%
Employment	Part time	13	12%
	Full time	29	27%
	Self-employed	4	3%
		46	42%
Not working	Employable	14	13%
	Elderly	20	18%
	Disabled	5	5%
		39	36%
Education	Pre-school	3	3%
	School	14	13%
	University	3	3%
	Post-graduation	4	3%
		24	22%

Out of the total of 109:
57% have a university or higher qualification
23% have A-level standard

With the passage of time, and after many years of talking and recording their testimonies, survivors of the Holocaust are now focusing more on their practical problems as they grow older. Fewer are referring themselves to Shalvata. Conversely, the Bosnian refugees, whom we have come to know informally and through the practical help which has been offered, now sometimes wish to speak to a member of the Shalvata team. There was never any pressure on them to do so, only an awareness that any could choose to do so if they wished.

One of the refugees asked to see me. I would now like to detail this encounter. I will illustrate, by the way I work with her, how my responses are linked to the lessons I have learned from Chava, Irena and others.

Listening to a Bosnian refugee

Background

Hannah is a woman in her forties. She had worked as a doctor in Sarajevo and had reached a prominent position in her career. She was married and had one daughter. She had been used to a good standard of living, and had enjoyed entertaining and going out with family and friends. Her position and her salary allowed her to dress well, and she loved socialising and enjoying cultural activities. Hannah was integrated into the Jewish community in Sarajevo, but was not born a Jew. Like many of the families, religion did not play an important part in her life and did not define her identity. Contact with her parents and care for their well-being was very much part of the life of Sarajevo. After her mother's death, Hannah remained close to her father, and he joined them in the UK and continued to live nearby.

I had seen Hannah in Shalvata on her numerous visits to meet Branko and to participate in the newsletter committee, of which she was a member. She had always struck me as an energetic, lively person with a sophisticated appearance and a ready smile. One day, she sought me out at Shalvata and asked if I could arrange to meet her.

The encounter

The war turned Hannah's world upside down. She soon revealed that the impact of that devastation brought to the surface the cracks in her marriage which were already forming before the enforced departure from her home. In marked contrast to Hannah's outward appearance, our first meeting brought into sharp focus the extent of her suffering, her helplessness, and her sense that she was losing control over her life. From the pinnacle of her career in which she had been involved in saving lives, she fell into the abyss of no status, no money, no home, no security, and was now herself having to ask for help. As Hannah sat in my room, in the same chair that many other refugees and survivors had occupied, I remembered the powerlessness of the victim, but I also recalled connecting to the strength that co-existed with the vulnerability. The stress was taking her beyond her own threshold of pain and was focused on her strained relationship with her husband. Transferred to another environment, without the support network she had known in Sarajevo, and without the escape routes through her work, the conflict presented itself head on. Hannah seemed paralysed, not knowing how to respond. At times she saw the only option as suicide.

I remembered Jack, I thought of Irena and Chava, and how, in the depths of despair, we had found a way of searching for other routes out of the darkness. Hannah spoke to me about the problems with her husband and how many times she had wanted to leave him. Perhaps she would never have done so if her life had remained the same. Her unhappiness may have been masked throughout her life and tinged with regret in its closing chapters. This rupture in her life through the war, perhaps surprisingly, opened a door which would significantly alter the pattern which had embedded itself. Out of the destruction of the war and her marriage, new possibilities would free her to move on in her life. I was aware how difficult it was for Hannah to find the words, in a language which was not her mother tongue, to express the emotional impact of what she was experiencing. However, an interpreter would have forced a wedge between us, and we laughed as we struggled to understand each other. The language of suffering, unlike the Serbo-Croat language, was now familiar to me, and my responses were an interpretation of what had been understood. In that interpretation were practical issues which needed attention – for example, opening up the choices available in how to deal with the separation from her husband. Negotiating ways around a labyrinth of unfamiliar institutions – whether this related to Hannah's housing problems or financial issues – became the focus of our discussions. We worked on these matters together. Hannah found a lawyer to represent her, and I liaised with him to support her case.

As the survivors constantly reminded me, I was working with someone who had been very successful, and I engaged that part of Hannah's ability to master complex situations. I became like a guide to Hannah in her new homeland, but I never forgot who Hannah was, or what was important to her in terms of her dignity and status. Sometimes she spoke to me about clothes she had been given by her employer for whom she worked as a domestic help. These clothes helped to connect her to an image of herself which lifted her out of her refugee label. She noticed my clothes, and commented on them. As two women, we shared this interest, just as I have done with Irena and others.

The regularity of her work, the purchase of a small car, the focus on her daughter and her adaptation to school life diverted energy into concrete events which could be dealt with, to balance the emotional powerlessness with which Hannah was dealing. Hannah returned regularly, though not weekly. She used the time between our meetings to implement the directions she wished to take. There was no pressure on her to make our meetings more regular. Her constant attendance at Shalvata for informal reasons, plus her participation in the club and the support of the community and Branko, meant that her dependence on me was not absolute.

Hannah, who had contributed to the newsletter, began to write short stories for publication. Her creative ability was encouraged and once more added to a sense of mastery and control over the turbulence which characterised her experience in the war, plus her more current upheaval due to her separation from her husband. The structure of the stories gave a form for containing the chaos, as well as an outlet for her talent and imagination. I had learned about the power of the creative process with the survivors and refugees from the Holocaust, and it helped me to seek out and encourage this aspect in Hannah.

It would have been easy to drown as trauma was heaped upon trauma. The translated model of the HSC/Shalvata was clearly effective in this situation with Hannah. There was a balance between her social participation in The Friends of 'La Benevolencija' club, and her meetings with me to share her pain and suffering. If the club did not exist, if there was not a social network to support Hannah outside of our meetings, I do not think she could have moved on in the way that she did. The path was not straight or smooth. The impact of the separation resonated throughout the community of refugees, and members took sides for or against the respective parties. Hannah felt unable to participate in the club if her husband was also there. However, she maintained personal links with members of the community, with Branko, as well as widening her circle outside of the refugee community.

As she made a new life for herself and her daughter, Hannah became increasingly interested in Jewish matters. She already attended the Passover Seder at the synagogue which welcomed the refugees into their midst. Hannah, like many other members of the community, developed an enhanced interest in the Jewish aspects of her life. The desire to alleviate suffering of both the Jew and non-Jew alike in this mixed community seemed to draw some of the refugees like a magnet towards the Jewish nature of the helping agencies – the Jewish Refugee Committee (World Jewish Relief) and Shalvata (Jewish Care).

Hannah appeared to be increasingly relaxed in my company and seemed to see me on many different levels. As a professional, as a woman, as a Jew, Hannah seemed to be identifying with me. It was therefore no surprise when she told me that she wished to train as a counsellor in order to work with other refugees. The experience of sitting together, having a drink together, meeting her informally in other settings, crossing boundaries, working in partnership with her on her practical problems, reflected an image to her which had meaning in her world. Through the mirror which I continued to keep close by us, she saw an image of herself and of me which she would later use when *she* became the therapeutic facilitator in another setting.

Hannah enrolled on a course to train as a refugee counsellor. The redeployment of her professional skills to help other refugees from Bosnia, to act as advocate for them, and to communicate in their mother tongue, gave her an opportunity to make a positive contribution to this new country in which she now lived. The training and personal therapy channelled the negative energy of her trauma in a more constructive way. At the point at which Hannah began to train as a counsellor, our work together drew to a close. However, she continued to see another member of the Shalvata team for the weekly counselling required for her training. She continued to use Shalvata as the backdrop to this venture, returning to the safety of this familiar environment as she embarked on this new phase in her life. Within the group of students and tutors on her course, she translated her own needs as a refugee and the help she had received at Shalvata into responses which would assist others going through similar trauma. Her own trauma was never far away. Her housing problem continued. Her concerns to make a home for her daughter and give her the opportunity to succeed remained paramount. Her father developed health problems. Nevertheless, she was now converting the dead feelings associated with events related to her uprooting into an energy which changed the direction of her life in a positive way.

On the successful completion of her two-year training, Hannah asked if she could come and see me again. As I listened to her telling me of her work with a Bosnian refugee, I was struck by the similarities in her approach to the way we had worked together. The elderly refugee with whom she met found it hard to talk, and so she would sit with him and give him time to find a more appropriate way of expressing himself. Her flexibility in terms of the venue, the informal way she would share tea with him, reflected a memory of those early days when she had felt overwhelmed by her pain and suffering. She returned with me to those early encounters we had shared, and commented that she had felt understood, listened to and respected – yet she also taught me that the difficulties of expressing her emotions in English remained a constant hurdle. She could overcome this problem when working with Bosnian refugees in Serbo-Croat. At the same time, she was clear that she would not offer such a service to those within the community of refugees of which she formed a part. She knew the boundary, and knew how to apply it for the benefit of the sufferer.

Hannah has managed to find ways of regenerating her life out of the destructiveness of her traumatic experiences. Her dignity and self-worth have been restored through her successful training and subsequent offer of a job on the staff of the training institute in which she had graduated. The connectedness between my work with her and the focus of her training were underlined when I was invited through Hannah to give a seminar at the training centre. She felt the students could learn from my experiences of working with the aftermath of war.

The ripple effect of this mastery in her life could also be seen in the success of her daughter in her academic achievements at school. She told me with pride that her daughter had been offered a place at Cambridge University. I knew of the sacrifices Hannah had made to ensure her daughter had every chance to make a new life and to feel integrated with the new friends she had made.

What did the work with Hannah teach me? What would have been the outcome if I had not had the opportunity to work with Holocaust survivors and learn from them about what has helped them to live differently with their trauma?

Hannah offered me a chance to try out the possibility of adapting the lessons I had learned over the years from survivors to a situation of more recent trauma. I had greater confidence. I was carrying less of my own baggage than when I began my journey into a world of unimaginable horror.

Hannah allowed me to get closer to this group of Bosnian refugees and to offer something which could be used. The outcomes contained in her last visit to me provide evidence of the possibility of relating to other war trauma.

In my work over the years with Holocaust survivors, they had fine-tuned my hearing to be able to listen to Hannah. As I sat with her I remembered what the survivors had taught me about what it meant to be a powerless victim. I remembered the concepts of empowerment and the freedom to choose. I remembered the importance of finding the strength within the traumatised person and releasing the creative potential to find another pathway. I remembered the importance of the sense of belonging and connectedness in the process of finding what would be meaningful in our encounter. Without these memories and the reminders of what could be, I do not believe my work with Hannah would have had the same outcome.

Rwandan refugees

When I first met Mary, who co-ordinates the Rwandan refugee project here, I recognised in her the confusion, the powerlessness and the isolation which I had experienced many years ago. Having escaped the genocide in her homeland, she felt compelled to help those who had suffered directly. Without structure and without form, she was being pulled into a vortex of overwhelming despair in her efforts to reach out. Her desire to relieve distress pulled her in many directions. Inadequate funding, lack of support and over-whelming demands on her time and energy challenged any notion of strategy and containment.

In the quiet of Shalvata's space, the chaos which refracted through her from the horrors of war found a listening ear. She had no air to breathe, no time to think, but reacted humanely and constantly to the bombardment of need and desperation. I was learning about new atrocity – not only of rape and bestiality, but of how the resultant HIV virus was slowly killing those widows in Rwanda who had not been murdered in the war. In her desperation, Mary turned to the Medical Foundation for Victims of Torture to ask for counselling for the overwhelming emotions which she could not contain in the traumatised refugees whom she was meeting. The dispersed refugees had no place to meet, no centre or community in which they could share their trauma, or learn how to adapt to this new environment. Without the possibility of strengthening each other, they turned to Mary. The endless stream of phone calls at home meant her time was never her own. Her voice was not strong enough to empower herself or the refugees she was trying to help. She travelled long distances to support refugees who were having difficulties with their asylum issues. Mary was exhausted.

I took Mary into the Holocaust Survivors' Centre. She heard about how these severely traumatised survivors supported each other. She saw the café and she witnessed the importance of food and eating together as a way of nurturing the emptiness of those who have been violated. We discussed the details of the programme, and how it has been made meaningful to the experiences of the trauma. I emphasised, however, that what she saw was not how the centre had started.

Mary could not undertake this work alone. Reaching out to Mary included my acceptance of an invitation to attend an event commemorating the genocide in Rwanda. I made my way across London to be there and to share that experience. Sitting in my office with Mary would have been too clinical. I needed to get a feel of the community of which she was a part and to which she belonged.

I needed to give Mary information which would help her to lay the foundation on which to build. I involved Branko, the Bosnian worker, in the meetings with Mary, to share with her, as a former refugee from another war, his own experiences of how his community had dealt, and were still dealing, with the aftermath of their suffering and displacement.

Developing an infrastructure was essential in helping Mary survive and contain the chaos which threatened her. This needed funding. Much of the publicised fund-raising was channelled to the work in Rwanda, but Mary needed resources here. Mary's work needed backing through the established organisations such as the Medical Foundation and ourselves.

Mary took away from our meetings the idea of developing an informal social group for the Rwandan refugees which she could initially facilitate. Mary managed to appoint an assistant to help her with the enormous task she had undertaken.

Another meeting was made with Mary to develop the ideas which were beginning to germinate. However, Mary did not return. I left messages on her phone when new information came to light about possible sources of funding, but there was no response. My concern led me back to my contact at the Medical Foundation for Victims of Torture, who informed me that Mary had become ill and had not been able to work. However, she would be returning, and he was encouraging her to make contact with me once more.

The difference between Mary's isolated and desperate attempts to cope with the trauma of the Rwandan refugees contrasted with the supportive, informed and co-ordinated responses we were able to make to the Bosnian refugees described. It speaks volumes in terms of the gulf which exists in the different responses to war trauma. Far from the therapeutic responses to survivors of the Nazi Holocaust being confined to that atrocity, I believe that what we have learned puts us at the forefront in terms of contributing to this specialist field of war trauma and its aftermath.

Chapter 13

Developing Co-Ordinated Therapeutic Responses to War Trauma

It is worth underlining the key features which span the therapeutic responses to different experiences of war trauma recorded here. Much suffering could be prevented for those seeking asylum now, and much enriching could result by making appropriate responses to those who have suffered.

Remembering the trauma

Throughout this book we have focused on the different world the traumatised survivors and refugees have emerged from; the 'altered state' that has resulted from the trauma; and the adaptation needed to live in a new environment which may be unfamiliar, hostile and disconnected from who they are. We must go back to the beginning of the book and remember to suspend all our assumptions and put the trauma at the forefront in our thinking about how to help.

In the current experience of asylum seekers arriving in the UK, Audrey Thompson (2001) writes, 'It is almost unimaginable what many asylum seekers and refugees have gone through before getting into Britain: persecution, imprisonment, torture, threats to themselves, their family and friends' (p.6). As we search among the rubble of the destruction which these traumatised people have experienced, we must be sensitive to the 'unique issues of loss, confrontation with an alien culture, and challenges to identity' (Richman 1998, p.170).

We have to remember the context and the culture which the traumatised refugees bring with them. The transition from one culture to another is eased by those helping them when there is acceptance of the refugees' desire to maintain links with features of their country of origin. Familiar food and language are, for example, powerful comfort factors in an alien environment. Claudia Roden, a well-known cookery writer, spoke on the radio about her experience of being a refugee from Egypt in the 1950s (2001). She remarked that when everything is taken away from you, food and the recipes which remind you of home become an important part of your heritage. The process of adaptation cannot be rushed. There are many variables which affect how the individual copes with the aftermath of trauma, as witnessed with the Holocaust survivors. As facilitators in the process of adaptation, we have to work in partnership with the traumatised refugees to create opportunities to strengthen them and help them to cope.

The reception of refugees

To be able to reach out and help newly arrived refugees, we must remember what we have learned from the survivors of the Holocaust about listening to them, seeing them as individuals rather than a collective mass, and being sensitive to who they are, and what they have been through. We need to understand the particularness of the traumatised person's experience and suffering. Listening helps the trauma to be believed, and consultation helps the responses to become more meaningful.

When the Bosnian refugees began arriving from their war-torn homeland, Branko would go to the airport and meet them. Someone who could speak the language familiar to them, who would guide them to their accommodation, and who would subsequently be the familiar face to help them with all the practical obstacles they had to deal with would seem a worthwhile model to copy. In contrast, many Holocaust survivors, while thankful to find a haven before or after World War II, nevertheless were not offered such assistance and still remember how isolated, frightened and overwhelmed they had felt.

In our work in Shalvata and the HSC, I put a strong emphasis on how people are received by staff. A warm, friendly, caring receptionist can make all the difference to a vulnerable person. Multiply this many times over, and one comes to appreciate the essential preparation that is needed on how to deal with the reception of newly arrived refugees. 'Refugee advocates are therefore essential as a way to access appropriate care, and as those who know the culture and language of refugees the best will be other refugees, it seems only logical that advocates should be found amongst the individual communities and trained' (Thompson 2001, p.7). Like Branko, they can become key figures in co-ordinating the necessary services.

The integration of those traumatised by war

Naomi Richman (1998) describes the process of integration of refugees as follows: 'The journey cannot be seen as a linear progression; rather the analogy could be life experienced as a fugue in which themes related to loss, culture, identity and the search for understanding recur and modulate throughout life' (p.171). The survivors of the Nazi Holocaust, as we have seen, were never really helped to integrate, and their suffering served to render them 'outsiders' to the host community. This sense of being different, and not really belonging, persisted until they came together in the HSC.

In contrast, the responses to the Bosnian refugee experience, mentioned throughout the book, recognised the primary importance of developing services which would assist in the process of integration. Bridging the world of trauma they had come from with the world in which they now lived needed careful and conscious thought, rather than reactive responses which may not be in tune with their needs.

The advantage of keeping this group of Bosnian refugees in close proximity was made possible through the intervention of the JRC working with the local authorities to rehouse people as near to each other as possible. Clearly, when dealing with large numbers of refugees arriving in the country, there are logistical problems compared to the smaller group with whom we have been working. Nevertheless, a policy of dispersal and attempts to assimilate refugees do not take account of one of the fundamental needs for refugees from a similar background. They want to be with each other, to share with each other and to strengthen each other rather than depending on professionals for help.

We have observed throughout this book the therapeutic value of mutual support groups and community projects, whether this be the SOS group and the HSC for Holocaust survivors, The Friends of 'La Benevolencija' club and the centre for Bosnian refugees or, on a smaller scale, the social group for Rwandan refugees. Those who have experienced war trauma have lost their social network, and sometimes their entire communities. There are no buffers to protect them in an unsafe and alien environment. These informal social groups become paramount as catalysts to assist in the process of adaptation and integration. Such social groups become a major factor in helping refugees preserve aspects of their life which are familiar to them. It gives them reassurance, preserves their identity and they feel they belong as 'insiders'. When these 'communities in miniature' are preserved, the emotional adjustments are softened. From the safety of these groups, it becomes possible to put one's foot outside the door and make links with the outside world. *Salon* (the Bosnian newsletter), the art exhibitions and the fund-raising concerts became ways of telling the outside world that this group existed, and had a positive contribution to make in enriching the culture of the wider community. 'Refugees need contact with others who reflect their values, prize their culture, and share common experiences. Studies suggest that when they are living within a vigorous community of compatriots, this support plays an important role in preventing mental distress' (Valtoren 1994, pp.63–78).

If 'Isolation, loneliness and bereavement are key problems' for refugees (Thompson 2001, p.6) then social informal groups need to become policy features in meeting their needs. This will demand a rethinking about dispersal programmes to spread refugees around the country where they may be cut off from the more established refugee communities.

Training facilitators from within these groups would be an urgent task that needs investment.

Practical responses to the needs of traumatised refugees

There are many practical adjustments which need to be made by those who have fled from war. It is like beginning again with a blank page to fill. The chaotic aftermath of war is at odds with the often bureaucratic machinery set up to deal with the refugees.

Uncertainties about refugee status, uncertainties about family left behind and the inability to communicate in the new language offer a very shaky foundation on which to build. Many Holocaust survivors arrived prior to the Welfare State, and struggled to make ends meet. However, what was positive for them was that they were believed and were offered asylum as refugees. The Bosnians had to wait in the UK with concerns about their security, even though other practical help was on offer. The stress of this 'no man's land' situation exacerbates other stresses which proliferate in the entry to the host country. Knowing how to respond to newly arrived refugees, as witnessed through the JRC, helped enormously in the short-term practical arrangements which needed to be made regarding benefits, housing, English lessons and schooling for the children.

Paying attention to the practical needs allows us to also deal simultaneously with the emotional impact of displacement. If we take work as an example, we have seen how loss of work or retirement for the Holocaust survivors was a major trigger to the re-experiencing of trauma. The Bosnian refugees, many of whom are highly skilled professionals, could not find work in their fields. The frustration and anxiety associated with lack of work compounded the other stresses they faced. Retraining opportunities, shadowing employed staff and help in preparing CVs were all ways of addressing this important aspect of their adaptation. Work assists in the process of integration as the refugees get to know fellow employees. Their skills can be observed and recognised. Not working adds to family stress and low morale.

In times of recession and high unemployment, competition for work adds to the refugees' difficulties in being accepted as part of the wider community. This increases tensions which, in turn, serve to separate and isolate the refugees still further.

The importance of work may require a creative shift in helping refugees enter a work environment. Many refugees from Germany in the 1930s had been in academic professions, and then had to sell eggs, for example, to earn an income. The staff I employ at Shalvata from Bosnia are skilled professionals in architecture and physics respectively. One is now the community worker/advocate, while the other is in the caretaker/security post. Both jobs have interestingly drawn out their capacity to care for others and they feel integrated into the workplace.

Thinking about how to offer work in a limited market becomes a necessary requirement for those responsible for integrating refugees. Dealing with crisis situations does not necessarily allow space and time for such thinking to occur.

Responses to the emotional impact of war trauma

'Emotions about loss and separation are controlled in order to manage what is most pressing. This is not denial, but a way of avoiding being submerged by the obstacles faced' (Richman 1998, p.179). While practical issues do need to be given priority, we know from the lessons learned from the Holocaust survivors that the impact of war trauma may be long term and profound.

The complex association between the emotional repercussions of war trauma and the often prescribed treatment involving talking about feelings has been addressed throughout the book both in terms of the Holocaust survivors and the Bosnian refugees. 'Counselling is often quite strange for many refugees not used to talking about deep feelings with a stranger' (Thompson 2001, p.7). To this Naomi Richman adds, when talking about asylum seekers coming to the UK, 'Refugees feel patronised and undermined when they are told they are traumatised and need treatment, especially as in many cultures psychological treatment is only for the 'mad'. Instead of being able to decide their priorities for themselves, they may be faced with a predetermined programme of therapy' (Richman 1998, p.180).

This book serves as a detailed example of how to adapt therapeutic services to be more meaningful to those who have experienced war trauma. Whether or not literally next door to each other like the HSC and Shalvata, the concept of promoting informal social-support groups alongside opportunities to share the experiences of war and its aftermath with specialist workers would seem to have wide application. Those who have been victimised have experienced powerlessness, vulnerability and despair. We need to maximise opportunities for empowerment, for building on the coping, healthy, strong aspects of the traumatised person rather than on treating symptoms. Some people want to talk, some prefer creative or recreational outlets, while others get most benefit from building a new community with those who have gone through similar experiences. Therapeutic responses with traumatised people must therefore offer choices which assist in helping regeneration emerge out of destruction.

Therapeutic language may be as much to do with fighting for justice and compensation as it is to do with mourning the massive losses the traumatised have experienced. For each age group, the language of therapeutic responses must be redefined – children, for example, have different ways of responding to trauma than older people. Fundamental and central to all the experiences of war trauma is the need to develop a therapeutic language which can be understood and used by those for whom the responses are intended. Working with them, we learn that the therapeutic responses emerge from the language of trauma itself. This book is a clear exponent of how this adaptation may be achieved and evaluated.

More training and education is necessary to promote this specialist area of work. The practical knowledge we have gained over many years needs to be formalised through programmes that both develop these skills in therapeutic workers trained in the UK and also, like Hannah, the Bosnian refugee, train people from within the refugee communities.

Framework and structure of therapeutic responses

Therapeutic responses need a framework and a structure in order to survive, as well as a dedicated person(s) to ensure its survival. This book has emphasised the organisational and managerial aspects of the work which promote the therapeutic services. Adaptation to the changing needs of the refugees necessitates strategic development in how the services are offered.

We need to look for markers of adaptation among those who were traumatised – for example, achievements at school, retraining in professions, facility with the new language, links with the host community, publications, number of refugees who are working. These are signs of new life which need to be publicised by the media, and which help to change the negative image which feeds the insensitive responses to those who have suffered. For the refugees themselves, the time may come when they no longer wish to be seen and labelled as refugees.

In addition, organisations working with refugees and survivors need to develop strategic responses which cross the boundaries that formerly separated them and disempowered them. To fight for the rights and needs of those who have suffered the effects of war trauma, the organisations have to gain strength from each other in order to give the traumatised people a louder voice. This is strongly in evidence between Jewish Care and the Jewish Refugee Committee as well as the Umbrella Group mentioned earlier. The organisations need to pool their knowledge to gain better understanding from each other about how therapeutic responses to war trauma can be adapted to different circumstances, whether the trauma takes place in this country or, for example, in Africa. Long-term studies, such as the one described herein with Holocaust survivors, need comparison with other examples. In this way, development may be accelerated. The advantages of this co-operation will, it is hoped, lead to policy developments for more recently traumatised refugees. This in turn may change the tide of their current distress.

Chapter 14

Closing the Final Page

What we call the beginning is often the end
And to make an end is to make a beginning.
The end is where we start from.

(T.S. Eliot's poem 'Little Gidding' [1] *)*

In this quotation, Eliot summarises for me a cycle of continuity which is present in the text of this book. As the description of the journey I have undertaken with Holocaust survivors was drawing to a conclusion, I realised I had already embarked on an additional journey. In a house next door to trauma, the impact of the survivor's suffering had drawn me closer to other experiences of war. The book therefore cannot end neatly with the termination of the journey. Instead I am challenged to seek out a more lasting legacy through which the Holocaust survivors can live on. When a traumatised person can begin to live differently with his/her trauma as a result of being listened to and responded to in more meaningful ways, then the possibility for that remembrance to happen is enhanced.

My task has been to document these lessons in this book. I hope I have been able to clarify some of the personal and professional challenges which need to be faced when adapting the therapeutic responses to make them more appropriate to those who have undergone the trauma. This has meant questioning our therapeutic assumptions so that new and innovative ways of responding to the aftermath of atrocity could be developed. It has been possible to observe the effect these changes have made in the lives of those who experienced the trauma.

The book can go no further than the confines of its cover. I was concerned that the ending should not become too abstract or removed. It therefore seemed appropriate that at the closing of the book one of the survivors who comes to the centre, Jacob, should ask to see me to include one last thought in my writing. His presence at the ending contains the essence of the way that I work.

In Buchenwald, he told me, during the endless hours of waiting in the Appelplatz as the Nazis counted how many of the prisoners had survived another day, classical music was being played. He felt nothing – neither joy nor sadness. Reflecting back on that time, he pondered over the incongruity of the situation in which pain and suffering could co-exist with sounds that emanated from another world with which he had lost touch. For Jacob, the paradox continues to exist today. Before falling asleep at night, he likes to listen to classical music. In this world, the sounds of the music offer him respite from the trauma which never leaves him.

The importance of this encounter has as much to do with its symbolism as its content. In his unanswered questions, Jacob reminds us to be challenged in our work by what we do not know. In his comments about the positive role that music now plays in his life, he encourages us not to give up hope. He reminds us that in our quest for understanding how to work with the aftermath of atrocity, we never reach our destination. The learning never ends. I believe he wanted me to convey this message to those who read this book. By so doing, the cycle of continuity can be kept alive and vibrant. I hope a new chapter is already beginning in the minds of those interested in developing this important work.

Endnote

1. Excerpt from 'Little Gidding' in *Four Quartets*, copyright 1942 by T.S. Eliot and renewed 1970 by Esme Valerie Eliot, reprinted by permission of Harcourt, Inc. Permission to reprint is also granted by Faber and Faber Limited, London.

References

Amery, J. (1999) *At the Mind's Limits*. London: Granta Books.

Bar-On, D. (1999) *The Indescribable and the Undiscussable – Reconstructing Human Discourse after Trauma*. Hungary: Central European University Press.

Bergman, S. and Jucovy, M.E. (1982) *Generations of the Holocaust*. New York: Basic Books.

Bettelheim, B. (1943) 'Individual and Mass Behaviour in Extreme Situations.' *Journal of Abnormal and Social Psychology 38*, 4, 417–452.

Bettelheim, B. (1971) *The Informed Heart*. New York: Avon Books.

Black, D. Freeman and Urbanowicz, M. (1983) *Family Therapy with Bereaved Children: Process and Outcome*. 4th International Congress of Family Therapy. Israel.

Bluhm, H. (1948) 'How Did They Survive?' *American Journal of Psychotherapy 2*, 1, 3–32.

Bond, E. (1991) 'Soup.' Poem part of a series called 'The Unfinished Line', produced in a National Theatre programme for Bond's play *The Sea*.

Bond, E. (1995) 'If.' From *Plays Four*. In H. Schiff (ed) *Holocaust Poetry*. London: HarperCollins.

Bowlby, J. (1982) 'Attachment and Loss.' *Retrospect and Prospect American Journal of Orthopsychiatry 52*, 664–678.

Bracken, P. (1998) 'Hidden Agendas: Deconstructing Post Traumatic Stress Disorder.' In P.J. Bracken and C. Petty (eds) *Rethinking the Trauma of War*. London and New York: Free Association Books.

Bracken, P.J. and Petty, C. (eds) (1998) *Rethinking the Trauma of War*. London and New York: Free Association Books.

Brainin, E. and Teicher, S. (1997) 'Time Heals no Wounds.' In L. Hunt, M. Marshall and C. Rowlings (eds) *Past Trauma in Late Life*. London: Jessica Kingsley Publishers.

Brook, P. (1990) *The Empty Space*. England: Penguin (originally published 1968).

Buber, M. (1958) *I and Thou*. Edinburgh: T and T Clark.

Carmi, T. (1977) 'Anatomy of a War.' *Jerusalem Quarterly 3*, 102, epigraph.

Cloyes, S. (1998) 'Presiding over Genocide: The Shame of the West.' *Illyria*, August 1–31.

Cooper, H. (1995) 'The Second Generation Syndrome.' *The Journal of Holocaust Education 4*, 2, 131–145.

Danieli, Y. (1984) 'Psychotherapists' Participation in the Conspiracy of Silence about the Holocaust.' *Psychoanalytic Psychology I*, 1, 25.

Danieli, Y. (1985a) 'The Treatment and Prevention of Long Term Effects and Inter-Generational Transmission of Victimization: A Lesson from Holocaust Survivors and their Children.' In C.R. Figley (ed) *Trauma and its Wake*. New York: Brunner/Mazel.

Danieli, Y. (1985b) 'The Use of Mutual Support Approaches in the Treatment of Victims.' A paper presented at a Services Research and Evaluation Colloquium. *The Aftermath of Crime: A Mental Health Crisis*. Washington DC.

Danieli, Y. (1989) 'The Survivor and Psychoanalysis.' In P. Marcus and A. Rosenberg (eds) *Healing their Wounds: Psychotherapy with Holocaust Survivors and their Families*. New York: Praeger.

Davidson, S. (1984) 'Human Reciprocity among Jewish Prisoners in the Nazi Concentration Camps.' *Proceedings of the 4th Yad Vashem International Conference 1984*. Jerusalem: Yad Vashem Publications.

Davidson, S. (1981) *On Relating to Traumatised Persecuted People. Israel and the Netherlands*. Symposium on the Impact of Persecution II. 14–18 April. Amsterdam: Rijsvijk.

Davidson, S. (1992a) 'Surviving During the Holocaust and Afterwards: The Post Liberation Experience.' In I.W. Charney (ed) *Holding on to Humanity*. New York: New York University.

Davidson, S. (1992b) 'The Transmission of Psychopathology in Families of Concentration Camp Survivors.' In I.W. Charney (ed) *Holding on to Humanity*. New York: New York University.

Des Pres, T. (1976) *The Survivor – An Anatomy of Life in the Death Camps*. New York: Oxford University Press.

Dodd, V. (2000) 'The Asylum Debate.' *The Guardian*, March.

Donat, A. (1967) *The Holocaust Kingdom*. London: Corgi.

Donne, J. ([1624] 1993) 'Devotions from Emergent Occasions: Meditation xvii.' In A. Partington (ed) *Concise Oxford Dictionary of Quotations*. Oxford: Oxford University Press.

Durst, N. (1995) 'A Child Survives…and Then What?' In J. Lemberger (ed) *A Global Perspective on Working with Holocaust Survivors and the Second Generation*. Israel: JDC/Brookdale Institute.

Edwards, B. (1981) *Drawing on the Right Hand Side of the Brain – How to Unlock Your Hidden Artistic Talent*. England: Fontana/Collins.

Eliot, T.S. 'Little Gidding.' *Four Quartets, Collected Poems 1909–1962*. London: Faber and Faber, 1976.

Fogelman, E. (1991) Paper at Hidden Child Conference, USA. (Fogelman is a psychotherapist as well as a child survivor. She has written about her group work with children of Holocaust survivors.)

Frankl, V. (1987) *Man's Search for Meaning: An Introduction to Logotherapy*. London: Hodder and Stoughton.

Freyberg, J. (1989) 'The Emerging Self in the Survivor Family.' In P. Marcus and A. Rosenberg (eds) *Healing their Wounds: Psychotherapy with Holocaust Survivors and their Families*. New York and London: Praeger.

Fried, H. (1997) 'Café 84: A Social Day Care Centre for Survivors and their Children.' In L. Hunt, M. Marshall and C. Rowlings (eds) *Past Trauma in Late Life*. London: Jessica Kingsley Publishers.

Gilbert, M. (1996) *The Boys – Triumph over Adversity*. London: Weidenfeld and Nicholson.

Gilbert, M. (2000) 'Hope, Resistance, Refuge.' In M. Gilbert (ed) *Never Again. A History of the Holocaust*. London: HarperCollins in association with the Imperial War Museum.

Giller, J. (1998) 'Caring for Victims of Torture in Uganda: Some Personal Reflections.' In P.J. Bracken and C. Petty (eds) *Rethinking the Trauma of War*. London and New York: Free Association Books.

Greenspan, H. (1998a) 'Making a Story From What is Not a Story: Constructing the Tellable in Recounting by Holocaust Survivors.' *International Journal: Studies on the Audio-Visual Testimony of Victims of the Nazi Crimes and Genocides 1*, June 1998. Brussels: Editions du Centre D'Etudes et de Documentation Foundation Auschwitz.

Greenspan, H. (1998b) 'The Tellable and the Hearable: Survivor Guilt in Narrative Context.' *International Journal: Studies on the Audio-Visual Testimony of Victims of the Nazi Crimes and Genocides 2*, December 1998. Brussels: Editions du Centre D'Etudes et de Documentation Foundation Auschwitz.

Gross, J.T. (2001) *Neighbours*. Oxfordshire: Princeton University Press.

Grossman, D. (1995) mentioned in H. Cooper 'The Second Generation Syndrome.' *Journal of Holocaust Education 4*, 2, 145.

Haas, A. (1996) *The Aftermath – Living with the Holocaust*. Cambridge, New York and Melbourne: Cambridge University Press.

Hadda, J. (1989) 'Mourning the Yiddish Language and Some Implications for Treatment.' In P. Marcus and A. Rosenberg (eds) *Healing their Wounds: Psychotherapy with Holocaust Survivors and their Families*. New York: Praeger.

Harris, K. (2002) 'The Importance of Developing a "Culture of Belief" Amongst Counselling Psychologists Working with Asylum Seekers.' *Counselling Psychology Review 17*, 1, 4–13.

Hart, K. (1962) *I am Alive*. London and New York: Abelard-Schuman.

Hassan, J. (2001) Talk given at the Holocaust Survivors' Centre to commemorate Liberation.

Hawkins, P. and Miller, E. (1994) 'Psychotherapy in and with Organisations.' In P. Clarkson and M. Pokorny (eds) *The Handbook of Psychotherapy*. London: Routledge.

Heimler, E. (1966) *Resistance Against Tyranny*. London: Praeger.

Herzog, J. (1982) 'World Beyond Metaphor: Thoughts on the Transmission of Trauma.' In S. Bergman and M.E. Jucovy (eds) *Generations of the Holocaust*. New York: Basic Books Inc.

Hoppe, K.D. (1989) 'Severed Ties.' In P. Marcus and A. Rosenberg (eds) *Healing their Wounds: Psychotherapy with Holocaust Survivors and their Families*. New York: Praeger.

Hoyt, M. (2000) 'Cognitive-Behavioural Treatment of Post Traumatic Stress Disorder from a Narrative Constructive Perspective – A Conversation with Donald Meichenbaum.' In M. Scott and S. Palmer (eds) *Trauma and Post Traumatic Stress Disorder*. London/New York: Cassell.

Huneke, D. (1988) 'Glimpses of Light in a Vast Darkness: A Study of the Moral and Spiritual Development of Nazi Era Rescuers.' *Remembering for the Future. Theme I*. These were the pre-prints of the papers presented at the International Scholars Conference in Oxford, 10–13 July 1988, pp.486–494. Oxford: Pergamon Press.

Hunt, L., Marshall, M. and Rowlings, C. (eds) (1997) *Past Trauma in Late Life*. London: Jessica Kingsley Publishers.

Into the Light (2000). London: Jewish Care/World Jewish Relief. (A collection of short stories by survivors, with a foreword by Alan Sillitoe.)

Jensen, B. (1973) 'Human Reciprocity – An Arctic Exemplification.' *American Journal of Orthopsychiatry 43*, 447–458.

Keane, F. (2002) Personal communication.

Kessel, S. (1973) *Hanged in Auschwitz*. Translated by Melville and Delight Wallace. London: Talmy Franklin.

Kestenberg, J. and Brenner, I. (1986) 'Children who Survived the Holocaust: The Role of Rules and Routines in the Development of the Super Ego.' *International Journal of Psycho-Analysis 67*, 309–316.

Kinsler, F. (1998) 'Group Services for Holocaust Survivors and their Families.' In J. Lemberger (ed) *A Global Perspective on Working with Holocaust Survivors and the Second Generation*. Israel: JDC/Brookdale Institute.

Klein, H. (1968) 'Problems in the Psychotherapeutic Treatment of Israeli Soldiers of the Holocaust.' In H. Krystal (ed) *Massive Psychic Trauma*. New York: International Universities Press.

Krell, R. (1989) 'Alternative Therapeutic Approaches to Holocaust Survivors.' In P. Marcus and A. Rosenberg (eds) *Healing their Wounds: Psychotherapy with Holocaust Survivors and their Families*. New York: Praeger.

Kren, G. (1989) 'The Holocaust Survivor and Psychoanalysis.' In P. Marcus and A. Rosenberg (eds) *Healing their Wounds: Psychotherapy with Holocaust Survivors and their Families*. New York: Praeger.

Krystal, H. (ed) (1968) *Massive Psychic Trauma*. New York: International Universities Press.

Krystal, H. and Niederland, W. (eds) (1971) *Psychic Traumatisation*. Boston: Little, Brown.

Levi, P. (1965) *The Truce*. London: Bodley Head.

Levi, P. (1988a) *The Drowned and the Saved*. Harmondsworth: Penguin Group.

Levi, P. (1988b) 'Passover.' *Collected Poems*. Translated by R. Feldman and B. Swann. London: Faber and Faber.

Luchterand, E. (1967) 'Prisoners' Behaviour and Social System in the Nazi Camp.' *International Journal of Psychiatry 13*, 245–264.

Mandelstam, N. (1970) *Hope Against Hope*. New York: Athenium.

Marcus, P. (1989) 'Jewish Consciousness after the Holocaust.' In P. Marcus and A. Rosenberg (eds) *Healing their Wounds: Psychotherapy with Holocaust Survivors and their Families*. New York: Praeger.

Marcus, P. and Rosenberg, A. (1988) 'A Philosophical Critique of the "Survivor Syndrome" and Some Implications for Treatment.' In L. Randolph Braham (ed) *The Psychological Perspectives of the Holocaust and of its Aftermath*. Boulder, CO: Social Science Monographs and The Csengeri Institute for Holocaust Studies of the Graduate School and University Centre of the City University of New York. Distributed by Columbia University Press.

Marcus, P. and Rosenberg, A. (eds) (1989a) *Healing their Wounds: Psychotherapy with Holocaust Survivors and their Families*. New York: Praeger.

Marcus, P. And Rosenberg, A. (1989b) 'Treatment Issues with Survivors and their Offspring: An Interview with Anna Ornstein.' In P. Marcus and A. Rosenberg (eds) *Healing their Wounds: Psychotherapy with Holocaust Survivors and their Families*. New York: Praeger

Meichenbaum, D. (2000a) 'What Can Be Done to Help Clients with PTSD and DES.' In M. Scott and S. Palmer (eds) *Trauma and Post Traumatic Stress Disorder*. London/New York: Cassell.

Meichenbaum, D. (2000b) 'Helping Clients with PTSD and DES.' In M. Scott and S. Palmer (eds) *Trauma and Post Traumatic Stress Disorder*. London/New York: Cassell.

Mombert, A. (1999) 'How Much Home Does a Person Need?' In J. Amery (ed) *At the Mind's Limits*. London: Granta Books.

Montefiore, C.G. and Loewe, R. (1974) *A Rabbinic Anthology*. New York: Schocken Books Inc.

Niemöller, Pastor M. (1995) 'First They Came for the Jews.' In H. Schiff (ed) *Holocaust Poetry*. London: HarperCollins.

Nietzsche, F. (1987) 'Introduction.' In V. Frankl (ed) *Man's Search for Meaning: An Introduction to Logotherapy*. London: Hodder and Stoughton.

Oliner, P. and Oliner, S. (1988) 'Rescuers during the Holocaust: Justice, Care and Religion.' *Remembering for the Future. Theme I*. These were the pre-prints of the papers presented at the International Scholars Conference in Oxford, 10–13 July 1988, pp.506–517. Oxford: Pergamon Press.

Out of the Dark (1996). London: Jewish Care/World Jewish Relief. (A Collection of short stories by survivors, with a Foreword by Alan Sillitoe.)

Paldiel, M. (1988) 'The Altruism of the Righteous Gentiles.' *Remembering for the Future. Theme I*. These were the pre-prints of the papers presented at the International Scholars Conference in Oxford 10–13 July 1988, pp.517–526. England: Pergamon Press.

Richman, N. (1998) 'Looking Before and After: Refugees and Asylum Seekers in the West.' In P.J. Bracken and C. Petty (eds) *Rethinking the Trauma of War*. London and New York: Free Association Books.

Richter, A. (1998) 'Sexual Violence in Wartime.' In P.J. Bracken and C. Petty (eds) *Rethinking the Trauma of War*. London and New York: Free Association Books.

Roden, C. (2001) Guest on *Desert Island Discs*, a BBC Radio 4 programme broadcast on 29 July. (Her writing can be found in *The Book of Jewish Food – An Odyssey from Damarkand and Vilna to the Present Day*. Viking Books, 1997.)

Rosenbloom, M. (1983) 'Implications of the Holocaust for Social Work.' *Social Casework. The Journal of Contemporary Social Work*. Family Service Association of America, 205–213.

Samer, H. (1997) *Rescue in Albania*. Cathedral City, CA: Brunswick Press.

Schreuder, J.N. (1997) 'Post Traumatic Re-Experiencing in Old Age Working Through or Covering Up?' In L. Hunt, M. Marshall and C. Rowlings (eds) *Past Trauma in Late Life*. London: Jessica Kingsley Publishers.

Scott, M. (2000) 'Assessment and Conceptualisation.' In M. Scott and S. Palmer (eds) *Trauma and Post Traumatic Stress Disorder*. London/New York: Cassell.

Shakespeare, W. (1988) *Shakespeare's Sonnets. Sonnet No. 3*. London: Guild Publishing.

Steinberg, A. (1989) 'Holocaust Survivors and their Children: A Review of the Clinical Literature.' In P. Marcus and A. Rosenberg (eds) *Healing their Wounds: Psychotherapy with Holocaust Survivors and their Families*. New York: Praeger.

Summerfield, D. (1998) 'The Social Experience of War and Social Issues for the Humanitarian Field.' In P.J. Bracken and C. Petty (eds) *Rethinking the Trauma of War*. London and New York: Free Association Books.

Thompson, A. (2001) 'Refugees and Mental Health.' *Diverse Minds Magazine, 9*, 6–7.

Turner, B.N. (1990) *...And the Policeman Smiled*. London: Bloomsbury.

Valent, P. (1993) *Child Survivors – Adults Living with Childhood Trauma*. Port Melbourne: Heinemann.

Vallejo, C. (1978) 'The Windows Shuddered.' *Cesar Vallejo. The Complete Posthumous Poetry*. Translated by Clayton Eshleman and José Rubia Barcia. Berkeley: University of California Press.

Valtoren, K. (1994) 'Adaptation of Vietnamese Refugees in Finland.' *Journal of Refugee Studies 7*, 63–78.

Wardi, D. (1992) *Memorial Candles: Children of the Holocaust*. New York: Routledge.

Wardi, D. (1995) 'Familial and Collective Identity in Holocaust Survivors and the Second Generation.' In J. Lemberger (ed) *A Global Perspective on Working with Holocaust Survivors and the Second Generation*. Israel: JDC/Brookdale.

Wheeler, C. (1999) *Evacuation*. A BBC Radio 4 programme presented by Charles Wheeler, broadcast 16 August.

Wiesel, E. (1970) *A Beggar in Jerusalem*. London: Weidenfeld and Nicholson.

Wiesel, E. (1981, first published as *Les Editions de Minuit*, 1958) *Night*. Harmondsworth: Penguin.

Wiesel, E. (1982) 'The Holocaust Patient.' Address to Cedars Sinai Medical Staff, Los Angeles.

Wiesel, E. (1990a) 'A Celebration of Friendship.' In E. Wiesel's collection of his essays: *From the Kingdom of Memory – Reminiscences*. New York: Schocken Books.

Wiesel, E. (1990b) 'Kaddish in Cambodia.' In E. Wiesel's collection of his essays: *From the Kingdom of Memory – Reminiscences*. New York: Schocken Books.

Wiesel, E. (1990c) 'Pilgrimage to the Kingdom of Night.' In E. Wiesel's collection of his essays: *From the Kingdom of Memory – Reminiscences*. New York: Schocken Books.

Wiesel, E. (1990d) 'Trivialising Memory.' In E. Wiesel's collection of his essays: *From the Kingdom of Memory – Reminiscences*. New York: Schocken Books.

Wiesel, E. (1990e) 'When Memory Brings People Together.' In E. Wiesel's collection of his essays: *From the Kingdom of Memory – Reminiscences*. New York: Schocken Books.

Wiesel, E. (1990f) 'Why I Write.' In E. Wiesel's collection of his essays: *From the Kingdom of Memory – Reminiscences*. New York: Schocken Books.

Wiesel, E. (1992) *The Forgotten*. New York: Summit Books.

Wiesel, E. (1996) *All Rivers Run to the Sea. Memoirs v.1 1928–1969*. London: HarperCollins.

Wiesel, E. (2000) 'It Would Be Impossible to Keep Silent.' *The Daily Telegraph*, 31 July, p.13.

Wilgowicz, P. (1995) 'The Effects of the Holocaust on the Children of Former Prisoners and Survivors.' In J. Lemberger (ed) *A Global Perspective on Working with Holocaust Survivors and the Second Generation*. Israel: JDC/Brookdale Institute.

Subject Index

Author Index